MIND IN COMFORT AND EASE

MIND IN COMFORT AND EASE

THE VISION OF ENLIGHTENMENT IN THE GREAT PERFECTION

Including Longchen Rabjam's
Finding Comfort and Ease in Meditation on the Great Perfection

His Holiness the Dalai Lama

FOREWORD BY SOGYAL RINPOCHE

TRANSLATED BY MATTHIEU RICARD,
RICHARD BARRON, AND ADAM PEARCEY

EDITED BY PATRICK GAFFNEY

WISDOM PUBLICATIONS • BOSTON

Wisdom Publications
199 Elm Street
Somerville MA 02144 USA

ISBN-13: 978-0-7394-9182-9

Cover design by Emily Mahon. Interior design by Margery Cantor. Set in Dante MT 11.5 pt/14.5 pt.

A commemorative edition of this book, under the title *The Vision of Enlightenment,* was published by Dharmakosha for The Tertön Sogyal Trust in London in 2006.

Printed in the United States of America

CONTENTS

VERSES OF HOMAGE

by Kyabjé Trulshik Rinpoche

Om svasti!

With merit and wisdom gathered over countless ages as the cause,
You gained the result—the ten strengths and four fearlessnesses of buddhahood.
Great guide of this fortunate age, appearing with the signs and marks of perfection,
Siddhartha, you who fulfilled your every aim, grant us virtue and excellence!

Amid the splendor of a hundred rays of light from Amitabha's heart,
You were born on the tip of a lotus stem upon the lake of Sindhu
And came as a second buddha to the Land of Snows.
Lotus-born guru Padmakara, grant us your protection at all times!

Embodiment of all the buddhas' compassion, holder of the white lotus,
Having set aside the apparel of the sambhogakaya,
You appear as a monk in saffron robes to protect this world.
Victorious lord Tenzin Gyatso, in heartfelt devotion, we bow to you!

In response to requests by the Rigpa Sangha of Lerab Ling in France for a prologue to this book, this was written and offered from Nepal by the one called Dzarong Shadeu Trulshik, Ngawang Chökyi Lodrö, in the Tibetan year 2133, the Fire Dog, on the 26th day of the 4th month (June 21, 2006).

PUBLISHER'S ACKNOWLEDGMENT

The publisher gratefully acknowledges the generous help of the Hershey Family Foundation in sponsoring the printing of this book.

FOREWORD

His Holiness the Dalai Lama of Tibet is one of the great spiritual leaders of our age. He has devoted his whole life to furthering the well-being of humanity and for nearly forty years has traveled all over the world, sharing his message of human values, universal responsibility, and compassion. It is a message that grows more pertinent and more vital as each day goes by. What His Holiness has shown, and so many people respond to with alacrity and joy, is that altruism and caring for others hold the very meaning of life and that by training and transforming the mind with compassion, we can become better human beings, we can treat others with love and respect, and we can find happiness and peace. With his sincerity and his humanity, for countless people His Holiness is the still center in a chaotic and violent world.

His Holiness the Dalai Lama's first visit to the West was in September 1973. He met Pope Paul VI in the Vatican, who declared in his welcome that His Holiness' presence would "contribute to the furtherance of mutual love and respect among the adherents of different creeds." I will never forget that occasion, as I had the honor of serving His Holiness and helping to organize his visit. But we could never have imagined then, as we welcomed him onto the soil of Europe, the impact and influence that he would have on the world. At that time, his message was one of universal responsibility, kindness, and the good heart, and it is a message he has tirelessly continued to deepen and expand, to address the many dimensions of our changing world. His Holiness' vision, which the Nobel Peace Prize Committee called his "philosophy of peace," embraces the whole theater of human affairs, encompassing understanding between religions, peace and reconciliation, the protection of the environment, human rights, economic equality, education, and science. I often feel that these deep concerns of his, to use a Buddhist image, are like the rays that stream from the blazing sun of his wisdom and compassion. The scale of both his vision and his achievements is simply staggering; you only have to look at the list of countries he visits, the amount he accomplishes, and the sheer number of people he reaches. His Holiness tends to describe his international activities modestly, in terms of sharing his understanding of the importance of basic human values, advocating interreligious understanding and harmony, and promoting the rights and freedoms of the Tibetan people. Yet of all the Dalai Lamas, I feel there has never been one who has accomplished anything comparable with what he has achieved.

One dimension in which His Holiness the Dalai Lama has played a unique and critical role is the development of Buddhism in the West. He has personally taken an extremely active interest in ensuring that the study and practice of Dharma flourish authentically in the West, as much as in the East. His continuous commitment to teaching in different countries has proved, for students of the Dharma, an unceasing source of inspiration. He is a master scholar whose teachings are studied like those of the learned panditas of the past, but at the same time his knowledge and experience allow him to translate and relate the Buddhadharma to modern life in a persuasively immediate and accessible way. His brilliant and far-reaching dialogue with the world of science has demonstrated unequivocally the extraordinary depth and power of the Buddhist teachings and what they have to offer. And he has taken a lead as well in building a road to real interaction and openness within Buddhism and between Buddhism and the other faith traditions. If over the last two decades Buddhism has won greater respect and acknowledgement in the world at large, it must be largely because of his leadership and example. Without him, the world of Buddhism would be quite different.

In September 2000, His Holiness visited our international retreat center, Lerab Ling, in the south of France, to give a major Buddhist teaching entitled "The Path to Enlightenment." We had invited him to map out the path of study and practice from the beginning up to the Great Perfection, *Dzogpachenpo,* with its key elements and reference points, and so provide a blueprint for a complete spiritual path for modern people. With his learning, his familiarity with the different Buddhist schools, and his ability to adapt and relate to the modern world, we knew that he was uniquely placed to give such a survey of Buddhist teachings and practice.

I remember so vividly the whole ten days of His Holiness' visit. It was the first time that he had been to Lerab Ling, and he arrived one day early in order to devote some time to quiet retreat in the rural surroundings. As he told us later, "I have found this to be a delightful place, secluded, beautiful, full of blessings, and with its natural environment well preserved..." This was 2000 and a year of anniversaries. As well as being the millennial year, it also marked the sixtieth anniversary of His Holiness' enthronement and the fiftieth year since he was invested, at the age of fifteen, with the rule of Tibet. Seeking to find a way to celebrate the importance of this occasion, I invited thirty of the seniormost monks of the Dalai Lama's own personal monastery, Namgyal Dratsang, to Lerab Ling to conduct a special Vajrayana practice, the complete *drupchen* (group practice) and *mendrup* (consecration of medicine) of Vajrakilaya, the yidam deity who embodies all the buddhas' enlightened activity. Never performed before outside of Tibet or Dharamsala in India, this particular practice is from a *terma* treasure called *Phurba Yang Nying Pudri,* concealed by Guru Padmasambhava and revealed by Tertön Sogyal, Lerab Lingpa, who conferred the whole of this teaching on the Thirteenth Dalai Lama and entrusted him as its custodian. What is significant about this practice, as His Holiness explained, is that it has a unique connection with the well-being of the Dalai Lamas, the future of Tibet, and the flourishing of Tibetan Buddhism.

His Holiness arrived to preside over the final day of the two-week drupchen, which included the receiving of the blessings of the practice and the consecration of a large quantity of medicinal *amrita*. On the following day, he conferred the empowerment of *Phurba Yang Nying Pudri* on the 1,400 people gathered in the drupchen tent situated at the heart of Lerab Ling. At that moment, I could not help feeling tremendous hope and promise that this very powerful practice, executed so perfectly by the Namgyal monks and presided over by His Holiness, would indeed have an effect for the long life of the Dalai Lamas and their work, the resolution of the question of Tibet, and the future of the teachings of Tibetan Buddhism in the West. A number of propitious signs accompanied the drupchen, and His Holiness confirmed how auspicious it had been.

How wonderful it was, too, that Kyabjé Trulshik Rinpoche, one of the most eminent and highly revered masters in Tibetan Buddhism, was also present at this time. A great upholder of the Vinaya lineage of the Nyingma tradition, he was a disciple of my master Jamyang Khyentse Chökyi Lodrö and the heart son of both Kyabjé Dudjom Rinpoche and Kyabjé Dilgo Khyentse Rinpoche. For a number of years he has been giving His Holiness rare teachings and transmissions from the Nyingma and Dzogchen traditions. Soon after His Holiness arrived at Lerab Ling, he paid a number of visits to Trulshik Rinpoche, from whom he was receiving the transmission of *The Trilogy of Finding Comfort and Ease* by the great Dzogchen master, Longchenpa. I remember that Trulshik Rinpoche auspiciously offered His Holiness a photograph of Gangri Thökar, the hermitage in Tibet where Longchenpa had composed his masterworks; I offered him a portrait statue of this great master made from life, which had been revered by Dilgo Khyentse Rinpoche and Nyoshul Khenpo, two of the foremost exponents of Dzogchen of our time. His Holiness seemed to decide spontaneously that he would teach on Longchenpa's *Finding Comfort and Ease in Meditation on the Great Perfection,* one of the texts in the trilogy, as a principal theme during his five-day teaching.

Over ten thousand people attended His Holiness' teachings, from twenty-one countries and from as far away as Australia and the United States. There were over a hundred lamas and geshes, and many were struck that His Holiness had chosen such a profound text on which to comment. All of us were moved by the depth, relevance, and accessibility of his teachings; there were those who considered them among the most remarkable they had ever heard him give. In a wholly original but always authentic way, His Holiness brought a sense of his own personal quest, as he explored the entire Buddhist path and particularly the pith instructions of the great masters of the Great Perfection. Like an expert jeweller, he set the teaching of Dzogchen within the context of the other traditions of Tibetan Buddhism, highlighting their parallels and their common ultimate aim of realizing the clear light nature of the mind; in so doing, he seemed to continue many of the themes from previous teachings on Dzogchen he had given in the West. During the course of the teachings, His Holiness conferred the empowerment of Padmasambhava and his Eight Manifestations from the pure visions of the Great Fifth Dalai Lama, which he had granted at our request in 1982 in Paris and in 1989 in San Jose, California. As Guru Padmasambhava is so often invoked as a powerful source of peace and transformation, this represented an immense blessing for the whole region and for France itself and seemed to seal the dedication of these extraordinary teachings to peace in the world.

One of His Holiness' great gifts is his ability to show the distinctive features of the teachings and practices of the different schools of Tibetan Buddhism. At Lerab Ling he spoke of his own deep commitment to the open-minded, unbiased spirit of Rimé, which I have always sought to make a defining feature of Rigpa's work, considering it as the legacy, in a way, of the great Rimé master Jamyang Khyentse Chökyi Lodrö. At the same time, too, His Holiness gave precious advice on the importance of maintaining the integrity and authenticity of the Buddhist tradition of Tibet. "At Lerab Ling," he said, "a center has been born that is destined to make Buddhist culture, as developed in Tibet, known in an authentic manner. For what counts is that it is an authentic representation of Tibetan Buddhist culture and so can provide an example and bring about intercultural exchanges in France and in other places. I am convinced that this center at Lerab Ling is already making a contribution and will continue to do so, more and more, toward a greater knowledge of the rich culture of the Tibetan Buddhist tradition." As ever, His Holiness' presence had an indelible impact on the hearts of everyone, whether experienced Dharma students, local people, politicians, VIP protection officers, or the local *gendarmerie.* And as often happens, it opened the door to a new sympathy and acceptance for Buddhism in the whole region.

For me it is the greatest possible privilege to introduce this book and also an immense blessing as His Holiness is one of my principal teachers; and for all Tibetans, he is our leader, our guiding light, and our inspiration. All His Holiness' precious teachings in September 2000 are included in this volume, which is being published to celebrate His Holiness' second visit to Lerab Ling and his inauguration of its temple and monastery. The temple was constructed on the very site where the drupchen took place in 2000, and I am certain that it is thanks to His Holiness' blessing that it came into being so swiftly and auspiciously. Kyabjé Trulshik Rinpoche has named this temple *Palri Pema Ösel Dargyé Ling,* after the Copper-Colored Mountain with its Palace of Lotus Light, the heaven of Guru Padmasambhava. It is here at Lerab Ling that I will be leading my students in a three-year retreat, beginning this year.

All of this, the temple and all our work, I dedicate to His Holiness' long life and good health, to the fulfillment of his aspirations for Tibet and humanity, and to the thriving of the Buddhadharma here in the West. I pray that, for all who read this book, the nectar of His Holiness' teachings infuses their mindstreams, inspires them with new understanding and enthusiasm, and leads them unerringly along the path to enlightenment.

SOGYAL RINPOCHE
LERAB LING
JULY 6, 2006

PREFACE

"CAN YOU TELL us something about your extraordinary destiny?" asked a journalist as His Holiness the Dalai Lama arrived at Lerab Ling on the morning of September 17, 2000. His Holiness turned to him and said, "All human beings have an extraordinary destiny! Sometimes things bring us joy and, at other times, sadness. But these ups and downs are part of everyone's destiny. I believe the most important thing in this existence of ours is to do something that can be of benefit to others. What we need more than anything is to develop an attitude of altruism—that is what truly gives meaning to life. The fact of having been recognized as the Dalai Lama allows me on various occasions to do a bit of good around me. This is the path I try to follow, to the best of my ability."

In these few words, the Dalai Lama captured the message of compassion and altruism that has made him known throughout the world and that figured prominently throughout his visit to the Languedoc-Roussillon region of southern France in September 2000. This was His Holiness' seventeenth visit to France, and in the course of the year leading up to it, three very different events took place that vividly displayed the scope of his compassionate action in the world. The first was in 1999 with the publication of *Ethics for a New Millennium,* in which the Dalai Lama distilled his sixty-year study and practice of Buddhism into a nonreligious, but fundamentally spiritual, vision for individuals and society, based on the training of the mind. He called for a spiritual and ethical revolution—"a radical reorientation away from our habitual preoccupation with self, toward the wider community of beings with whom we are connected." *Ethics for a New Millennium* is a handbook for human survival, which begs to be put into action with imagination and rigor, by being translated into a practical program of training and education.

The second was in March 2000, when His Holiness met with a group of neuroscientists, psychologists, philosophers, and Buddhist practitioners in Dharamsala in India, for the eighth in the series of conferences organized by the Mind and Life Institute. These ground-breaking meetings have constituted the most profound and important collaboration ever to have taken place between Buddhism and the sciences. The 2000 dialogue studied destructive emotions and led directly to a number of far-reaching initiatives in research into the effects and applications of meditation training. Experiments took place the following year in the United States in Madison, Wisconsin, on the effects of meditation practices on brain function, which involved experienced Tibetan Buddhist practitioners and received attention not only from the world press but also from prestigious scientific journals. Many people began to realize the extraordinary repercussions if the universal value of Buddhist contemplative techniques for training the mind in meditation and compassion were to become more widely recognized. The momentum of this seminal meeting in 2000 continues still; in 2005 His Holiness addressed the Society for Neuroscience in Washington, DC, and the following year published *The Universe in a Single Atom: The Convergence of Science and Spirituality,* wherein he describes this encounter of science and spirituality as having "far-reaching potential to help humanity meet the challenges before us."

Lastly, after visiting Poland, Germany, Norway, Denmark, and Sweden in the early summer of 2000, His Holiness traveled to the United States on his last trip abroad before going to France in September. He took part in the massive Folklife Festival, "Tibetan Culture Beyond the Land of Snows," in Washington, DC. There, on July 2, in an hour-long free public speech to fifteen thousand people on the National Mall, he made a powerful plea for inner values, basic human qualities, and concern for others: "In modern times, I feel it is vitally important to promote basic human values. Otherwise in the future, material development will be our only goal, and inner values will be neglected. Then humanity will face many more problems." But what most people there will remember is His Holiness' uncompromising words on the damage to the environment caused by the richer nations and by those striving to copy the American lifestyle and pattern of wealth and consumption. He warned of the long-term global dangers of economic and social inequality at its present scale, and he spoke explicitly about Washington's poor. To a mounting tide of applause, he said: "This is the nation's capital, in the richest country in the world, but in some sections of society here people are very, very poor. This is not just morally wrong, but practically wrong...We need to close the gap between the rich and poor."

A revolutionary formula for a saner and more peaceful world, a groundbreaking collaboration of science and spirituality, and a deep and outspoken concern for humanity and the planet—these powerful examples of the Dalai Lama's compassionate involvement with the world all formed part of the background to his visit to France in 2000.

THE CONTEXT OF THE TEACHINGS

Beginning in 1991, His Holiness the Dalai Lama began to give a regular series of Buddhist teachings for a federation of the Tibetan Buddhist centers in France, and in 2000 it was the turn of the centers grouped geographically in the Golfe du Lion region, near Montpellier in southern France.[1] The honor of arranging His Holiness' teachings fell to Lerab Ling, which is Rigpa's main international center, founded by Sogyal Rinpoche and now at the heart of his work. Chosen and blessed by Kyabjé Dilgo Khyentse Rinpoche and consecrated in 1991 by Kyabjé Dodrupchen Rinpoche, Lerab Ling became the site for Rigpa's summer retreats from 1992 onward, since when many eminent Tibetan Buddhist masters have been invited to teach and retreats have taken place continuously. In the ancient Occitan language, the original name for the site means "the place of springs," and its wooded slopes, streams, and meadows lie on the edge of the immense Larzac plateau, most of which is national parkland.

In September 2000 for two weeks, monks from the Namgyal Monastery led by Khamtrul Rinpoche and their abbot Jadho Rinpoche, conducted an intensive group practice at Lerab Ling, a drupchen of Vajrakilaya according to the terma revelation of Lerab Lingpa, Sogyal Rinpoche's previous incarnation. His Holiness' arrival was timed to allow him to preside over the final day and culmination of the drupchen and to grant the empowerment for this practice the following day. Also present was Kyabjé Trulshik Rinpoche, from whom His Holiness was receiving the transmission of *The Trilogy of Finding Comfort and Ease,* an important work by the great Dzogchen master Longchen Rabjam (1308–64). This was the context for his choosing to comment on and explain one of the texts in the trilogy, *Finding Comfort and Ease in Meditation on the Great Perfection,* in Tibetan *Samten Ngalso.*

The teachings of Dzogchen, or Great Perfection, are treasured at the heart of the "Ancient," or Nyingma, tradition of Tibetan Buddhism, which dates back to the eighth or ninth century, when Buddhism was established in Tibet by the great Guru Padmasambhava, King Trisong Detsen, and the scholar-abbot Shantarakshita. The origins of Dzogchen are traced to the primordial buddha, Samantabhadra, from whom a living heritage of wisdom has been transmitted from master to disciple in an unbroken lineage down to the present day. Dzogchen is described as "the primordial state, that state of total awakening that is the heart-essence of all the buddhas and all spiritual paths, and the summit of an individual's spiritual evolution."[2] While considered the very pinnacle of all teachings, the practice of Dzogchen is also renowned as particularly clear, effective, and relevant to the modern world and the needs of today.

His Holiness divided his teachings into two sections. First, he gave an introduction to the key principles of the Buddhadharma. Second, to demonstrate how to take the teachings to heart and practice them, he began to explain the root text of *Finding Comfort and Ease in Meditation on the Great Perfection.* At the same time, he gave the oral transmission for the whole of the root text.

In choosing to teach on a text by Longchenpa, His Holiness was going to the very heart of the ancient Nyingma tradition and its Dzogchen teachings. The "omniscient" Longchen Rabjam was one of the greatest scholars and realized masters of Tibet, who gathered and synthesized all the traditions of Dzogchen in Tibet, setting out a complete foundation for the study and practice of Dzogchen in his extraordinary writings such as *The Seven Treasuries, The Trilogy of Finding Comfort and Ease, The Trilogy of Natural Freedom,* and *The Three Inner Essences.*[3] The great Dzogchen master Patrul Rinpoche (1808–87), to whom His Holiness often refers in his teachings, wrote:

> So did this omniscient master reveal in his sublime works
> The entire range of the Victorious One's teachings.
> Never before had any of the wise masters of India or Tibet
> Left such a legacy to the world.

Nyoshul Khenpo (1932–99), who was such an authority on Longchenpa and his works that many of his students regarded him as Longchenpa in the flesh, wrote: "Longchenpa appeared in this world as a second primordial buddha Samantabhadra, transmitting teachings with the lion's roar of the three categories of Dzogchen...His works are indistinguishable from the words of the Victorious One and constitute an inconceivable body of secrets. Simply to read them causes realization of the wisdom mind that is the true nature of reality to arise in one's mind."

Longchenpa composed *The Trilogy on Finding Comfort and Ease* at his hermitage of Orgyen Dzong, located at Gangri Thökar in central Tibet to the south of Lhasa, where he taught and composed many of his works such as *The Seven Treasuries.* In his own catalog of his writings, dividing them into outer, inner, and secret, he placed *The Trilogy* in the secret category and within the more general explanations that, he said, "serve to show how the Dzogchen path, together with its fruition, is in accord with, and incorporates, all the other vehicles, so that one can understand the ultimate point of these vehicles: that they are simply skillful preliminary paths leading to the path of Dzogpachenpo."[4]

Nyoshul Khenpo gathered Longchenpa's works on Dzogchen into three groups:[5]

> First are those that represent the extensive, scholarly, or pandita's approach, principally *The Seven Treasuries* and *The Trilogy of Natural Freedom.* This group also contains commentaries such

as Longchenpa's overview of the tantra *The All-Creating Monarch,* which constitute the portion of his writings concerning *the category of mind.* The portion of his writings related to *the category of space* in this extensive scholarly mode includes a short text known as *The Vast Array of Space,* along with his commentary.

The second group is that of the profound, *kusuli's* approach, that is, the streamlined approach of a Dzogchen yogi. This group consists of the three Yangtik cycles that Longchenpa revealed: *The Innermost Heart Drop of the Guru (Lama Yangtik), The Innermost Heart Drop of the Dakini (Khandro Yangtik),* and *The Innermost Heart Drop of Profundity (Zapmo Yangtik).* These teachings are designed for the very unelaborate lifestyle of a wandering yogi or someone in retreat.

The third group consists of the teachings that are the underpinnings of both the extensive, scholar's approach and the profound, yogi's approach. These are Longchenpa's teachings on the graduated path—*lamrim.* The most well known is *The Trilogy of Finding Comfort and Ease,* which comprises *Finding Comfort and Ease in the Nature of Mind (Semnyi Ngalso), Finding Comfort and Ease in Meditation (Samten Ngalso),* and *Finding Comfort and Ease in the Illusoriness of Things (Gyuma Ngalso).*

Longchenpa explains the sequence of the three works in *The Trilogy of Finding Comfort and Ease:*

> In the beginning, when we first set out on the path, it is important that we establish a good foundation in the Dharma, and that is why the thirteen chapters of *Finding Comfort and Ease in the Nature of Mind* offer an elaborate explanation of the bases for *the view* that is beyond the two extremes, from the difficulty of finding the freedoms and advantages onward. At the same time, they also explain aspects of the stages of the path and fruition.
>
> Once we have understood the ground, we can begin *meditation* on the path, and so the four chapters of *Finding Comfort and Ease in Meditation* offer a step-by-step explanation of the places where *meditation* can be practiced, the types of individual

suited to the practice, the techniques we can use in meditation, and the types of concentration that can be achieved.

While this path is being practiced it is important to have teachings on nonattachment and nonclinging toward phenomena. So, as a support, a clear and elaborate presentation of the stages of *action* is given in the eight chapters of *Finding Comfort and Ease in the Illusoriness of Things.* These chapters reveal, thoroughly and without any error, how to relate to all phenomena, and how to experience them as the eight similes of illusoriness.[6]

His Holiness frequently quotes Longchenpa's works in his teachings on Dzogchen in the West and in 1989 based his teachings in San Jose, California, on sections from *The Precious Treasury of the Dharmadhatu.*[7] When he visited the Dzogchen monastery in south India in December 2000, at the invitation of His Eminence the Seventh Dzogchen Rinpoche, he also gave a transmission and teaching on both *Finding Comfort and Ease in the Nature of Mind* and *Finding Comfort and Ease in Meditation.*

THE SEQUENCE OF THE TEACHINGS

The Dalai Lama's five-day teaching, entitled "The Path to Enlightenment," took place close to Lerab Ling on a site that was given the name Lerab Gar. An enormous teaching tent stood surrounded by other tents housing restaurants, information resources, publications, an exhibition on the history of Rigpa, services, and the press. Seventy percent of the audience of over ten thousand came from France and the rest from twenty-one other countries. Over a hundred lamas and geshes, monks from the Namgyal, Gomang, and Gyutö monasteries, and two hundred Western monks and nuns attended, along with a hundred friends of His Holiness and Tibet.[8] Two hundred people from the surrounding villages were invited to attend the teachings for a day. Sogyal Rinpoche conveyed the feeling of those present in his welcome to His Holiness:

Here in France we know you will feel at home and among

friends. France is a land that has been touched deeply by the Dharma and its healing message, and that has opened its arms to embrace Tibet and the Tibetans...People have gathered here from all over the world. They realize that you are one of the greatest scholars and Buddhist teachers of our time, and so they know that to receive these teachings from you is the opportunity of a lifetime. We rejoice that these teachings are taking place in the year of the sixtieth anniversary of your enthronement and also in the millennial year 2000. It seems to remind us of your importance for the world, the human race, and its future.

His Holiness began by apologizing for the late start due to the unusual weather conditions. "We have started slightly late on this first day of the teachings," he announced. "This has been because of all kinds of difficulties due to the climate. I am sorry about this, although it is not really my fault. You seem to be in some difficulty; I probably look more comfortable, but it's not very warm up here either." In fact, a devastating storm had hit the south coast of France the previous afternoon, causing severe flooding and damage in Montpellier. Driving rain and gale force winds had flattened the smaller tents on the site, flooded the main tent, and turned much of the area into a quagmire. However, the audience had been so intent on getting there that the teaching was able to begin after a delay of merely an hour.

His Holiness then set the scene for his teachings by speaking about the common objectives of the different religions and the value of maintaining one's tradition and learning from other faiths. He dwelled on the themes of personal transformation, human intelligence and reason, and the importance of altruism and love, speaking of the power of the mind in attaining true happiness. From time to time throughout his teachings, he would strike a personal note or tell an anecdote, as he deftly introduced the key principles of Buddhadharma in a way that was accessible for those present. The topics he explained were: the four noble truths, interdependence, absolute and relative truth, shunyata, the nature of consciousness, the continuity of mind and matter, the disturbing emotions, and enlightenment. These all form the first part of this book: Key Principles of the Buddhadharma.

It was on the third day that His Holiness started to give a commentary on Longchen Rabjam's *Finding Comfort and Ease in Meditation on the Great Perfection,* and these teachings comprise the second part of this book. He began by speaking on the schools of Buddhism in Tibet and the great scholars and realized masters of the Nyingma tradition. This led him to present the unique features of the Great Perfection as compared to other vehicles and the distinction made between ordinary mind and the pure awareness of rigpa, quoting the Great Fifth Dalai Lama as he did so.

Longchenpa's text is composed of three parts: the *locations* for cultivating meditation, the individual *meditator* or practitioner, and the *Dharma* to be practiced. His Holiness commented on the first two parts in detail. Here he spoke on renunciation, following a spiritual teacher, overcoming and transforming the negative emotions, mindfulness and vigilance, the different views of selflessness, anger and patience, impermanence and death. He then came to the third part, the main practice, and the four kinds of preliminary: (1) renunciation, (2) compassion and bodhichitta, (3) pure vision, and (4) guru yoga.

In connection with the preliminary of bodhichitta, on the following day His Holiness gave a teaching on compassion and bodhichitta, which grew progressively more moving till he spoke very personally of the value and benefit of bodhichitta, at which point he wept for a few moments. He then conferred the bodhisattva vow, in the most beautiful ceremony based on Asanga's *Bodhisattva Stages.* During the series of questions and responses between the master and disciples that form part of the ceremony, His Holiness introduced an air of lightness and comedy by improvising a set of wry, but probably truthful, replies on behalf of the audience. For the bodhisattva vow ceremony, His Holiness' throne and table had been garlanded with white and yellow Tokyo lilies, and at the conclusion of the transmission of the vow, His Holiness stood on the throne and cast flowers to the buddhas and bodhisattvas in all directions, imploring everyone not to let their aspirations be mediocre or ordinary but to make the most heartfelt prayers to reach buddhahood for the benefit of both themselves and others.

That same afternoon, in light of the teaching on the preliminaries of pure vision and guru yoga, His Holiness conferred the empowerment of Padmasambhava and his Eight Manifestations, the mind sadhana of *The Union of All Innermost Essences* from the cycle of pure visions of the Great Fifth Dalai Lama (1617–82), an empowerment he had granted when giving Dzogchen teachings at Rigpa's request in 1982 in Paris and in 1989 in San Jose. His Holiness spoke about the Great Fifth Dalai Lama and his pure visions, which are entitled *Bearing the Seal of Secrecy.* The eight manifestations of Guru Rinpoche, or Pema Tötreng, as listed in the empowerment are: the lotus-born vidyadhara Padmakara, the bhikshu Padmasambhava, the learned Loden Choksé, the magnificent Padma Gyalpo, the yogi Nyima Özer, the enlightened lord Shakya Sengé, the wrathful Sengé Dradok, and the embodiment of "crazy wisdom," Dorjé Drolö. In Dharamsala in 2004, when explaining the importance of invoking and praying to Guru Rinpoche, His Holiness spoke of the unique inspiration that the Great Fifth Dalai Lama drew from Guru Padmasambhava:

> The precious guru Padmasambhava—*Lopön Rinpoche*—was not only endowed with all the true qualities of a great spiritual guide—knowledge, compassion and infinite capacity—but he was also a great master who commanded extraordinary power. Most of the great historical figures of Tibet, both spiritual and secular, have placed themselves under the compassionate protection of the great master Padmasambhava and received his blessing. The Great Fifth Dalai Lama, for example, clearly had a very special link with Guru Rinpoche, and the thirteenth Dalai Lama, too, quite evidently enjoyed a unique connection with the precious master.[9]

Immediately after the empowerment, His Holiness then embarked on the main practice from the third part of *Finding Comfort and Ease in Meditation on the Great Perfection*: the Dharma to be practiced. Straightaway he taught on the Great Perfection, the clear light, and the ultimate nature of the mind, introducing the *higher two truths,* identifying the clear light as the profound feature of both highest yoga tantra and Dzogchen, and clarifying the place of analytical meditation and the Middle Way view. At this juncture, he quoted from Longchen Rabjam's

Seven Treasuries and referred to instructions by the third Dodrupchen, Jikmé Tenpé Nyima (1865–1926), for whose writings His Holiness always expresses the deepest admiration and whom he invariably quotes when teaching on Dzogchen. Dodrupchen Jikmé Tenpé Nyima was one of the foremost masters in the Nyingma tradition in the early twentieth century and was himself a student of legendary figures such as Patrul Rinpoche and Jamyang Khyentse Wangpo. In shaping his own understanding of the profound correspondences between highest yoga tantra and Dzogchen, the Dalai Lama wrote, "reading Dodrupchen was as if he were stroking my head in confirmation, giving me confidence that my insight was not unfounded."[10]

On the morning of the final day of the teachings, Kyabjé Trulshik Rinpoche led everyone present in a long-life ceremony for His Holiness. This was especially meaningful, as every year Kyabjé Trulshik Rinpoche accomplishes a retreat for His Holiness' longevity at the Maratika Cave in Nepal, where Padmasambhava attained the stage of *vidyadhara of immortal life.* The actual ceremony, entitled *Sublime Vase of Nectar of Immortality,* was compiled by Trulshik Rinpoche himself from the long-life practice *Light of Immortality,* a terma revelation from the Northern Terma tradition, along with elements from Lhatsün Namkha Jikmé's pure visions, a dream revelation of Minling Terchen Gyurmé Dorjé, and the Sangwa Gyachen visions of the Great Fifth Dalai Lama. It was chosen for this occasion by His Holiness, and it was performed, for the first time in the West, with meticulous perfection and grace by the Namgyal monks, just as it would have been in Dharamsala. Two features stood out: the deep rapport and devotion between Trulshik Rinpoche and His Holiness and also the quality of completeness created by the combined presence of His Holiness, Trulshik Rinpoche, the Namgyal monks, His Holiness' associates from Dharamsala, supporters of Tibet, and the whole assembly. This was the only longevity ceremony of such scope carried out in the West to mark the sixtieth anniversary year of the Dalai Lama's enthronement.

It was the weekend, and, learning that there were some people who had just arrived, His Holiness presented a masterful summary of the teachings so far, including themes such as happiness and suffering, understanding interdependence, altruism and love, the essence of religion, the view and conduct of the Buddhadharma, caution on the spiritual path, and the need to maintain authenticity.

His Holiness then continued to deepen the teaching on Dzogchen, clarifying the wisdom of rigpa, the introduction to the nature of mind, the view of Dzogchen, essence, nature and compassion, and many other key points of Dzogchen practice. As well as quoting from Dodrupchen Jikmé Tenpé Nyima, His Holiness read a passage from the writings of Tulku Tsullo, or Tsultrim Zangpo (1884–1957), a disciple of Dodrupchen and Tertön Sogyal Lerab Lingpa. Speaking later to the directors of studies at Lerab Ling about how to implement a Rimé, unbiased, approach in practical terms, His Holiness made mention of Tulku Tsullo:

> In my own experience, when I read a Nyingma text written by a great Nyingma teacher who does not know the terminology of other traditions, it can create confusion for me. When I read a pure Geluk lama, who only knows about the Geluk tradition, it is not much help either in developing a deeper understanding of other traditions. However, as I mentioned earlier, there are some remarkable teachers such as Dodrupchen Jikmé Tenpé Nyima, and particularly his student, Tsullo. His background was Nyingma, but at the same time he was familiar with the Geluk tradition. Tsullo knew all about Lama Tsongkhapa's way of presenting things and the terminology involved, and so he often makes the connections in his writings.
>
> There is another author who has a similar grasp of the different traditions. I just received a book from Tibet by Nyengön Tulku Sungrap. He was a lama from the Geluk tradition, who at the same time received teaching from the previous Tertön Sogyal Rinpoche and other Nyingma lamas. He had a real experience and through this experience developed a deep respect and admiration for the Dzogchen tradition. In his work, he draws out comparisons, and so it becomes very clear.
>
> Say, for example, individuals who are already familiar with the Nyingma and Dzogchen teachings, and especially *trekchö,* study such comparative explanations. If they then come across

the explanation of emptiness or clear light according to the work of Lama Tsongkhapa, they will be able to connect and correlate one with the other. Once these students have a more complete picture, if they receive teachings from a Geluk scholar, they will already have the basis for understanding. Subsequently they can receive further explanation from a Geluk lama, or from a Sakya lama on "the inseparability of samsara and nirvana," for example. Even though the lamas may not know all these different traditions, at least on the student's side there will already be some background. Then, with the help of these different teachers, the student's knowledge can increase. That is the way, I think, to create genuine Rimé practitioners.

His Holiness concluded the teachings by granting the oral transmission for the remaining part of the main practice and concluding practices from *Finding Comfort and Ease in Meditation on the Great Perfection.*

Throughout these five days, His Holiness gave the impression of being impelled by a singular inspiration, and he did not allot any time for questions and answers. His closing words were: "To sum up, I think that the main point is to try to be a good human being. This is the way to give meaning to our present existence and to all the existences to come… At any rate, as the Buddha said, it is up to us to travel the path. It is entirely in our hands: we are our own guide and our own protector. So, be diligent in your spiritual practice." Finally, Sogyal Rinpoche thanked everyone and dedicated the whole event: "By the truth of these teachings, may Your Holiness' deepest aspirations and hopes for the Tibetan people be fulfilled. May they find freedom, may their suffering be ended, and may you return soon to Tibet." The entire audience gave His Holiness a standing ovation.

When it came time for His Holiness to depart from Lerab Ling, a squad of stout uniformed policemen scrambled into line to have their photo taken with him. Catching sight of one of the officers who had a handlebar moustache worthy of Salvador Dalí or Kaiser Wilhelm, His Holiness leaned over and tweaked it, a playful glint in his eye.

His Holiness then took part in an interreligious gathering in the neighboring town of Lodève, an event that became a milestone in interfaith understanding for the area and was widely covered in the national newspapers. He spoke on "Human Values, the Heart of Religion." From there, he went to Montpellier, home to one of France's oldest universities (the medical school is Western Europe's oldest center of medical learning), and now a city known for new industries and information technology. His Holiness gave a public talk, entitled "Peace of Mind, the Source of Happiness," which was attended by over five thousand people. On this occasion he was introduced by Jean-Claude Carrière, the well-known scriptwriter, author, and dramatist, who has written a book, *The Power of Buddhism,*[11] based on a series of dialogues with the Dalai Lama in Dharamsala. Once again, His Holiness made the link between inner and outer peace and in particular emphasized how vital it is to develop mastery over the emotions and to nurture the true qualities of a human being. At the end of the talk, His Holiness visited the adjacent hall where he had been relayed on video to another thousand people or more. Striding briskly toward the hall, with his security team sprinting to catch up, he climbed onto a podium and, in two minutes, encapsulated the heart of his talk. The atmosphere in the hall was alive with appreciation at his gesture of coming to address a second audience, and, as he left, he kept plunging into the crowd to shake hands, as if he were somehow attached to each of the people in the room, and each step he made toward the door took him no nearer. If the applause in the main hall had been rapturous, here it bordered on the overwhelming.

His Holiness' teaching "The Path to Enlightenment," given on September 20–24, 2000, was translated live into French by Matthieu Ricard, and the transcript was then translated into English by Ane Samten Palmo. A Tibetan transcription of the teachings was made in Dharamsala under the supervision of Ven. Geshe Lhakdor, the main English translator at the teachings in France. On the basis of this, the translation was then revised, with reference to the recording of His Holiness' own words, by Richard Barron (Lama Chökyi Nyima) and Adam Pearcey. For the sake of completeness and with His Holiness' blessing, a translation of Longchenpa's *Finding Comfort and Ease in Meditation on the Great Perfection* has been included here at the end of His Holiness' teaching. This translation is by Adam Pearcey, based on an earlier translation made jointly with B. Alan Wallace in 2000. A number of difficult points and references from the teachings and this text have been graciously clarified by Tulku Thondup Rinpoche, Ringu Tulku Rinpoche, Geshe Thupten Jinpa, and Geshe Tashi Tsering.

The appendix offers a historical perspective, based on His Holiness' own explanation of the history and significance of the Vajrayana practices—the empowerment, the drupchen, and the mendrup—that took place at Lerab Ling.

All in all, His Holiness' teachings and his visit to the south of France surpassed everyone's expectations and had repercussions on various levels. For France, this visit by His Holiness witnessed a deepening and maturing of the interest in the Buddhist teachings. His Holiness himself and others commented on the rapt attention and appreciativeness of the audience, who frequently applauded and at the end rose in a long, standing ovation. With the largest gathering to date for a Buddhist teaching by His Holiness in France, news of Lerab Gar was broadcast as far away as Korea and Tibet. For Europe and beyond, these events underlined the respect that Buddhism has increasingly won in the modern world as a great source of wisdom, offered with no notion of conversion but simply to benefit human beings and bring them ever closer to their ultimate nature.

PART ONE

KEY PRINCIPLES OF THE BUDDHADHARMA

CHAPTER 1

INTRODUCTION

FIRST OF ALL, let me tell you how happy I am to be able to spend these few days here with you, my spiritual brothers and sisters, and speak about the Dharma. You have come from every corner of the world, which probably has not been so easy as you are doubtless all very busy, and you have had to overcome difficulties of many kinds in order to get here. There are a number of you as well who have worked to make this event possible. So let me welcome and thank you all.

I would like to say one thing at the outset. You have all come here to meet me, and if your purpose in doing so was because you expected to hear me say something quite amazing or to receive some kind of blessing from me that would instantly remove all your suffering and grant you true happiness—I'm afraid you were mistaken. Here we are basically all just human beings, and we are all the same. Our minds work in the same way, and we experience the same kind of emotions and feelings. There is one other thing we have in common and which we need to be aware of: that we all possess the capacity to become good human beings and to make our lives happy. It is up to us. Equally, we have the power to render our lives unhappy, and not only to experience individual misfortune and sorrow but also to cause pain and misery to those around us and bring ruin to others. Looking at it like this, there is no difference between us.

So what do *I* have to offer? I am just a practitioner of the Buddhadharma, a simple Buddhist monk. I am now sixty-six years of age. Ever since I was about ten or fifteen years old, I have felt a conviction and a sincere interest in the teachings of Buddha. Over the years I have not been able to practice a great deal, but still I have tried, as much as possible, to persevere in the practice. What it has taught me is that all of us are the same, in wanting to find happiness and to avoid suffering. Since we wish to be happy and to steer clear of suffering, naturally we will be keen to know what will truly be of benefit as we live our lives. We will want to know the causes and conditions that lead to either a happy life or an unhappy one. And this is where I do have some slight experience, which is what I would like to share with you now. It is possible that some of you may benefit from my words, and if you do find something helpful, please take it into consideration. But if you find no benefit in what I say, forget it. There's no harm in that, is there?

THE COMMON OBJECTIVE OF ALL RELIGIONS

During the course of my life, on account of my training in the Buddhist teachings, I have gained some experiential understanding; I have thought a lot about these topics, and this is what I would like to share with you. However, if, as I speak, I relate my experience to the Buddhist teachings, it is not in order to propagate Buddhism. That is not my intention, not even in the slightest. I have reasons for this.

First, among human beings there is an enormous variety of mentalities and interests, and over the last three to four thousand years, numerous great religious and spiritual traditions have flourished on earth. Many of them are still alive and active on the planet. Throughout their history, they have served the spiritual needs of millions of people. They still do so and will certainly continue to do so in the future. If, on account of our diverse capacities and inclinations, there are these different spiritual traditions with their individual views and philosophies, it can only be of immense benefit to the individual. This is why I feel convinced that people who adhere to the spiritual tradition of their parents, and live according to its view and philosophy, will find that it suits them very well.

Second, while the spiritual traditions of the world do have different views and philosophies, whatever their differences—and some of them are quite major—we find that the ethical training is mostly the same. For example, when it comes to cultivating love, compassion, patience, and contentment, or the observance of self-discipline and ethical principles, most spiritual traditions seem to be more or less the same. This is why I feel that, from the point of view of their potential to benefit people and help them develop into good human beings, most spiritual traditions are indeed the same, and this remains my firm conviction. This is a good reason for staying with the religion we have inherited from our parents.

Otherwise, changing one's religion is a serious matter and can be problematic; in some cases it can lead to real difficulties. Whenever I give talks in Western countries to people of different religious backgrounds and I explain the Buddhist teachings, my aim is never to proselytize on behalf of Buddhism. In fact, from time to time, I do have slight misgivings about teaching Buddhism in the West. Why? Because in these countries there are already established spiritual traditions, whether Christian, Jewish, or Muslim. If someone appears and talks about something like Buddhism, in certain cases it may cause people to have doubts about their own faith that they never had before. That is why I feel a little uneasy and apprehensive.

As for the spiritual traditions and religions that do exist around the world, two dimensions or aspects can be discerned. One aspect consists of the metaphysical or philosophical views. The other aspect comprises the precepts we need to follow in order to put these views into practice. This means the regular practice of training the mind, day by day, together with the appropriate kind of speech and physical behavior that go along with it. I believe that the major faith traditions generally exhibit these two aspects.

Sometimes you might wonder: What is the point of having such a diversity of metaphysical views and philosophies? Their aim is to tame this mind of ours and help us develop into good human beings. From the point of view of training the mind, all spiritual traditions are more or less the same and possess this same potential. It is only when we discuss them from the standpoint of the views and philosophies themselves that their differences stand out.

DIFFERENT PATHS

From the point of view of the actual training of the mind, I feel that it is difficult to say that one particular religion is better or worse, or higher or lower, than another. They are all there to suit our various capacities and interests, and it is because of these differences that someone can say, "For me, personally, this spiritual tradition is the most profound and the most appropriate." But it would be difficult, I feel, to make the claim that any one religion would be just as profound, or not so effective, for everyone as a whole.

On the other hand, if we talk about the views and philosophies of the various religious traditions, I think we can describe one tradition as being vast and profound and another as being more concise or succinct. So from the standpoint of metaphysics and philosophy, it would seem permissible to establish some kind of hierarchy. And yet, however vast and profound it may be, when it comes to putting a given view or philosophy into practice, if it does not suit a particular individual's mind, it will not inspire any profound experience nor frankly will it be of much use. Conversely, even though a philosophical view may not be labeled profound and vast, if it helps a person to develop his or her mind, then truly it is profound as far as that person is concerned.

Let me give you an example. Even within the Buddhist teachings, there are numerous philosophical systems. In the Mahayana tradition there are two principal systems—the Mind Only (Chittamatra) school and the Middle Way (Madhyamaka) school. These two schools both convey the ultimate intention and vision of the Buddha, and both are based on his words. Yet at first glance, they might seem to be in complete disagreement. The Mind Only school considers certain aspects of the Middle Way school of philosophy to be a kind of nihilism, while from the latter school's point of view, the Mind Only school falls into the extremes of either materialism or nihilism. So there do appear to be contradictions, even great differences, between these two schools. But they were taught by the same teacher! So you might well wonder, "How are we to reconcile this? What are we to make of it?"

The point is that when Lord Buddha taught the Dharma, he recognized among his followers a diversity of capacities and inclinations and saw just how important it was for his teachings to adapt accordingly. It was to address this need that he taught different kinds of view, and so this is how we can understand and explain the seeming contradiction.

ONE TRUTH, ONE RELIGION

The same principle can help us consider another important point. Individual practitioners of the various religions need to believe and have faith that their religion is for them the ultimate truth and the only authentic teaching. They might call it "the one and only truth, the one and only religion." Yet since all the various spiritual traditions and philosophies exist on account of people's diverse mentalities and interests, it follows that they must all, in a sense, be "true." But if there are all these authentic religions and philosophies, and yet now only one of them is regarded as correct, isn't this a contradiction? It seems we have to accommodate two ways of thinking simultaneously: the idea that all religions are good and the idea that the religion we practice is the authentic one.

As I mentioned earlier, within the framework of the Buddhist teachings, a person for whom the Mind Only school is the most appropriate and whose mind is inclined toward this approach will be a follower of this school and therefore reckon it to be the best. Adherents of the Mind Only school will employ the view of their school to assess the ultimate point of view of the Middle Way school, namely, the ultimate state of buddhahood, and they will conclude that the meaning of the Middle Way school, as explained by its followers, is not authentic. That is what they are bound to say, because they feel that the Mind Only school is the approach most suited to their capacities and inclinations. Since this view serves them in such a way, they will think: "This is the most profound; *this* is the best. And so ours must be the unmistaken and ultimate explanation of the state of buddhahood." They would have to feel this way, wouldn't they?

At the same time, someone who is more impartial will know that the followers of Lord Buddha, whichever of the four schools of Buddhist philosophy they uphold—Vaibhashika, Sautrantika, Mind Only, or Middle Way—are all followers of one and the same teacher, all of them dependent upon his kindness. So this impartial person will view the followers of any Buddhist school with equal faith, devotion, and respect.

Therefore, we can say that the statement that there is only one truth is entirely valid and authentic for a given individual, from his or her own personal point of view. But from a global point of view, referring to a group of many individuals, we have to say that there are many truths and many authentic paths. In this way, I feel that there is no contradiction. To sum up: From the point of view of a single individual or of your own spiritual practice, there can be one truth. But from the point of view of a multitude, there can be many.

I believe the different religions and philosophies of the world—Christianity, Judaism, Islam, or any of the many branches of Hinduism—are all extremely beneficial and truly help many people. And so I admire and respect them all. It is never my intention to denigrate or find fault with other traditions. Of course, sometimes if I meet a very sectarian or stubborn person, I may feel they are exaggerating and be slightly irritated, but these are isolated cases! Overall, I have a deep reverence and appreciation for all the great religious traditions of the world. So I would like to invite you, my spiritual friends, to think likewise. We should recognize that all the different religions are truly wonderful and serve to help many people. There is a benefit for us, as well, in developing such appreciation for other religions. This is an important point.

Having said all this, it can happen that someone whose parents follow one religion may decide to adopt another. We could take the case of an individual from a Christian family who becomes a Buddhist practitioner, because he or she finds that this tradition suits his or her mentality and inclinations. He or she might even seek ordination as a Buddhist monk or nun and choose the path of a "homeless one" over that of a householder. This person's family tradition was Christian, but among the millions of Christians in the world, there must, of course, be a wide variety of capacities and inclinations. But what is important is that those who decide to take up the practice of Buddhism maintain respect for the traditions of their parents. It would not be desirable for people to take up a new religion and use that as a reason to act and speak as though their former religion were useless. Their former religion is still benefiting countless people now.

LEARNING FROM OTHER SPIRITUAL TRADITIONS

I believe that there is an obvious benefit to learning about spiritual traditions and religions other than our own. For one thing, we can find in other religions a great inspiration that deepens our understanding of our own faith. I find this so often to be the case. Some of my friends who are Christian practitioners have told me how they incorporate certain points of Buddhist contemplative practice into their spiritual life and how this has helped deepen their own practice. In the same way, too, I think that the Buddhist community, and especially the monastic community, can learn from their Christian brothers and sisters—particularly from their example of community service, in the fields of education and healthcare, and in providing humanitarian aid, all of which they do with such great dedication and commitment. This is definitely an example from which our Buddhist community can learn, and I believe this is extremely important.

So it is with this background of acknowledging our need to foster harmony among the different religious traditions and cultivate a pure and positive attitude toward them, that over the next few days I will speak a little about the teachings of Buddhism. Of course, when I speak from the Buddhist standpoint, I will express philosophical views that are quite different from those held by other religions, for example, the belief in a Creator, which is not accepted in Buddhism. However, in explaining these views, my aim is to clarify the Buddhist philosophical point of view and in no way to create controversy or refute the points of view of other religions.

THE PRELIMINARIES TO THE TEACHING

Usually, when I give general Buddhist teachings, I sit on a chair, and I tend to prefer it that way. In that case, there is no need to begin with prayers. However, today, as you will have seen, I am seated on a throne. The reason for this is purely out of respect for the words of the Buddha, the vast and profound teaching he gave more than two thousand five hundred years ago, and not because of any sense I may have of being someone important. You may have noticed that before sitting on the throne, I made three prostrations in front of it. In so doing, I was paying homage to the words of the Buddha that I am going to interpret. If I were really some very important person, there would be no need for me to perform such prostrations. It would be enough for me simply to sit up here and look impressive. But if the truth be known, I consider myself just a very simple Buddhist monk, a follower of the Buddha who interprets and shares his words.

Traditionally, whenever a teacher takes his seat on a throne to teach, he recites this verse from the sutras:

> Regard all compounded things in this way—
> Like stars, hallucinations, and flickering lamps,
> Like illusions, dewdrops, and bubbles on water,
> Like dream images, flashes of lightning, and clouds.[12]

The teacher climbs onto the throne, recites these lines, and then snaps his fingers. At that instant, he recalls the impermanence of everything; he reflects on suffering and brings to mind the lack of identity in things. Otherwise, when you sit on a throne, there is a risk that you might start to feel proud of yourself. The mind of the one who explains the teachings must be peaceful, tamed, and free from any trace of arrogance or pride.

Of course, some of you here may have been following your spiritual practice with great perseverance and sincerity and gradually progressed through all the levels that lead to spiritual realization. So you may have reached a much higher stage of realization than I have. In which case, it is from you that I should be receiving blessings!

The main point, for each and every one of us, is to tame and train our minds and to put the teachings into practice. In that light, for me to sit on a high throne and fancy myself someone special and different would be a huge mistake. Incidentally, I am not particularly comfortable with all the ostentatious kinds of ceremony we tend to indulge in. In fact, I feel we would be much better off without it. Long ago, after the Lord Buddha had awakened to perfect enlightenment and began turning the wheel of the Dharma, apart from on a few special occasions, as a rule he did not indulge in any ceremony whatsoever. He simply went about barefoot, carrying his alms bowl, walking here and there, as he taught the Dharma. We hear no accounts of the Buddha being chauffeured around in splendor in some ornate chariot.

It was the same in the case of Nagarjuna, who was known as the "second Buddha," and his spiritual son Aryadeva, and with Asanga and his brother Vasubandhu. They were all fully ordained monks, who carried their bowls as they went about begging for alms. Apart from that, it does not seem that they went in for any fuss or ceremony. I often joke that we don't hear about the glorious protector Arya Nagarjuna's business manager or his treasurer or private secretary. It is most likely he did not have any. However, in Tibet a custom slowly developed whereby spiritual and political roles merged, so that people were at one and the same time lamas and chieftains. This gave rise to a lot of elaborate ceremony and spectacle. Nevertheless, there have been many learned and highly accomplished Tibetan masters, from all traditions—Sakya, Geluk, Kagyü, and Nyingma—who were impeccable upholders of the victory banner of the Dharma. For the most part, these masters acted quite ordinarily and lived as pure and simple monks. All the more reason, I feel, for us not to let ourselves get carried away with ceremony and ostentation but to exercise restraint and caution.

The scriptures state that the Dharma, or spirituality, does not depend primarily on some kind of physical expression, like attire or deportment, nor on some verbal expression, such as recitation and chanting, but is experienced, first and foremost, on the basis of the mind. They say that, rather than emphasizing some outward expression, the Dharma consists principally of special methods for analyzing and watching the mind so as to transform it.

It is true that the methods given in the Buddhist teachings do not focus predominantly on external verbal acts such as reciting prayers and mantras, or on physical acts such as prostrations, and the like. Rather, the teachings are put into practice by means of your mind. This makes the process a little more difficult. Another scripture says,

"For this reason, the tradition of the Buddha is a subtle one." Why? you might ask. Because it is always possible for people to behave outwardly like spiritual practitioners, while at the same time harboring negative thoughts unworthy of a real practitioner. Similarly, it is possible for people to recite prayers and mantras continuously, while their minds are simultaneously polluted by all kinds of destructive thoughts. However, if we are practicing something positive in our mind—say we are cultivating faith or compassion, for example—at the same time as that positive quality is generated in our mind, it is quite impossible for us to give rise to a harmful state of mind. By the same token, where there is a negative state of mind, a positive one cannot coexist. So the important point here is that everything is accomplished on the basis of our mind.

Now, to begin with, I will be reciting certain traditional prayers—a homage that calls to mind the qualities of the Buddha's body, speech, and mind; a recitation from the sutras; and a dedication. These are the "three regular prayers" that come before a teaching. Then I will recite the *Heart Sutra* in its Tibetan translation, the homage from *The Ornament of Clear Realization*—its prayer in praise of the "mother" Prajnaparamita—and a prayer of praise from *The Root Verses on Wisdom,* which honors our unsurpassable teacher, the Lord Buddha, as the one who revealed the truth of dependent origination. Those of you who are Buddhists may not know exactly how to chant these verses along with me, but it will be fine if you reflect on the qualities of the gracious Lord Buddha's body, speech, and mind and rest the mind for a moment with a sense of vivid inspiration. If you are not a Buddhist, then just take a moment now to relax.

> Homage to the teacher, the conqueror, the tathagata, the arhat, the perfect Buddha, the glorious and victorious one, the sage of the Shakyas.

Praise to the Prajnaparamita

Through knowledge of all, you guide the hearers who seek for peace toward perfect peace,
Through knowledge of the path, you enable those who benefit beings to bring about the welfare of the world,

Through being endowed with you, the omniscient sages can teach in various ways—
Homage to you, mother of the buddhas and of all the hearers and bodhisattvas.[13]

Homage to the Buddha

He who taught dependent origination—
No cessation and no origination,
No annihilation and no permanence,
No coming and no going,
Neither different nor same—
This thorough calming of conceptual elaborations:
To you, who are supreme speaker
Among all fully enlightened buddhas, I pay homage.[14]

TAKING REFUGE AND GENERATING BODHICHITTA

Someone teaching the Dharma should do so with a completely pure motivation, and someone listening to the teachings should also do so with a completely pure motivation. If the teachings are explained and heard in this authentic way, they can have a beneficial effect in guiding your mind, but, without this pure motivation, there is no such benefit. So let us now, teacher and students, recite this prayer together three times:

In the Buddha, the Dharma, and the Supreme Assembly,
I take refuge until I attain enlightenment.
Through the merit of practicing generosity, and so on,
May I attain buddhahood for the benefit of all beings.

This prayer includes both the taking of refuge and the generation of bodhichitta. Without taking refuge in the Three Jewels, this would not qualify as a Buddhist teaching, and without generating the altruistic aspiration of bodhichitta to seek enlightenment for the sake of all sentient beings, this would not count as a Mahayana teaching. So at the outset of my explaining and your listening to the teachings, we should recite this prayer and so take refuge and arouse bodhichitta.

CHAPTER 2

TRANSFORMING THE MIND

THE TEACHINGS over the days to come will be divided into two parts: a general introduction to the Buddhist teachings, followed by an explanation of how to take these teachings to heart and practice them.

THE THREE JEWELS

As we just saw, without first taking refuge, this teaching does not qualify as a Buddhist teaching at all. This makes it all the more important for us to come to a precise understanding of what is constituted by these "three refuges"—the Buddha, Dharma, and Sangha. The Lord Buddha is said to have been a very special and holy being, who appeared in India about two thousand five hundred years ago. However, we cannot confine our definition of *buddha* simply to this remarkable historical figure. In order to explain "the jewel of the Buddha," first of all we need to introduce the jewel of the Dharma. Once we have grasped what the jewel of the Dharma represents, we will understand that a buddha is someone who has put that jewel of the Dharma into practice and become a holy being endowed with all the consummate qualities of the Dharma that result from renunciation and realization. In fact, it is on the basis of the jewel of the Dharma that we can truly comprehend what is meant by the *Three Jewels*.

To understand what is meant by "the jewel of the Dharma," we need to be aware that the Dharma is twofold—the Dharma of scripture or transmission and the Dharma of realization or experience—and the more important of the two is "the Dharma of realization or experience." We can also say that the jewel of the Dharma refers to two of the four noble truths: the truth of the cessation of suffering and the truth of the path to that cessation. So an understanding of these two truths will naturally form a basis for introducing what is meant by the jewel of the Dharma.

Given that the jewel of the Dharma consists of the qualities of both cessation and the path, let us look at the qualities of the cessation of suffering. This phrase "the qualities of the cessation of suffering" refers to cases in which a given flaw is eliminated and removed through applying an antidote. It follows, then, that we have to understand what exactly has to be eliminated and removed, what are the antidotes that we use to free ourselves, and what means or methods will bring us freedom. It was to help us understand this that, when the Lord Buddha turned the wheel of the Dharma for the first time, he began with the teaching on the four noble truths.

The four noble truths are the cornerstone and the foundation of the Buddhist teachings. They are: the truth of suffering, the truth of the origin of suffering, the truth of the cessation of suffering, and the truth of the path that leads to that cessation. The systematic presentation of these four noble truths is something we need to understand. Given that I intend to go into some detail concerning the four noble truths, I will begin by referring to the twelve links of dependent origination.

The first of these twelve links is fundamental ignorance. To what does this term *fundamental ignorance* refer? In this context, *ignorance* does not mean just a dull confusion nor a simple absence of knowledge. Of course, the term *ignorance* can have many shades of meaning. But the ignorance referred to here is the ignorance that serves as the root cause of conditioned existence and signifies a mistaken or distorted state of mind. Now, whether a state of mind is mistaken or not depends on whether what it takes to be the truth is in fact true. This is the criterion for distinguishing a mistaken from an unmistaken state of mind and also for determining what is helpful and what is harmful.

Given that ignorance, as we define it, is principally a misapprehension of the true nature of things, it means that we need to know what that nature actually is. And because of this need, we have to take all phenomena, both in the outer world and within us, and ask ourselves the following questions: "Is the way they appear actually the way they are in their true nature, or not? Are these two modes—how things really are and how they appear to be—identical or not?" Whichever way you look at it, there is a discrepancy between how things appear and how they truly abide. So it is on this basis that there are what we call two truths—relative or conventional truth and absolute or ultimate truth.

There are a number of ways to explain the meaning of these two truths, but in my remarks I will refer principally to the Middle Way, or Madhyamaka, approach. According to this approach, we need to understand what the ultimate nature, or ground, of reality is. With this understanding, we can then identify the state of mind that confuses and misapprehends the true nature of things as ignorance. And so, to help us understand correctly the systematic arrangement of the four noble truths, we first need to understand the relationship of these two truths, relative and absolute.

TRANSFORMING THE MIND: THE PLAY OF OPPOSITES

Now let me explain things from a different angle. The purpose of the Buddhist teachings is to transform the mind. How is it then that our mind can be transformed? If we are to change or transform something in the external world, we start by understanding how two incompatible items work against, or act in opposition to, one another. So if a certain feature or result is required, what we have to do is reduce whatever its opposite may be. Or if one element is not required, it can be eliminated by enhancing its opposite.

Let us take illness as an example. Of all the chemical substances and organisms in the body, certain ones are beneficial and others are harmful. Once we identify which these are, and how they act upon and undermine one another, then we can introduce a new substance to counter the one that is causing the illness or the pain and so destroy its power. Otherwise, we know that simply reciting, "May the cells that are causing my suffering be eliminated!" will not make them disappear, nor will it do any good to sit there thinking, "May they be gone!" You have to seek out the counter-agent and reinforce it so as to reduce the strength of the disease.

Transforming the mind proceeds along the same lines: by seeking out the counter-agent within your own mind. Given that mind is intangible, you might ask what could this "counter-agent" possibly be? What it amounts to is a different way of perceiving things, an alternative attitude or mental focus. We can take an everyday example. When we see or hear something, depending on our state of mind that day, we can perceive it as either wonderful or horrible. These two states of mind belong to the same consciousness, and they are both focusing on the same object. Yet their ways of perceiving are complete opposites.

Now, if any given state of mind is to be diminished or weakened, this must be achieved by seeking out a state of mind that is its opposite. For example, take anger, covetousness, or malice. Once you are conscious of the drawbacks of such states of mind, and you are keen to reduce them, you need to cultivate their opposites, which are love and affection. If you think about covetousness and malice, they are states where you wish harm upon other people and feel aggressive toward them. The antidote to such attitudes is to focus on others and develop a sincere feeling, "If only they could be well! If only they could be happy! If only they could be full of joy!" This frame of mind is the complete opposite of something like anger or malice, and so it will have the effect of undermining it.

As a rule then, where you have two attitudes that are contrary to one other, one will undermine the other. As much as states of anger or malice increase, to that same extent love and affection will diminish. And to the extent that attitudes of love and affection become stronger, malicious states of mind will be reduced. Therefore, just as we can identify the opposite of something in the external world and use it to change or transform that thing, so we need to transform our minds by seeking out such counter-agents inside our own minds.

PREEMPTING PROBLEMS BEFORE THEY ARISE

One method of achieving this is to prioritize an approach that anticipates and stops something before it can happen. For example, suffering is something that nobody wants, but once some kind of suffering has already set in, it is good to have a method to diminish it. Even more fundamental and effective, however, is to take action *before* the suffering strikes and so ensure that it need not occur in the first place. Whether we are talking about problems in the world around us or about our own psychological or emotional problems, we can preempt them and stop them from happening, thereby avoiding something we don't want.

Let's see how. Regardless of what we are discussing, whether external or internal, there is nothing that is completely independent and that does not depend on causes and conditions. Whether it is some inner experience or whether it is a question of outer, material things, they all come about solely thanks to causes and conditions. Given that this is the case, in order to eliminate a problem or some kind of suffering, first of all you have to identify its causes and conditions and then ensure that either they do not become complete, or that they do not ripen. With such a method, you are preventing the result that is otherwise inevitable.

Just as nothing in our external world or inner experience happens independently, without causes or conditions, so nothing occurs as a result of one solitary cause or condition. Things depend in fact on a vast number of causes and conditions. Therefore, as we are looking for the way to dispel suffering or attain happiness, we have to ask: "What is the nature of suffering? What is the nature of happiness? What are their causes and conditions?" We need to fathom out their causes and conditions and in the case of suffering stop them, before they can occur. If we are unable to intervene and preempt something before it happens, its result will inexorably continue to ripen, and when it matures, we will have no option but to fall back on a method for simply reducing the suffering.

That is the way the Buddhist teachings work. Of course happiness and suffering are primarily feelings and emotions experienced by our inner consciousness. To a certain extent external stimuli, like visible objects that we see, can act as conditions that cause happiness or suffering. But in the main, happiness and suffering are feelings experienced in the domain of our consciousness. This is why it is so important to understand their causes and conditions and the whole nature of these feelings and emotions. The systematic investigation of our minds can turn up quite a lot of detail!

Once we have found the counter-agents that we mentioned earlier, we can use them as remedies through which we can strengthen whichever aspect of the mind we desire. This is how we can transform the mind.

WHAT IS REQUIRED TO TRANSFORM THE MIND

Yet for all this to come about, we need to make an effort. We cannot expect our minds to change by simply sitting back and waiting for it to happen. If we take stock of the negative elements in our minds, they can be summarized as three—desire, aversion, and ignorance—the so-called three poisons or pollutants. For a long time, our minds have been habituated and inured to these poisons, which are now deeply ingrained. As much as we might talk about "having no desire," "having no aversion," or "having no ignorance"—being free, in fact, from the three poisons—up until this point we have almost never experienced such a state. In fact, we have virtually no idea what it might be like. Because we are so very unfamiliar with the antidote that we need to strengthen in order to transform our minds, it requires a correspondingly determined effort on our part. Otherwise, it will be very difficult for transformation to happen easily or just occur at random.

To make this kind of effort, we need perseverance and diligence. And before we can develop diligence, we need to have an eager, inspired sense of willpower, so that we say to ourselves, "This is something I must accomplish." If we have this kind of incentive deep in our hearts, we will press on, persevering whatever the hardships. Once you understand the dangers of not transforming your mind and the qualities and virtues of transforming it, you will have the grounds for inspiring diligence. This underlines the importance of understanding, on the one hand, the kind of disasters and suffering that the negative elements in our minds inflict on us and, on the other hand, the kind of benefit that the positive qualities of our minds can bring.

If transforming the mind requires effort, effort demands interest and involvement; for that sense of involvement to be strong enough, you have to be motivated from the depths of your heart. If you do not have this drive yourself, it is extremely difficult for something external or someone else to force you to transform your mind. In fact, if they tried, it might make things even worse. After all, what we call this mind of ours is a very curious thing. On the one hand, a very minor condition can bring about a change in our minds. But on the other hand, if someone else tries to bully us, no matter how hard they try, our mind just gets more and more stubborn. Yet if we ourselves are motivated, in both our hearts and our minds, we will be able to forge ahead with indefatigable effort and without paying too much attention to any difficulties.

MOTIVATION, REASON, AND BELIEF

As our motivation is what drives and inspires our actions, we need to take a good look at the reasoning or thinking that it is based on. This means comparing the relative advantages and disadvantages associated with our motivation or its opposite, as well as the possible short- and long-term impact, especially that of long-term harm. In either case, our mind tends to rely on whatever it is familiar with. If it has a reason for depending on something, we must reflect on, and repeatedly check, what that reason is. Then the mind will feel a steadily stronger and more stable sense of certainty. If, on the other hand, there is no valid reason for us to place our trust in something, all we are doing really is simply cultivating a belief. Apart from mere assumption that such-and-such is so, we are unable to marshal the certainty that comes from having thought through the underlying reasons for something. My point is that we need to make sure our actions have valid reasons behind them.

The key to this certainty is to know the true nature of things. Whether it be from the relative or the ultimate point of view, we need to understand the way in which something is what it is. Without such an understanding, none of our assumptions about things, that "such-and-such might be the case," will actually reflect reality.

Basically, whether or not our beliefs are based on valid reasoning, there is a tendency for them to grow stronger and more vivid in direct proportion to our familiarity with them. Yet if a certain belief does not have valid reasons to support it, it will be all the more difficult for us to deepen our conviction in it simply through familiarity. Therefore it is critical that we understand how things are in reality.

THE POWER OF REASONING

Thinking about what brings us well-being or causes us harm, it is a fact that all of us, no matter who we are, wish only to be happy and not to suffer. This phenomenon is not restricted to the population alive during our generation. From the time that human life began until the present day, every single human being has wished only to be happy and to escape suffering. What is more, any living creature that can feel pleasure and pain wishes only to find happiness and avoid suffering.

Now there is one kind of suffering and happiness that comes predominantly from our sense consciousnesses, for example, from what we see or hear. This type of pleasure or pain is one that we have in common with animals. On account of the forms we see, sounds we hear, odors we smell, flavors we taste, or textures that we touch, we can have all kinds of undesirable experiences, from which we try to distance ourselves. Or we can enjoy pleasant and desirable kinds of experiences, which afford us satisfaction. To pursue this sort of satisfaction is a motivating force among all animals; for example, relishing the enjoyment of food and drink, seeking sexual pleasure, or dealing with the pleasure or discomfort due to heat and cold are all things that human beings experience in common with animals.

If we wonder, then, what the difference is between human beings and animals, it would seem to be our powers of thought. We have an enormous capacity for thinking and reasoning and, in conjunction with that, a strong capacity for long-term memory. Not only can we recall the experiences we have had in this human lifetime, in some cases many years' worth, but we can also comprehend and remember the history of generations of human beings in the past. Similarly, we can foresee the future, and we are not limited to an awareness of the present moment. Mind you, certain animals do have an ability to recall past events and to some extent anticipate the future. When animals rear their young, for example, they seem to know over a period of months what will be needed. That is quite something, isn't it? Nevertheless, they are not like human beings. To be able to recall the significance of many years or of many generations of history seems to be a singularly human trait. What sets human beings apart from other living things seems to be this capacity for intelligent thought.

So let us discuss things from the point of view of this critical intelligence. Ironically, it is this great capacity for intelligence that accounts for much of our suffering. Animals live in the moment, experiencing only the pleasure and pain that come mainly from their sense consciousnesses. In contrast, we human beings are always thinking about countless different concepts, we have all kinds of memories of past events that can upset us, and we have no end of expectations and fears about the future that haunt us with anxiety. Just a moment's personal reflection is enough to recognize how this is true. It explains how some people have all they need to get by in life, everything is perfectly adequate, yet their minds are basically in a jumble, and they are depressed and miserable.

At the same time, then, as we human beings have this enormous capacity for intelligent thought, that very thinking can plunge us into all kinds of suffering and destabilize our minds. The kind of suffering that comes about through the five senses is fairly easy and straightforward to eliminate. But the kind of unhappiness that is due to all the thoughts and concepts that stem from the human intellect can only be done away with by harnessing that very same power of reasoning. When you are unhappy because your mind is in turmoil, it is very difficult to overcome that unhappiness with some kind of physical pleasure due to your sensory consciousness of, say, a lovely sound. This is why someone can be extremely well off, with abundant possessions, a perfect family, and wonderful friends, but still be unhappy. Psychological and emotional unhappiness that comes from deep inside, as a result of our thinking, cannot be overturned by the kind of happiness that is provided by external things.

But we can turn things around. If we can discover a sense of well-being, fulfillment, and satisfaction *within our minds,* even though external conditions might not be ideal and make us ill at ease on the level of our senses, still our peace of mind will prevail.

Let us take the example of a physical illness. We will find it easier to cope when we are physically sick if mentally we know that it is affording us some protection or immunity from something worse. A vaccination against smallpox can cause short-term side effects and discomfort, but if we understand that it will help prevent us succumbing to the disease and therefore suffering in the future, we will feel a sense of relief and contentment. It is for the same reason that a soldier might be proud of his war wounds as testimony to his bravery on the battlefield. Spiritual practitioners, too, may have to endure temporary hardships while practicing, but knowing that these hardships are serving to purify harmful actions strengthens their resolve. So your mental attitude toward physical pain allows you to accept some slight feeling of discomfort and tell yourself, It's worthwhile; it's serving a greater purpose. So it's all right. It is clear that the pleasure or pain we feel in our minds can prevail over the pleasure or pain connected with our senses. This pleasure or pain that is related to our conceptual, thinking mind is of greater consequence and has greater power to affect us, for better or for worse.

THE FIXATION ON MATERIAL PROGRESS

The sensory level of pleasure and pain we were talking about is intimately bound up with material progress. Up until the present day, there has been an immense amount of such progress, and it must only increase in the future. Given the degree to which sensory pleasure or pain does affect our lives, we have to acknowledge that material development is extremely useful and constructive. At the same time, however, we have to recognize that the mental well-being or distress that we bring upon ourselves by our way of thinking has a dominant and powerful effect on us, for better or for worse. And to eliminate such mental distress through some external device is extremely difficult.

After all, peace of mind is not something we can buy or manufacture with material ingredients. It is very difficult for peace and happiness to arise in the mind as a result of some medical intervention. Of course, when our minds are distraught with so much thinking, we often resort to tranquilizers as a way of simply finding some rest for our minds and a break from the excessive mental churning. Then, without a thought in the world, we do relax, but like a pig snoozing in the mud! Our minds may experience a modicum of ease and rest, but aside from that, finding peace and happiness in our minds with the aid of some outside ingredients is highly unlikely.

This is the main point: of all the kinds of pleasure and pain we feel as human beings, the most crucial are those that come from the mind. External, material progress for the most part alleviates the suffering and ensures the pleasure we can feel through our senses. But it is very hard for it to have any real effect in removing the kind of suffering and bringing the kind of pleasure associated with our mental processes.

In our society, we are led to believe that we can fulfill all our desires through external, material things; money and possessions, especially, have come to be regarded as a refuge that we run to for protection. But "happiness" and "suffering" are individual feelings and experiences, which are intimately connected to the way we think. However, we do not seem to take this into account at all. Instead, we invariably put all our hope, and take refuge, in something external, believing that it will alleviate our suffering and guarantee our happiness. We entrust everything to material things, which is why they inevitably arouse in us such tenacious attachment and fixation.

When our habits and our whole way of life depend exclusively on material things, one inevitable result is that we are robbed of any feeling of contentment. If we just continue on blindly, without ever thinking about what we are doing, then no matter how many material possessions we surround ourselves with, our minds are never satisfied. The consequence of this lack of contentment, at the level of society as a whole, is the enormous damage that we have done to our natural environment.

THE IMPORTANCE OF HUMAN AFFECTION AND LOVE

Our general condition in human society is that we all depend upon each other. We are social animals, and we must live and interact with one another. Yet it seems that we have lost any feeling of basic human affection or a sense of relatedness and closeness to others. Our society does not place any value on the idea of love or indeed show much interest in it. With material things being prized above all else, nothing is said, is it, about the importance of love for our fellow human beings? Lacking any such feeling of love, instead we put all our energy into making yet more money. And if we are concerned solely with exploiting others whenever possible, exerting control over them whenever we can, forever hoarding and competing, we will end up using any kind of situation whatsoever to further our own ends. In such an eventuality, the principle of loving our fellow human beings will have no currency whatsoever. Yet without this ideal of human affection, there is no happiness in the family, no happiness between couples, and no happiness between parents and children. However many millions of us there are all living here together, in our hearts each one of us will feel lonely and isolated.

What about the feeling of joy in one another's company? What about caring for other people and feeling they are our friends? What about trust and confidence in our dealings with others? They all seem to be cooling off. They seem to be lacking, don't they?

The reality is that we all have to live together on this one small planet of ours, and, in this day and age especially, we have to depend on one another to an enormous degree. Circumstances dictate that we have to think of the good of the whole planet and of all humanity. Yet we stay stuck in our limited personal views, dominated by ideas of "me" and "us." In the worst of cases, this leads to open conflict. What is missing, or never occurs to us, is a sense of cooperation or pulling together, and this is a recipe for all kinds of disaster. With the world population being what it is, it means we are facing real problems.

THE MARK OF A GOOD HUMAN BEING

For us as human beings, then, I believe our priority is to look into ways of getting rid of suffering and finding happiness within our own minds. Imagine if we were able to make significant inner, mental progress alongside all our material progress and development. This, I feel, is what would truly give a purpose to our lives as human beings and at the same time definitely make a positive contribution to society as a whole.

In my own life, I have experienced many joys and sorrows, and I have encountered many difficulties. But when I think about the difficult times, I can see there has always been one thing that has given me hope, whatever the circumstances. The main reason I can feel, in my heart, that my human life has had a purpose and been worthwhile is that I have based my life on the wish to help others. This is something that I know has definitely proved very helpful to me throughout my life. When I have encountered difficulties, this attitude has given me courage and a feeling that hope is never lost, that hardship is manageable and worth going through. And this has brought me a kind of satisfaction through which I am able to find, quite naturally, some small degree of relaxation—peace of mind and happiness, too. Without a doubt, it has also contributed to my physical well-being.

Now, one of the main conditions for us to allow our minds to relax is unquestionably the attitude of love and affection we touched upon before. This attitude is neither absent from our natural make-up as human beings nor something fundamentally new, which has to come from somewhere else. People say, for example, that while a baby is still in its mother's womb, it can recognize her voice. That ability to recognize the unique sound of its mother's voice is something that is naturally just present, it seems, and something that it will need for its survival. And because the child possesses a natural feeling of intimacy with its mother, it can recognize her voice from the start.

Take another example. Generally the first word that an infant gurgles, in any language, is "mama." It is a word that is so easy to say. Just the syllable "ma"—"mother"—seems to evoke that feeling of closeness. Not many words are needed; just one will convey that understanding instantly.

In any case, mother and child feel a mutual love for one another. The baby is born and grows up surrounded by the special kind of love that exists between mother and child, and this creates the beginnings of a good and happy life.

The reason we can say that we all possess love and affection is that they are naturally and inherently part of us. So we have to enhance them, rather than ignore them and let them disappear. This is of vital importance, because this love is one of the most essential qualities of our mind, something truly precious and crucial for a human being. Once we recognize how vital it is, then we can cherish and enhance it, although the basic potential that we are accentuating is already naturally ours.

Now, when a person embodies that attitude of love and affection, his or her conduct in life will be admirable and what we call that of "a true human being." In fact this is the mark of a good human being, rather than whether or not he or she is a spiritual practitioner. It also lies at the root of a happy and peaceful human society. How important it is, then, that we recognize this and do everything we can to enhance that attitude of love and caring for others.

Human beings naturally possess this love and affection, and so I feel it is the role of the religions of the world to bring out their potential and make these wonderful qualities grow. Isn't this why so many different spiritual views and philosophies have indeed evolved—so that we can develop these wonderful, natural qualities more and more? In a nutshell, this is the whole reason that we undertake spiritual practice: to become a good human being, someone who is patient, tolerant, altruistic, compassionate, contented, and self-disciplined. We practice because that is the kind of person we want to become.

CHAPTER 3

APPEARANCE AND REALITY

As I EXPLAINED BEFORE, in the case of the Buddhist teachings, you have to proceed primarily by using your powers of thought and through analysis and investigation. When it comes to identifying the true nature of reality, we need an unerring and undistorted state of mind. In other words, this means a state of mind that is not deceptive at all, one where whatever is perceived accords with reality. This is called *valid cognition.* Throughout the Buddhist teachings in general, and especially in the scriptures concerning the bodhisattva path in the Mahayana teachings, this *valid cognition* is held to be of great importance. All the objectives we are seeking to achieve—higher rebirth, liberation, and omniscience[15]—come about as a result of valid cognition. In the study of logic and epistemology, we speak of *the indirect fruits of valid cognition* and *the direct fruits of valid cognition.*[16] What we call the indirect fruits of valid cognition are all the attainments of the higher realms, liberation, and omniscience. The essential point here is that it is only on the basis of an unmistaken state of mind that the levels of liberation and omniscience can be achieved.

In order for us to arrive at a definitive conclusion about the nature of reality—whether it is a question of the actual nature of things or of things in all their multiplicity—we have to find out what things are in themselves, or what their ultimate nature is. To know this is extremely important. Why? Because our ordinary state of mind is usually mistaken and deluded. Our way of perceiving things involves just so many errors and distortions, all of which we take to be true, and this continually leads us into mishaps and failure. Imagine, for example, that someone is trying to trick us. If we know, right from the beginning, that there is no substance to what he is up to—that however valid it looks in fact, appearance simply does not match reality—he will have no chance of duping us. Given that there is a profound disparity between how things really are and our perceptions of reality, as long as we place our trust in the way things appear, we will end up deceived. Generally speaking, if someone manages to fool us day after day, it is because we choose to trust whatever he is telling us and take it at face value, just as it appears. Similarly, rather than relying simply on the way things seem, we must probe into the ultimate nature of things and discover what it really is.

SUBTLE AND OBVIOUS IMPERMANENCE

One of our most deeply entrenched beliefs is that things remain the same over time. Take a range of mountains, for example. They have been there for millions of years. We think that the mountains we are looking at today are the same as those we saw yesterday or the day before. This kind of attitude, of holding things to be the same from some earlier point in time to some later point, seems instinctive. Of course, when we talk about the most obvious way that things appear, it is in fact quite correct. The mountains we see today have been there for centuries. What, however, if we investigate their true reality, beyond all their appearance of continuity? These cliffs, for example, at a subatomic level are constantly changing and in a process of flux. There is never an instant when they are not changing. However many millions of years they have been there, a time will come when their material mass will disintegrate. Yesterday's mountains are still there, maintaining all their appearance of continuity, but if we think about them more precisely, their subatomic particles have changed a great deal since yesterday. In fact, if things were not continuously changing, none of the changes we see in the world around us could happen. Nor could anything disintegrate when its end had come. Consequently, in the way things seem to be, they appear as though they were exactly the same as they were in the past; but look at them from an ultimate point of view, and they are changing constantly every instant.

What this demonstrates is that the way we perceive reality is not the way it actually is; in other words, the manner in which things *appear* does not accord with how they really *are.* Let us take another example. We could choose an experience we are going through in our minds or just something like this flower I can see in front of me. But whether it is a mental experience or some solid object in the outer world, sooner or later it will disintegrate and cease to be. This is a fact, not something that we have to prove with our powers of reasoning. The flower will wither, dry out, and die. We can see it happening. This continuous process of disintegration and impermanence is the more obvious kind of impermanence—something that we can see directly with our own eyes. It is due to changes that take place moment by moment, which eventually result in the destruction of the object in question. If something did not change moment by moment, it would never cease to be.

DEPENDENT ORIGINATION

What is the key to this process of change? When we speak of continuous change, it does not imply a moment-by-moment disintegration in the sense that an object in the first moment encounters some new cause for its disintegration in the next moment, whereupon the thing that existed in the first moment disintegrates. Rather, it implies that the cause that initially produces something ensures that it comes into being as something that, by its very nature, will disintegrate. Things are perishable on account of their nature. Let me reiterate: we are not saying that things are first produced by one particular cause that brings them into being and then later made to disintegrate by meeting another cause that brings about their destruction. The cause of their arising is *itself* the very cause of their destruction. They come into being already possessing the character of perishable things. That means that the cause for their arising turns, moment by moment, into the cause of their destruction.

So any phenomenon produced by causes in this way is dependent on those causes. If things were existent in their own right, if they existed naturally, they would be innately and independently existent. And something that was innately or independently existent would have to be unalterable. Yet we can actually see that things are susceptible to change; we can see how they are dependent on causes and conditions other than themselves. Whatever we take as an example, something with a tangible form or an inner experience, it only comes about through the power of causes other than itself.

That is not all, however. If we think further about any item, a flower, for instance, it has so many aspects—its shape, color, scent, taste, and more. If we speak of these as the properties of something, in this case they are the properties of our flower—the flower's shape, the flower's color, the flower's scent, and the flower's taste. With the single flower as the basis of these specific properties, we can assign to it these specific attributes of shape, color, scent, and taste. It possesses these properties. This is a fact. Specific properties can only be assigned to some basis for them, and, if there are specific properties, there has to be some basis on which these properties can be assigned. Now the basis of the properties and the properties themselves do seem to be distinct from one another, but if we think it through another step, once we have eliminated the specific properties of something—such as its shape, and so on—if we then seek further for the thing itself that is the basis of the properties, we cannot find it.

A LOOK AT TIME

In a similar fashion, we accumulate experiences from our *past,* and in our present actions we develop new attitudes and ways of doing things informed by those past experiences. So what took place in the past becomes useful in our current behavior. But right now the past is just a thought flitting through our minds. If we search for the past, it has already ceased to be. There's nothing to be found, nothing at all that we can put our finger on.

The same holds true for what will happen in the *future.* Our present actions, which are based on our experiences from the past, will have an effect upon our future. They will either benefit or harm us. Even so, what will happen in the future is at present just a thought taking shape within our minds, a thought concerning what is yet to come about. If we try to put our finger on some future "thing," we find there is only the present.

Therefore, all the many things we categorize as "past" or "future" are simply ideas we have now about what has already happened or what might happen. We use the terms *past* and *future* so that we can think and talk about them, and in that sense they can affect us, for better or for worse, but in fact, it is very difficult to find anything from the past or future that we can actually point to. What we talk about in the present as having occurred in the past is just an object of memory. What we talk about as the future is just a prediction about what might happen that arises in our mind. Apart from what we can say about the past and the future, they do not exist.

Finally, what we call the *present* does seem to be something we can pinpoint, but if we think about what we call the present moment and analyze it into its earlier and later phases, what we will find is that, aside from the past and the future, there is in fact no present at all. We can break things down from years into months, days, hours, minutes, and seconds; everything up to the present second will constitute the past and everything beyond it the future. So there is no present, is there? It is hard to find or establish.

This holds true with so many of our other notions and ways of apprehending the world. The categories we invent are not inherent properties of the entities themselves but labels arrived at through consensus and then applied through the power of language. They are conventional ideas derived from our thoughts about what happened in the past or what might happen in the future. In fact, this is how we arrive at all our conventional notions. How many of them would survive if they had to be inherent properties of things or exist independently of anything else?

This is why Lord Buddha said in the sutras that all phenomena exist by virtue of their names and their conventional designations. They amount to nothing more, he said, than names or symbols.

THE ULTIMATE AND THE RELATIVE: THE TWO TRUTHS

When the Buddha first turned the wheel of Dharma and taught the four noble truths, he spoke of suffering, its origin, its cessation, and the path to that cessation. How are we to relate to these four noble truths? Suffering must be understood; its origin must be removed; its cessation must be actualized; and the path must be cultivated. This is how we should engage with them, but are these truths things in themselves, we might ask? No, they are not. Suffering is to be understood, but if we search for it and think about it, there is no such "suffering to be understood." The origin of suffering must be removed, but if we look for or contemplate some "origin to be removed," there is no such thing to be found. So while the Buddha taught that we should relate to the four noble truths by removing some and enacting others, and this is the way they are presented, at the same time he taught that there is nothing in itself to remove or enact.

It is similar if we look at the skandhas, or mind-body aggregates, which are dependent on karma and disturbing emotions. Being dependent in this way, these aggregates are impermanent, they have no true identity, they produce suffering, and they are impure. If we see them as such, it means our apprehension of them is an unmistaken and authentic one. But if we view these aggregates—dependent as they are on karma and disturbing emotions—as permanent, truly existent, a source of pleasure, and pure, then our apprehension is a mistaken one. On the other hand, we might examine these aggregates and try to find something with some ultimate status behind the labels. On an ultimate level, both these views—mistaken and unmistaken—are transcended altogether, and neither one exists.

So there are these two modes: first, the way things appear, and, second, the way they actually are. From the point of view of how things appear, we classify them into many categories—mountains, fences, buildings, flowers, and so on. These things, and their effects, all come about contingent upon causes and conditions. They also cause us to experience feelings of pleasure or pain, since their connection with us can be beneficial or harmful. Because of its "seeds," everything produces its own "fruit," and these things affect us in beneficial or harmful ways.

Now what is the ultimate way of being of these helpful or harmful phenomena? If we refuse to be satisfied merely by the way things appear, and we look deeper, we discover there is nothing to be found. The more we examine the way things really are, underlying the way they appear, the clearer this fact becomes. Say we catch sight of a mirage in the desert, far off in the distance. If it were actually there, it would appear in greater detail the nearer we got. Yet the closer we come, it does not become any clearer but fades away and vanishes, till there is nothing left to see.

The same applies to the whole spectrum of phenomena, all functioning as causes and conditions, interconnected with one another, for better or for worse. If we are not content with appearances, and we examine their ultimate essence, their absolute way of being, their fundamentally unconditioned nature, we discover it is unfindable. The appearance of things, then, does not correspond to their true nature.

So the *two levels of truth* refer exactly to these two: the way things appear and the way they really are. To a mind that is not examining or investigating the true nature of something, there appears to be some essence to things that we can identify. On the other hand, if we are not content with superficial appearances, and we delve deeper to determine the primordial or fundamentally unconditioned nature of something, what we discover is said to be its ultimate reality, or its innermost primordial nature. Therefore, for any given phenomenon there are two aspects—its apparent reality, which is conventionally true, and its intrinsic nature, which is ultimately true. On this basis we can talk about there being two levels of truth.

With any thing or event that can appear or be possible, if we search beneath the surface for its innermost identity, and we find a discrete, individual essence of its very own, then we can say that it is *truly existent* or *ultimately existent*. If something really is the way it appears to be, then appearance and reality are in harmony, and that thing truly exists in the way it appears to. However, this is not the case; things are not really the way they appear to be, and so they are not truly existent. Their appearance and their true nature do not match. This disparity is due to the fact that the things in question manifest in a false way. If they manifested in a truly authentic way, there would be no such discrepancy.

This is how phenomena are said to be *false* and are not found to be truly existent. Their true existence, which is what is being refuted here, has never actually been the case. The very nature of things is such that they are there, but they cannot be established as existing.

However, it is not that they do exist only as long as we are not investigating them but become nonexistent as soon as we scrutinize them!

There is a verse in Maitreya's *Ornament of Clear Realization* that says: "In this, there is not a thing to be removed."[17] This means that what is being refuted, namely true existence, is not a property that is initially present and then is somehow done away with through reasoning. Rather, it means that phenomena are, and always have been, dependent by their very nature, and so they have always been devoid, or "empty," of autonomy or independence. If things were not "empty" of independent existence, they could not come into being in the first place. Phenomena have to depend on other things in order to come into being; they must depend on conditions. Only autonomous entities would not need to depend on conditions.

True existence, then, is not something that previously existed but was eliminated later on. Since things are empty of true existence, what we call *emptiness* or the *ultimate aspect* is not something new that has been superimposed by the mind.

The next verse in the quotation continues, "Nor is there the slightest thing to be added." This indicates that the two levels of reality, the relative truth or conventional way of being and the absolute or ultimate way of being, do not come about as a result of the Buddha's enlightened activity or as a result of ordinary beings' karma. It is simply the way things naturally are.

Therefore, the mind that investigates what something really is, without being satisfied with mere appearances, is a mind engaged in investigation on the ultimate level. We could call it an *ultimate mind*. And whatever that *ultimate mind* finds to be true is called *ultimate truth*.

Among the phenomena that appear to an ordinary mind that does not analyze or investigate, whatever is found to be true when investigated on the conventional level is what we call *relative truth*. The term *relative* also refers to the factors that obscure or conceal reality. That is to say, the *relative* is applied to the ignorance that obscures our perception of the ultimate, intrinsic nature of reality. So whatever is true from the perspective of this relative ignorance, which obscures our perception of ultimate reality, is called *relative truth*.

EMPTINESS OF INHERENT EXISTENCE

Any kind of thing or event that can appear or be possible, whether in samsara or nirvana, appears to us as though it could exist by virtue of its very essence, or be truly existent. But if it did exist just as it appeared, some basis for its name or designation would have to be ascertainable. Also, the way things appeared would have to accord with the way they actually were, whereas it does not. For when they are scrutinized, things cannot be found to be just as they appear to be, and this fact shows that, even while they are manifesting, they are empty of any status as existent.

So *empty* means "empty of any intrinsic essential existence," which is what is being refuted. The suffix *ness* in emptiness simply has the connotation of "only that." With all this being the case, we can refer to this ultimate truth as emptiness.

As we already saw, whatever we perceive appears to us as if it does in fact exist, in its own right. Regardless of whether it is some inner experience or some object in the world outside us, in each and every case, it seems to us as though things really do exist in the way that we label them conventionally. Now if things actually existed in the way we perceived them, it would stand to reason that the more we looked into them, the clearer they ought to become. But when we do examine them, not only do they fail to become any clearer, but we cannot actually even find anything there. This is a sign that things do not exist in the way they appear.

Therefore, things are *empty* of existing in the way that we perceive them to, *empty* of any true existence, and empty of any intrinsic existence. And so when both outer and inner phenomena are in their own right empty of existence, they are said to be *empty of inherent existence.*

In *The Descent to Lanka Sutra,* the Buddha speaks of seven different senses in which something can be said to be empty. The seventh is where one thing is empty of something else. The example given is of a temple that is empty of monks. The emptiness of the temple is something different or separate from what is being negated—the presence of the monks. The Buddha described this as a lesser instance of emptiness.

We are not using the term *empty* in the sense where a pillar, for example, is empty of something else, like a vase. Rather, a pillar itself is empty of any intrinsic existence as such. Occasionally the term *self-empty,* in Tibetan *rang tong,* is used to describe this. *Self-empty* is a term used to signify that something is empty of any intrinsic existence, as opposed to being empty of anything "other" than itself. However, *self-empty* does not literally mean it is empty of *itself.* When we say that a flower is empty of inherent existence, we are not denying the reality of the flower. If the flower did not exist at all, there would be only an absence: no seed to germinate, grow, and blossom into a flower, nothing to produce its buds and fruit and so nothing to provide feelings of pleasure or dislike at seeing and smelling the flower or pricking our finger on its thorns.

Self-empty, in relation to the flower, means that it is empty of intrinsic existence. To think that the flower was empty *of itself* would be tantamount to proposing nothingness and slipping into a nihilistic extreme. Rather, we should understand that any given thing, since it is produced in dependence on other conditions, is empty in the sense that it has no inherent existence of its own. And for this reason, it is self-empty.

So whether it is a feeling or an actual object that we perceive, there is always that distinction between how things appear to us and how they actually are. If we examine whether something actually is the way it appears to be, it is not. With any object we care to investigate, we can never find some core identity of which we can say, This is it! When we look for it even in minutest subatomic particles, there is nothing to find. This seems to reflect the same general position as that of modern quantum physics—that however deeply you research into an object, finally there is nothing to be found.

THE WAY THINGS EXIST

Does this imply, then, that things are simply nonexistent? No, they do exist, in a sense. Things can have a beneficial or harmful effect on us. So in what way do they exist? With anything, on a conventional level it exists in the sense that it performs some function, be it positive or negative. It has its distinct properties, and there is something to which we can assign a name. It exists, but this kind of existence is not due to having some ultimate or inherent existence. And this is just what the term *self-empty* means—that things do not possess such ultimate, inherent existence.

So *self-empty* does not imply nonexistence, because things do exist, in the sense that they have their own specific properties. This whole discussion of whether things exist inherently or not hinges on the fact that they have such properties. If they had no such distinguishing properties, we could not discuss whether or not this constitutes having *inherent* existence. But even though things possess individual identities, this does not signify that they exist inherently.

All right, then, you might say, how exactly do they exist? They exist only through the power of conditions other than themselves. So they exist through being labeled or designated in dependence on other things. They are *produced* as well in dependence on other factors. This being so, in many of the sutras and tantras, the Lord Buddha stated that things are found to exist only in dependence on causes and conditions that are other than themselves. And since they do not exist independently, or without relying on these other conditions, the Buddha taught that all phenomena arise *dependently* and are by nature emptiness.

Nothing in the universe either arises by itself or possesses any inherent existence, and since every single thing arises solely through its relationship to other phenomena, it proves that nothing occurs without the play of causes and conditions. These causes and conditions can affect things, positively or adversely. Were things truly to exist in themselves, causes and conditions could not affect them one way or the other. But since phenomena lack inherent existence, it necessarily implies that they occur in dependence on causes and conditions.

According to the Buddhist teachings, then, all these things that can affect us for better or for worse and that are changeable by nature—any thing either within us or in the world around us, absolutely everything, in fact—occur only in dependence on causes and conditions. All their various transformations occur simply because of causes and conditions. Other than this, things do not occur without cause nor do they occur on account of some eternal cause that is completely different from them. This is how the Buddhist teachings explain things and so lead us to the position that there is no Creator of the world.

The teachings explain that we have to investigate the fact that things are subject to change owing to their causes and conditions through a fourfold method of reasoning.[18] In so doing, we will arrive at the fundamental quality or intrinsic nature of any given phenomenon, whether it be matter or consciousness.

By the way, we are not talking about emptiness here. Let's take an example to illustrate this. The element earth is hard and unyielding, while the element air is light and mobile. Each of these two phenomena possesses its individual basic nature—its special set of characteristics, which is not shared by the other. But when their fundamental qualities or characteristics combine, it provokes change, which is explained as the result of their mutual interaction.

Every material substance in fact has its own individual potentialities, and when these are combined in various ways, it can instigate change, serve a function, and give rise to different potentials, causing things to interact in beneficial or harmful ways. Earth is hard and unyielding. Since its very nature is such, it will have a particular kind of effect, won't it? Generally speaking, the elements each have their own individual qualities, which allow them to exert different kinds of influence and serve different functions. When things that have different functions combine, new potentials will emerge.

Now, when we examine and investigate any given object, whether within us or in the world around us, we should already be aware of its characteristics. And we should also understand its specific way of functioning and the sort of changes that can occur when it interacts with something else.

On the basis of this kind of approach, if there is something that will naturally benefit us, we can work out how to achieve it, and if there is something that is naturally harmful, we can take steps to eliminate it. We have to think it through along these lines. And this, in fact, brings us right back to our discussion about happiness and suffering.

Quite naturally, we all wish to be happy and not to suffer. And we all have the same right to achieve happiness and avoid suffering. This is based on reason; after all, we have every reason to want to be happy.

CHAPTER 4

THE QUESTION OF CONSCIOUSNESS

SENSATIONS AND PERCEPTIONS

When we speak of happiness and suffering, we are mainly referring to sensations of pleasure and pain. Together with these pleasurable or painful sensations, we also have to consider the factors that cause them. So let us look at sensations and perceptions. For the most part, sensations arise based on material things. There is something that triggers off a sensation, whether pleasurable, painful, or neutral. We say that it is responsible for the sensation, but it does not necessarily mean that just because this particular factor is there, a sensation will arise. Other conditions have to coincide as well, and if one of them is lacking, the sensation cannot happen. In any case, it seems that there needs to be first some tangible basis for a sensation.

When we talk about sensations, and perceptions as well, we are talking about consciousness—consciousness in the sense of the awareness of objects. The word *awareness* here does not refer to the *rigpa* that is differentiated from the ordinary mind, which we will discuss in some depth later on.[19] It is simply awareness of objects. It is this kind of consciousness that experiences sensations: we come into contact with an object, next we are aware of it, and then we experience pleasurable or painful sensations. Then, as we are aware of things, so we have ideas about them: This is such and such. This is what is meant by perception.

Sensations come in different kinds. There is one type of everyday sensation, either pleasant or painful, which is not caused by our way of thinking. Say, for example, I bang my hand against the table. It will cause me a feeling of pain, and I will think, "Ouch! I hit my hand!" The act of hitting my hand and the pain involved then spark off various thoughts in my mind. So this is one category of sensations, those which are instigated by some kind of external circumstance.

Then there is another category, which comprises those sensations that are not due to this kind of contact with objects through the five senses but are caused by a change in consciousness itself, as a result of some memory of the past or some thought about the future. This change at the level of our consciousness or awareness can provoke a physical sensation, however. If we examine this, does it mean that first there is an idea, a thought, or a memory, which is then followed by some kind of physical change, such as the activation of neurons or an electrochemical reaction in the brain? Or must ideas or memories, which are changes in our awareness, always be the result of some subtle change at a physical or neurological level? This is a question, I feel, that really needs to be investigated.

It is said that consciousness arises based on the sense faculties. There is indeed this dependent relationship, but, if there were absolutely no consciousness that was separate from the physical senses, it would be difficult to account for many events that happen to us in the course of our daily lives—in particular, the amazing physical changes that can come from practicing meditation. These changes are not due to some drug or a medical procedure. There is a physical transformation that takes place because of a change in consciousness itself. Therefore, it is much more convenient, and much easier, for us to account for this kind of thing, if we explain consciousness as something that is primarily dependent on the physical body but also capable of bringing about certain changes by itself. If we don't accept a role such as this for consciousness, many of these phenomena are difficult to explain.

CONSCIOUSNESS DEFINED

When we speak about sensations and perceptions, we are talking exclusively about sentient forms of life. Of course, flowers and plants are alive, their chemical makeup is similar to other forms of life, and they are subject to cycles of life, growth, death, and destruction. But while their cells are alive, plants do not have sensations or perceptions. So when we talk about sentience, or consciousness, I think there is one fundamental defining property common to all sentient forms of life and that is movement. Even tiny insects exhibit this kind of movement. They can use the power of their bodies to move from place to place. A plant can move as it grows, and it can be swayed by the wind or the rain, but it cannot move *intentionally* from one place to another. So when we talk about *sentient beings,* we mean that, in addition to the basic characteristics of life, which are common to plants and animals, there is also this ability to move intentionally from one place to another. The definition of a living or sentient being is one that possesses consciousness. Whatever lacks consciousness is classed as nonsentient or inanimate matter.

Consciousness is described in terms of its function, which is to know or cognize objects. It is therefore defined as "clear and knowing," or "luminous and cognizant." How do we explain this? *Clarity* here refers to the clear arising of appearances to consciousness. It does not make any difference whether or not this perception corresponds to the actual nature of things. A particular appearance arises to consciousness, along with an awareness of its aspects or features. Now that appearance is always valid and direct. This is what is meant by *clear*—the fact that this appearance is reflected *clearly*. Once this appearance has been made clear, there is a "knowing" or awareness that apprehends that appearance, along with its various aspects.

For example, even when we are fast asleep, in our dreams there are all kinds of different perceptions, sights, sounds, smells, tastes, and tactile sensations. Our consciousness in the dream is aware of these countless appearances and their different aspects. They all arise to that consciousness, which is the capacity for clarity and cognizance, and as these experiences appear, we are aware of each of them, along with their respective features.

During the course of our lives, in fact, we go through various levels of consciousness: from the coarser level of ordinary sensory experience, to the subtler mode of consciousness during dreams, which functions independently of the sense faculties, and then to the even subtler mode of consciousness that prevails during deep sleep.

As for the coarser level of consciousness, if we take the example of a visual cognition, the mere interaction of the eye faculty with some visual form will not necessarily produce a visual awareness. There also needs to be the *immediate condition,* meaning that the mind is not distracted by thoughts of something else. If the mind is lost in thought, then the contact between the visual faculty and a form will not necessarily lead to a visual cognition. That is why we say that in order to produce a clear knowledge or awareness in which external forms are clearly cognized, there must be this third factor, the immediate condition.

Whatever the case, any act of cognition or consciousness, from the subtle down to the more coarse, must occur on the basis of the continuous stream of subtlemost consciousness, which is by nature clarity and cognizance, the capacity to be aware.

THE CONTINUITY OF PHYSICAL MATTER

Looking at the external world around us, of course there are changes and transformations that occur due to particular causes and conditions, but still there is something like an underlying continuity of substance or matter. We could take the example of a flower or the physical body of any living being. The physical matter that makes up this flower or our body is part of a continuity, in which each instance depends on what came before, stretching all the way back in time to the formation of the universe. The potential for this flower must have been present in the subtle particles that were present at the beginning of the universe.

Buddhist cosmology speaks of four different periods, or eras, in the history of a particular universe system: a period of formation, an era of abiding, a period of destruction, and a time of voidness between two universes. During this period of voidness, it is explained that "space particles" subsist. These particles are like the building blocks from which all the physical matter of a new universe is formed, including the physical bodies of living beings. Whatever has physical substance must derive from something with similar characteristics—in other words, it must be preceded by something that also has physical substance.

If we turn to consciousness—which is immaterial, has no physical form, color, or shape, and is nothing but the capacity for experience—

this must also come about from something similar to itself. Consciousness changes on the surface, but underlying these changes there is a continuity, the fundamental capacity for clarity and knowing that arises from an earlier instance of the same capacity.

Let us trace back the continuity of matter. We can explain it using a very simple example: this flower here in front of me. It came from a seed. That seed came from another flower, which came from its own respective seed...and so on. We can almost speak of the former "incarnations" of this flower. On a subtle level, there is just a single continuity, but of course it goes through all kinds of manifestations. According to particular causes and conditions, it will change in terms of its appearance from one "incarnation" to the next. It may have a different color or a different size. But if we were able to trace its ancestry, we would find a continuity of similar type. This is how inanimate matter evolves, through ongoing cycles of physical matter in which one manifestation depends on a similar manifestation that preceded it.

Nevertheless, this physical continuum fails to account for our conscious experience, the capacity for sensation and perception. As we saw, the physical body we have now, which is the support for consciousness, is based on preceding causes of a similar type and comes from a continuity of physical substance present since the very beginning of the universe. But we can hardly say that our consciousness, although it depends on this coarse physical body, derives from that same continuum of matter. As I explained earlier, it is much more likely that this consciousness comes from a subtle continuum of consciousness.[20]

DEGREES OF SUBTLETY IN CONSCIOUSNESS

The different degrees of subtlety in consciousness are determined by the subtlety of that which supports it. The more subtle the support, the more subtle the consciousness that depends upon it. For example, waking consciousness is relatively coarse, and its functioning is based upon a coarser type of wind energy, or *prana*. Consciousness during dreams is slightly more subtle than waking consciousness and is based on correspondingly subtler movements of the wind energy. When we faint or black out, there is only very slight movement of the wind energy.

So I think it is possible to account for these variations in consciousness on the basis of the differences in their respective supports.

In any case, when we get to the very subtlest level of consciousness, it is still dependent on the physical body to some degree, but, in terms of its actual essence, it is distinct and independent. This is supported by the experience of certain meditators. Of course, I don't think everything we hear about this is necessarily true. There may be false or exaggerated accounts, but some people definitely claim to experience what they describe as a "dream body" that is quite separate from their ordinary physical body. There is someone I know myself whose mother had this type of experience and for several days underwent an "out of body experience," of which later she gave a clear description. This does happen. People experience traveling outside their bodies and are able to describe things that happened far removed from where their ordinary physical body was left behind. This indicates that for the most part the mind relies upon the body, but not exclusively. On some level it can function independently—when we get to the subtlest level of consciousness. At that level, mind seems to be independent of the coarse physical body.

THE CONTINUITY OF CONSCIOUSNESS

If we were to sum up, then, in the case of inanimate matter, there exists a continuity of similar type. As far as sentient beings are concerned, there is a continuity of physical substance that accounts for the physical body. However, the consciousness that identifies with this physical body has to be accounted for separately. If this were not the case, we would share the same conscious experiences as our parents. Our physical bodies have developed from the egg and sperm of our mother and father, or, in other words, from their physical bodies. If our consciousness also arose from the same physical substance, it would be the same as that of our parents. We would share the same experience. But we don't.

So in the case of the physical body, we can say that it is similar to inanimate matter, insofar as it comes about based on a continuum of physical substance stretching back in time. But we have to say that the consciousness that relies upon this physical body is different.

If we try to pinpoint the precise origin of the continuity of physical matter, it becomes extremely problematic. Likewise, it is very difficult to posit a precise beginning for consciousness, which is defined as clarity and knowing, the basic capacity for experience. If we were to posit a beginning for either physical matter or consciousness, then that would be likely to entail origination from something with a different nature. Or it would entail origination without a cause. Both possibilities are unsatisfactory and unlikely to withstand logical investigation.

When we apply the label "living being," we do so primarily on the basis of consciousness. The terms *human being* or *animal* are used to make a distinction based primarily on the type of physical form. But when we say "living being" or "person," we are talking about a thing that has the capacity to experience pleasure and pain. Our notion of "I" or a personal self is related primarily to our stream of consciousness. If the physical body alone were the basis for this sense of self, we might as well consider inanimate objects as living beings. So it is the capacity to feel and to perceive things that sets sentient beings apart from inanimate matter. This is what makes the difference.

In the case of a sentient being, that "I" or sense of self is identified with the stream of consciousness, and since we cannot posit a beginning to this stream of consciousness, equally we cannot speak of a beginning for the self or the individual. Since there is nothing capable of obstructing the flow of consciousness, it does not have an end either. In fact, the stream of consciousness is beginningless and endless. So the individual or self that is identified with this stream of consciousness is likewise beginningless and endless.

However, we see that this continuum leaves room for a process of transformation. The principle is that there is a continuity, but it is always changing. Take the example of the body we possess in this life. Admittedly, there is a continuity, in that it is the same body more or less regardless of age. Yet a transformation takes place. We will say of people that they are young; then when they have aged and their bodies have changed in appearance, we will say that they are old. So there are characteristics that have changed, while there is a continuity that allows us to tie the different stages of this person's life together. At one and the same time, there is both continuity and transformation.

Likewise, in terms of the stream of consciousness, there is a certain continuity between when we are young and when we are old. At the same time, there will be one stage of life when we don't know very much and have not learned anything; then another when we have been educated, and this stream of consciousness has become enriched with knowledge and experience. We can therefore identify different stages or moments in this stream of consciousness. From a larger point of view, we can say that just as there is a state of ignorance and one of knowledge, there can also be some instances when the consciousness is linked to a human physical support and other states when consciousness is associated with other kinds of physical form. We can talk as well of different states that concern the quality of the stream of consciousness: it can be obscured to varying degrees, and similarly the preoccupation with disturbing emotions may vary. Then there can be states of consciousness, whether human, animal, or of other kinds, where slowly these destructive mental factors are diminishing and disappearing, while positive and constructive qualities are becoming prevalent. So it is evident that we can go from one state to another, from the state of ignorance and confusion that characterizes beings of the conditioned world, to a state that is gradually approaching enlightenment, until finally we reach enlightenment—the perfect knowledge that characterizes buddhahood. Our consciousness, too, manifests this dual quality of continuity and transformation.

CHAPTER 5

OVERCOMING THE CAUSES OF SUFFERING

THE FOUR NOBLE TRUTHS

There are two observations that we can make from our discussion so far:

- There is a discrepancy between our perception and reality, in that things are naturally empty of inherent existence and yet manifest dependently, according to the law of causality.
- There is a self or individual that is identified with the stream of consciousness and who experiences pleasure and pain.

These two observations lead us quite naturally to the Buddha's teaching on the four noble truths. The self, which is identified with the stream of consciousness, has the capacity to experience sensations—a capacity automatically accompanied by an aversion to unpleasant sensations and a desire for pleasant ones. But it is not enough simply to have a dislike for pain and suffering, we must actively remove them and, by eliminating suffering, bring about lasting happiness. That this is possible to achieve is shown by the four noble truths:

- The *truth of suffering* refers to all our unwanted pain and suffering, which occur as a result of causes and conditions and depend on them. What are these causes and conditions?
- They constitute what we refer to as the *origin of suffering*. This origin has two aspects: (1) karma and (2) mental afflictions, or disturbing emotions. *Karma* means "action"; disturbing emotions are

states of mind that motivate our actions, afflict us, and prevent us from ever finding inner peace.

- If we were to eliminate this kind of suffering entirely, in that *cessation of suffering,* we would find true and lasting happiness.
- Genuine, lasting happiness, which is achieved through getting rid of whatever has to be eliminated, is not something that will just happen on its own. It will only come about through creating the right causes and conditions, or, in other words, through applying effort. It is because this can only be achieved through effort that we speak of the *truth of the path.*

This is how the four truths are explained. Since they concern dependent origination, they are connected with the law of causality: if we seek the goal of happiness we need to identify the causes that will lead to happiness; if we seek to avoid suffering, we need to identify the causes that will eliminate it. When we say that suffering is the *result* that comes from the origin that is its *cause,* this means that it is governed, just like everything else, by the laws of dependent origination. Everything comes about as a result of causes and conditions.

So the truth of this origin of suffering possesses two aspects—karma and disturbing emotions. Karma, or action, refers to actions carried out with a specific motivation. Once there is the self that is identified with a stream of consciousness, then there are perceptions and ideas, and, on the basis of these ideas, there are different motivations. These various types of motivation create their own unique causes and conditions; actions carried out with a particular intention create new and further conditions of their own, which then become part of the general process of causality. The point is that actions undertaken with a particular motivation will influence the process of causality in a specific way, and because the motivation behind an action is a unique cause in its own right, different types of motivation will yield different types of result.

That which motivates the actions that lead to suffering is the mental afflictions.

THREE KINDS OF SUFFERING

When we discuss suffering in the context of the truth of suffering, we are not talking about painful sensations alone. Painful sensations are referred to as *obvious suffering,* or *the suffering of suffering.* But then, all our ordinary, tainted feelings of pleasure or happiness are also, by their very nature, suffering. This is known as *the suffering of change.* Where do these two kinds of suffering come from? They are the results of karma and disturbing emotions, which govern and control them. Our enslavement to karma and disturbing emotions is known as *the pervasive suffering of conditioning.*

All of these kinds of suffering ensue as a result of ordinary positive or negative samsaric actions. Incidentally, there are also *untainted actions,* which do not perpetuate samsaric existence, but they form a different category. If we confine our discussion to ordinary samsaric actions, they fall into three types: nonmeritorious, meritorious, and what are called *nontransferable.*[21] These three possible types of action function as causes and conditions, dictated by the particular motivation with which they are carried out.

Here, that motivation is the origin of suffering: the three afflictions of attachment, aversion, and ignorance. The root source of all these is fundamental ignorance. This in fact corresponds to the first of the twelve links of dependent origination, *the ignorance that is confused as to the nature of reality.* This ignorance is the fundamental basis. But on top of it there is a further delusion with regard to the workings of cause and effect, called *the ignorance that is confused about causality;* it is this that drives us to accumulate *nonmeritorious* actions, then undergo the suffering of suffering and eventually take rebirth in the lower realms, where this form of suffering is at its most violent and terrible.

Alternatively, we might have some understanding of cause and effect, so that we are free from this additional delusion regarding causality, but still we are under the power of the fundamental ignorance that is confused as to the nature of reality itself. In this case, we may accumulate *meritorious* or *nontransferable* actions, which will eventually result in rebirth in the higher realms of existence. In other words, such actions would bring the wonderful conditions of the higher realms; however, they would still be within the domain of the suffering of change and, in particular, the suffering of conditioning.

IGNORANCE THAT IS CONFUSED AS TO THE NATURE OF REALITY

All of this in the end comes down to ignorance, or delusion, meaning the fundamental ignorance that is confused as to the nature of reality. The actual nature of reality, or suchness, is what we called earlier *the ultimate truth.* Then we had identified two levels of truth: the way things appear and the way they truly are. Here we are talking not about how things appear but about the way they are, in terms of their ultimate, absolute nature. So what is the actual nature of things? They are empty of any intrinsic existence. But this is not how things appear to us or how we perceive them. Everything—from our own inner experiences, to the phenomena in the external world—appears to us as existing somehow independently and in its own right. And the mind that takes them at face value, as possessing some ultimate kind of existence, is what we call the *ignorance that is confused as to the nature of reality.*

So as we have seen, this deluded clinging to true existence, which is the fundamental basis for the mental afflictions, is a mistaken state of mind. The way the mind perceives things is not how they are in reality. However, it is not simply a matter of failing to recognize how things actually are. Although in reality things are empty of intrinsic existence, the ordinary mind perceives them *as if they did* actually have some intrinsic reality. What we are dealing with here is a perception that is completely distorted and mistaken.

Now there could not be a starker contrast between the misperceiving mind that clings to things as if they had some intrinsic reality and the mind that perceives the emptiness of intrinsic reality. They are two modes of perception that are diametrically opposite. At the moment the tendency to misperceive things as real is strongly established in our minds, because we are so familiar with it. It seems almost natural or instinctive. No sooner do we see something than automatically we think, "That *is* really there. It really does exist." But that is just our assumption. The more we reflect on the actual nature of things, the less clear this kind of assumption will begin to seem. And the more intently we examine things, the less entrenched this misperception will become.

It is true that we react almost instantaneously, saying to ourselves, "Of course this is real. It's here. It can actually do me some good, or harm. It works." We are simply taking things at face value and trusting in how they appear. If this were an accurate perception of things, then the more we investigated them, the clearer their reality would become. But this is not the case. So our perception of things as real or inherently existing is fortified solely by its familiarity; once examined and put to the test, it will not hold up. It can only ever give us a semblance of certainty but never a deep and genuine conviction.

Now, a mind that perceives the lack of true reality in things will not be in accord with how things appear, while by contrast a mind that takes things to be real does agree with how things appear. Yet despite the fact that the perception of the lack of true reality simply does not seem to tally with appearances, when you investigate and examine to see whether it does correspond to the actual nature of things, you will find a real certainty. So these two ways of perceiving are fundamentally at odds with one another. One of them is backed up by valid reasoning, while the other is not. And whatever is backed up by valid reasoning, will only grow stronger the more we become accustomed to reflecting on it.

TWO TYPES OF AFFLICTIONS, TWO KINDS OF ANTIDOTES

Let us turn now to the afflictions or disturbing emotions. We can distinguish two separate categories:

- afflictions that are linked to distorted views
- afflictions that are not associated with views or beliefs.

Anger and desire, for example, are among those afflictions that are not due to distorted views. The "view of the transitory collection," extreme views, and wrong views are among the afflictions that are linked to distorted views.[22] These are also collectively known as *deluded intelligence,* because they do have the power to engender a degree of apparent certainty about things.

The division into two types of afflictions—those associated with a distorted view and those not specifically linked to belief—will naturally be reflected in their respective antidotes. For example, the antidote to anger is meditation on loving-kindness, and the antidote to desire is meditation on repulsiveness. Both of these function as antidotes because they are states of mind that are complete opposites of the disturbing emotions in question, and they are what we call *confrontational antidotes.* When we meditate on love as an antidote to anger, we are suppressing that anger through love. This is a way of confronting the emotion, but it is not the same as an antidote that eliminates the emotion altogether.

Consequently two different types of antidote are discerned: antidotes that work against emotions and antidotes that eliminate them. In this case, love will diminish our anger to a certain extent, and so it is a *confrontational antidote.* But the real root of anger is ignorance and clinging to true existence, which boils down to *deluded intelligence.* So in order to get rid of this distortion of our own intelligence and wisdom, the antidote we have to apply is the wisdom that is the realization of selflessness.

Neither loving-kindness, which is the wish that beings might be happy, nor compassion, which is the wish that they be free from suffering, is based on this realization of selflessness. This is why they cannot eradicate the kind of afflictions that are connected with distorted views.

THE LIMITLESS POTENTIAL OF MIND

At the same time, there is another dimension that must be understood. Love, compassion, and the realization of selflessness are all qualities of the mind. They are based on the mind. So they are unlike athleticism, physical strength, or skills, which are based on the body. Or, if we consider an activity like boiling water, the heat generated is again based on coarse material elements. The qualities of the mind do not rely on coarse physical matter. This means there is an all-important difference. Properties that rely on physical matter, such as the heat of the water or our physical strength and skills, cannot be developed to infinity but are constrained by the limitations of the physical basis on which they must depend. Once water is taken off the boil, it cools down again, and its heat disappears; it will not go on increasing. Qualities that rely on consciousness, on the other hand, can be developed indefinitely—the support they are based on does not degenerate but is beginningless and endless. This means that if we exert ourselves and try to cultivate certain qualities of the mind, they will endure and continue.

Of course, in our practice we might develop certain positive experiences, but without stabilizing them through familiarity, they will last no more than a few days, weeks, or months. They will disappear like our physical strength when we don't keep in training or like the water that has gone off the boil. But once we manage to gain some stability, the qualities we are trying to develop in our training will become natural properties of our mind, which will then remain, even without any effort on our part. This is what it means to develop a quality to its fullest extent—to reach the point at which a property has become so familiar that it is simply present without us having to apply any further effort.

Our physical bodies age and lose their strength. Despite all our anti-aging creams and pills and rejuvenating treatments of every kind, slowly the wrinkles creep across our face and our hair turns grey. Regardless of what we do to care for our bodies, eventually they grow old, and we can do nothing to stop that process. In the case of consciousness, there are certain states of mind that have become familiar to us over the years and that continue even as we grow old or live with illness. If we have always been cheerful and calm, for example, we will continue to be cheerful and calm even in our old age. So the qualities of the body will eventually disappear no matter how much we might do to try and safeguard them, but the qualities of the mind, if we have really trained and cultivated familiarity with them, will remain for as long as the mind itself continues. That is why we can say that the qualities of the mind can be developed infinitely and boundlessly.

IGNORANCE AND AFFLICTIONS ARE PURIFIABLE

Consciousness itself, which is defined as "mere clarity and knowing," is entirely without any kind of fault or flaw. When discursive thoughts occur, attachment and aversion arise toward objects that we take to be good or bad. But what underlies these thoughts is the mind that believes objects to be as real as they appear to be. This is where the fault lies.

However, the attitude of clinging to things as real is not an inherent property of the mind. If it were, then the mind could never be free from attachment, aversion, and ignorance. Yet that is not the case. The essence of mind, which is its capacity for cognizance and awareness, is never stained by these flaws. As it is said, "The nature of mind is clear light."[23]

It follows then that we can say these two things:

- the nature of mind is clear light,
- and the flaws are only temporary.

Now "temporary" here does not imply that these flaws were not there before and then suddenly appeared. It means that they can be removed through the use of powerful antidotes, and they do not in any way stain consciousness at the level of that basic capacity for cognizance and awareness.

The key point here is that the fundamental ignorance is purifiable. We can put an end to it. And by putting an end to the cause, namely the origin, we will also put an end to the result, which is suffering. In other words, because we have established that fundamental ignorance can be eliminated by applying a powerful antidote, this implies that all the unwanted suffering it causes can also be eliminated. Basically, the wisdom that realizes selflessness is the powerful antidote to the ignorance that is the cause of karma and afflictions and all that they in turn produce.

In a sense it matters less what the effects of something may be, when we can employ some powerful force to destroy their root cause and so eliminate the effects. Why? Because the effects can only occur in dependence on the cause. Applying a powerful antidote to the cause will get rid of it, and once the cause is eliminated, the effects due to that cause will also cease. That is why this can be called *the truth of cessation.*

In general, the truth of cessation is within our mindstream; in particular, it refers to the wonderful quality of freedom that comes from having eradicated afflictions and disturbing emotions. After all, we do not want to suffer, and when we can use an antidote to get rid of the cause of suffering, the freedom it gives us is indeed a wonderful quality. Just as when we rid ourselves of something we really do not want, that is something precious. It is a good sign. It might not be what we would call an actual sensation of pleasure, but in fact it is true and lasting happiness.

THE QUALITIES OF FREEDOM AND REALIZATION

We mentioned earlier that this quality of cessation and the path that brings it about are what constitute *the jewel of the Dharma.* Progressively, in stages, we rid ourselves of obscurations, starting with the coarsest or the most apparent and applying steadily more powerful antidotes. First, we direct the antidotes to whatever flaws we have in our minds, so that eventually they no longer arise. Then we rid ourselves of even the latent tendencies of these afflictions. So gradually we are developing the qualities of freedom from these obscurations, along with their seeds. Until we gain all the qualities of having got rid of all the afflictions and everything that has to be eliminated, we have to continue training on increasingly higher paths.

This means there is a "stage of training" and then finally a "stage of no further training," where we have eliminated all that has to go and realized one of the various forms of awakening, leaving no need for any further training. According to the Mahayana, when we attain ultimate freedom from not only the disturbing emotions but also the subtle cognitive obscurations and habitual tendencies left behind by the disturbing emotions, that is the level of buddhahood. Until this stage is reached, you have to practice ridding yourself of the obscurations, beginning with the coarsest and most apparent, so that this freedom from the obscurations increases from what is a slight freedom at first to an ever-greater freedom. And from the moment you first actualize the truth of the path in order to bring about a genuine cessation of a particular flaw, you are said to be a member of "the sangha community of those in training."

So to bring these threads together, both the jewel of the Sangha, who are those in training, and the jewel of the Buddhas, that is, those who are beyond training, arise from the Dharma, meaning the two aspects of cessation and the path. When we talk about the jewel of the Sangha and the jewel of the Buddhas, we are not making a distinction based on how splendid they look, or who is seated on a higher throne, or even how fancy their hats are! The jewel of the Sangha and the jewel of the Buddhas are explained in terms of the untainted qualities manifest in their mindstreams. Therefore the jewel of the Dharma is in fact the most important of all. For if there is the jewel of the Dharma, there can be the jewel of the Sangha in training, and if there is a sangha in training, there can be a sangha of those beyond training.

If we really think about it then, we can come to understand that the jewel of the Buddha does not simply refer to a great historical figure but rather is to be explained in terms of qualities: the qualities of freedom from what has to be eliminated and the qualities of realization. This is a key understanding. It is in this light that we can see that the jewel of the Dharma is the most important of all. Based on the Dharma, the Sangha comes into being, and once training is completed and ultimate liberation is attained, that creates the jewel of the Sangha beyond training, or in other words, the jewel of the Buddhas.

If we were to explain the Buddha simply in terms of the splendor of his appearance, then of course he does have a crown protuberance, which is something we do lack. Otherwise, Buddha Shakyamuni was just a simple monk, as were Nagarjuna, Aryadeva, and his followers. So they would not seem so special compared to many of the lamas of today, who look very splendid indeed. I often joke that in the recent past in Tibet people used to judge a lama or a *tulku* according to how many horses and attendants he had in his entourage. Whenever a lama arrived followed by a great procession, everyone would think he must be a great master or important incarnation, present offerings of incense and all kinds of gifts, and make a big fuss. But then if a simple pilgrim turned up, someone who was truly learned and accomplished like Dza Patrul Rinpoche,[24] at best he might be given a little bit of roasted barley flour, but beyond that no one would pay him any attention at all. But once he had left to continue on his way, if something was found missing, they would all say, "Oh, that pilgrim must have taken it! He looked like a sneaky one!"

THE CHARACTERISTICS OF THE DHARMA

Generally, when we speak of the Three Jewels—the three objects of refuge—they are mentioned in the following order: Buddha, Dharma, and Sangha. This reflects the chronological order of their appearance. The Buddha, the master of the teachings, was the first to appear. Then, after attaining enlightenment, he turned the wheel of Dharma, so that there appeared the Dharma of transmission. His disciples put these teachings into practice and manifested the Dharma of realization. As they gradually gained the truth of the path of the sublime ones, the *aryas*,[25] the jewel of the Sangha, came into being. Therefore we speak of Buddha, Dharma, and Sangha.

When we say Dharma, or the teaching of Buddha, we understand that it mainly concerns *nirvana* or enlightenment. In fact, you could say that the defining characteristic of the Buddhadharma is nirvana, which is described as "the peace of passing beyond sorrow, the supreme freedom from passions." The practices of the three higher trainings of discipline, meditation, and wisdom, which enable us to achieve nirvana, are also part of what we think of as the Buddhadharma, but our overriding goal is the attainment of liberation and what is termed definitive goodness. Although this remains our ultimate objective, in order to achieve this goal, we also seek to attain a favorable rebirth in the higher states of existence;[26] but this is just a temporary objective, a way to obtain conditions conducive to the ultimate aim of definitive goodness.

It is because the attainment of these higher states is a temporary objective on the path that the methods for attaining them appear within the Buddha's teachings. But I don't think that they are really what characterize Buddhism. For one thing, similar teachings on attaining higher realms can also be found in other religions. Take the instruction on abstaining from taking life, for example, which is included within the Buddhist teachings in the discipline of avoiding the ten negative actions. There it is taught that we must refrain from taking the lives of others, avoid taking what has not been given, avoid sexual misconduct, and the rest. But simply to abstain from taking life does not necessarily count as a Buddhist practice. The injunction against killing is found in many other religions, and it is even to be found in secular laws that have nothing to do with religion or spirituality. Remember that the Buddhadharma is always concerned first and foremost with liberation. If you are observing the discipline of avoiding the ten negative actions so as to get a favorable rebirth, but you are doing this specifically in order to attain liberation, then it becomes Buddhadharma. That is why I maintain that the Buddhadharma is mainly concerned with nirvana.

What then is nirvana? When we say that nirvana means passing beyond or transcending sorrow, that mainly indicates transcending the causes of suffering, which are the afflictions. As we have seen, all phenomena are devoid of true existence; clinging to them as real is the ignorance that lies at the root of samsara and keeps us circling within cyclic existence. The basis or foundation for complete liberation from samsara is the *natural nirvana,* which is the fact that all phenomena are *naturally* empty of inherent existence. So the reason it is possible to attain nirvana is that it accords with the actual nature of things, which we call *natural nirvana.* We can gain complete freedom from this cycle of samsaric existence, since the reason we are here is our delusion about the actual nature of things.

It is because of the natural nirvana that the other types of nirvana are possible—the lesser nirvana, which is spoken of as *nirvana with remainder* and *nirvana without remainder,* and the greater or so-called *nonabiding nirvana,* which means transcending both samsaric existence and the limited quiescence of the lesser nirvana.[27]

As we saw, we can rid ourselves of the afflictions by applying antidotes, which means we can also use antidotes to rid ourselves of the habitual tendencies left behind by the afflictions.

The attainment of nirvana can also be termed *victory over the four maras or obstructive forces,* namely the afflictions, the aggregates, death, and desire.[28] When we refer to the Buddha as *Bhagavan* in Sanskrit, or *Chomdendé* in Tibetan, this refers to the fact that he "has vanquished *(chom)* the four and possesses *(den)* the six."[29] The most important point is that he has conquered the four obstructive forces. In fact, the Buddha Bhagavan has vanquished both coarse and subtle forms of these four obstructive forces. The arhats, by contrast, have conquered only the coarser forms of the four *maras.* Among these four obstructive forces, the most formidable of them all is the obstructive force of the afflictions. It is ultimately because of them, for example, that we are under the control of the obstructive force of the Lord of Death.

Therefore, recognizing the afflictions as our real enemy, applying antidotes to them, and seeing them not as something to indulge but as something to overcome—these are the hallmarks of the Buddhadharma. That is Buddhism. Someone who does not regard the afflictions as an enemy, but indulges in them, cannot be counted a genuine practitioner of the Buddhadharma.

In all the different vehicles of the teachings—"the vehicles leading from the origin," "the vehicles of Vedic asceticism," and "the vehicles of supreme and powerful transformative methods"[30]—we have to apply antidotes to the afflictions. There is a difference in the way the antidote is applied: whether the emotions are confronted directly, or transformed through skillful means to help accomplish the welfare of others, or liberated through recognizing their nature. Still, all the various approaches are alike in regarding the afflictions as something to be overcome by the use of antidotes.

So as we can see, the Buddhadharma is primarily concerned with recognizing afflictions as our real enemy and then applying antidotes to them. Because when we say that the Buddhadharma is about attaining nirvana, what is it that prevents us from attaining nirvana? It is the afflictions. So they have to be vanquished and overcome. As soon as we say that nirvana is the ultimate objective, it means we must not only recognize the afflictions that prevent us from reaching it but also become expert in how they work. Then, applying that newfound understanding about their workings, we must take care not to succumb or yield to them in any way.

THREE STAGES OF OVERCOMING AFFLICTIONS

The way to train in this while on the path was explained by the great master Aryadeva, Nagarjuna's main disciple, in his *Four Hundred Verses on the Middle Way:*

> At first, turn away from nonvirtue,
> In the middle, dispel misconceptions of self,
> Finally, go beyond all views—
> One who understands this is wise indeed.[31]

1. *Turning away from nonvirtue*

Our prime focus is the attainment of definitive goodness, but what prevents us from reaching it is the emotional obscurations. However, we cannot simply apply the antidotes to these afflictions and remove them at the outset, just like that. We need to practice lifetime after lifetime in order to gain complete freedom from them, so the first thing we need to do is secure a positive rebirth as a basis for practice. That is why we begin by practicing the discipline of avoiding the ten unwholesome actions, as a means to reach the higher states of existence. "Nonvirtue" in the first line of the quotation means the ten negative or unwholesome actions. We must turn away from these nonmeritorious actions, meaning that we refrain from negative conduct that is motivated by the afflictions. As a result, we will be reborn in the higher states of existence. That is the first stage.

2. *Dispelling conceptions of a self*

Then, at the second stage, since liberation is gained through applying antidotes to the afflictions, we need to become skillful at dealing with these afflictions. Of course, there are many different types, and we could apply a specific antidote to each one. As we saw earlier, there are antidotes that challenge the emotions head on, overwhelming them or reducing their intensity for a while, but they will not enable us to eradicate afflictions entirely. If we really look into what lies at the root of an affliction, apply the antidote to that fundamental, underlying cause, and remove it, then we will find that the very same antidote can automatically avert all the other afflictions, whether coarse or subtle. Therefore, as the root of the afflictions is our deluded clinging to true existence, the text says, "In the middle, dispel misconceptions of self." In other words, we have to eliminate clinging to a self by meditating on the wisdom that realizes selflessness.

3. *Going beyond all views*

Aryadeva's third line, "Finally, go beyond all views," indicates that we must rid ourselves not just of the afflictions but also of the habitual tendencies they create. Ridding ourselves of the afflictions alone is sufficient for reaching the level of definitive goodness that is liberation, but it is not enough to gain the ultimate level of definitive goodness, which is complete omniscience. To reach omniscience, we need to clear away the obscurations that obstruct the knowledge of all that is to be known. That is why it says "go beyond all views," meaning that we must cultivate the view of emptiness, accompanied by a vast accumulation of merit, as an antidote to the cognitive obscurations. It means that we must totally eliminate all distorted views, together with their habitual tendencies. Finally, Aryadeva says that if you practice in this way, you are "wise indeed."

GREATER AND LESSER VEHICLES

So there are two kinds of obscurations that we need to eliminate: emotional and cognitive. Now, the approach that focuses on abandoning just the emotional obscurations—gaining freedom from them and thereby attaining liberation and the level of arhat for oneself alone—is known as the *Lesser Vehicle.* It corresponds to the vehicle of shravakas and the vehicle of pratyekabuddhas. This is one approach, which prioritizes seeking liberation for oneself alone, and it is the path that is called the Hinayana.

Then there is another approach, which takes this first approach as its basis but goes further and applies the antidote to the cognitive obscurations, including the habitual tendencies left behind by the emotional obscurations. This is the approach that seeks the ultimate level of omniscience and buddhahood, and it is called the *Greater Vehicle,* or Mahayana. In both cases, the word vehicle implies a means for traveling along the path.

When we speak of greater and lesser vehicles, this is based on the scale of the motivation involved, the extent of the conduct to be practiced, and the magnitude of the result to be gained. The term *lesser vehicle* is not used in the teachings of the Lesser Vehicle itself; it occurs only in the texts of the Bodhisattva Vehicle, because of these differences when compared to the Basic Vehicle—the vastness of the motivation, the vastness of the conduct such as generosity, and the vastness of its result. It is because the Basic Vehicle thus seems lesser by comparison that it is called the Lesser Vehicle.

However, the term *lesser vehicle* is not intended to be derogatory in any way. Sometimes it may seem as if we, as followers of the Greater Vehicle, are making claims of superiority and dismissing the Basic Vehicle as inferior. People might even make this kind of judgment about the Theravada school. But that is not the case at all. The Theravada derives from the Sthaviravada, one of the main groups into which the eighteen early Buddhist schools were divided.[32] It would be a grave mistake to view this school as in any way inferior. In fact, the path that is taught in the scriptures of the Basic Vehicle is the foundation for the path taught in the texts of the Bodhisattva Vehicle. The Mahayana approach is predicated upon the teachings of the shravakas; in no way is it an entirely separate path.

According to one way of classifying the different vehicles, there are three: the vehicles of the shravakas, the pratyekabuddhas, and the bodhisattvas. More simply, you can identify two vehicles: the Basic Vehicle and the Mahayana. Then, within the Mahayana, there are the causal vehicle of the transcendent perfections and the resultant vajra vehicle of secret mantra, or Vajrayana. In Tibet, the Land of Snows, the complete spectrum of the Buddha's teachings was to be found: that is, the Basic Vehicle, Mahayana, and Vajrayana.

As the root text of the *Guhyasamaja Tantra* says:

Outwardly, maintain the discipline of the shravakas,
While inwardly delight in the practice of Guhyasamaja.

As this quotation indicates, there is a tradition of adhering to the discipline of the Vinaya in one's outer conduct, inwardly following the bodhisattva path, and secretly applying the Vajrayana. In this way, one individual can practice the Basic Vehicle, Mahayana, and Vajrayana at one and the same time.

THE THREE WISDOMS

As we bring all the levels of the teachings together like this, we must also combine the paths of study and practice. As it is said:

Learning does not guarantee saintliness,
Nor does saintliness guarantee learning.

This means that we must begin by studying, so that we know the characteristics of the path we intend to practice, we are prepared for any potential pitfalls, and we have some clear and thorough understanding of all that it entails. This comes from studying texts and receiving teachings and explanations from our teachers and Dharma friends, so that we develop the *wisdom born of study.* Then we can use this insight or intelligence to reflect on what we have learnt. It was Tsongkhapa who pointed out:

Examining thoroughly, by day and by night,
With fourfold reasoning, the meaning of what I have heard,
May I banish every doubt with the keen discernment
That is born of such contemplation.[33]

When we investigate and think deeply about what we have heard, after a while we begin to understand the main points of the teachings for ourselves and gain confidence in their truth and validity. This confidence is based on our own process of reflection and on what we have understood for ourselves. It is quite different from a theoretical knowledge of, and unquestioning reliance upon, what is said in the texts and teachings. It is the point when we begin to say to ourselves, "Ah, this is really true. This is actually how it is." This is known as *wisdom born of reflection.*

If we have nothing but the wisdom born of study, we may have some understanding, but this understanding will not be stable. For example, if we hear something we haven't heard before, we will get confused. Yet once the wisdom of study has developed into the wisdom born of reflection, we will have more confidence and certainty because of having thought things through deeply for ourselves. Then even when we hear something we have not heard before, we will be in a position to reflect on it and compare it with our own understanding. We won't be thrown straightaway into a state of confusion and begin to doubt all that we heard before. If we have really thought about the main points of the teachings and come to some understanding about them, then we will be able to reflect on anything else we hear in the light of that understanding. We will be able to put whatever we hear to the test and judge for ourselves whether it is valid or mistaken. We will have the confidence to do this. This is what we call the *wisdom born of reflection.*

Then, as we meditate more and more on these topics of reflection, which we have understood to be true, our understanding of them grows in clarity, until eventually it develops into an unshakable confidence and certainty. This is the *wisdom born of meditation.*

This shows the importance of combining study, reflection, and meditation. First we must study the texts; this is vital. Then we need to think deeply about what we have studied. Finally, we must integrate our understanding into our experience through practice, so that it really touches us and has a profound effect. This is the tradition as it was practiced in the past in Tibet.

DEEPENING LEVELS OF EXPERIENCE

We can also think about this process in terms of how it brings about increasingly profound levels of experience. First, we reflect again and again on what we have studied. Then, as we gain some stable confidence in our own understanding through this process of reflection, at some point we realize that by familiarizing ourselves with this understanding through meditation we will be able to transform our minds. To put it another way, we come to know that by meditating we will be able to gain for ourselves the qualities of realization mentioned in the teachings. This is known as *mastering experiences.*

Then, as we continue in the process and progressively familiarize ourselves with this understanding, we arrive at a point where, whenever we practice well, we are able to transform our minds, so that we actually experience what is mentioned in the texts. Yet whenever we are not deliberately applying the practice, these qualities are no longer there. This is known as the stage of *experience through effort.*

Eventually, as we continue to integrate our understanding through repeated practice and ever-deepening reflection, we reach the point at which our minds can be transformed automatically, whenever we are confronted with the appropriate conditions, whether good or bad. This is the stage where we enjoy *effortless experience.*

DISPELLING MISCONCEPTIONS

Furthermore, we can also think of this process in terms of how we dispel misconceptions. In the very beginning we have an unequivocal conviction in what is actually a mistaken and deluded viewpoint. But we don't even question it. We just believe that this is how it is. However, if we do start to question this viewpoint, then our conviction lessens and we begin to doubt it. There are actually three types of doubt: incorrect doubt, uncertain doubt, and correct doubt. The first type involves starting to think about the truth but still doubting it is correct. The second is more open but ambivalent and unsure of what is correct or incorrect. The third is when we start to believe in the truth.

Beyond doubt, the next stage is reached when we gain some understanding through analysis and investigation. Then we really start to believe in the truth. But we do not yet have the confidence that comes from contemplation using genuine logic. Eventually, however, by applying logical reasoning, we arrive at a valid cognition through what is known as *valid inference.* This happens when we have looked at something from every conceivable angle, and, having ruled out every possible alternative, we come to the firm conclusion that "this is it": this is the only possibility. With this, we gain complete confidence in the validity of our conclusion. If we continue to meditate on this understanding, it will develop into a clear experience, one that is non-conceptual, and this is what we call *valid direct perception*.

PART TWO

FINDING COMFORT AND EASE IN MEDITATION ON THE GREAT PERFECTION

CHAPTER 6

THE ANCIENT TRADITION OF THE NYINGMAPAS

THE WHOLE SPECTRUM of the Buddhist teachings, consisting of the Basic Vehicle, the Mahayana, and the Vajrayana, existed in Tibet. Over the course of time, on account of the historical dates and specific geographical location, different traditions gradually came into being. The masters of these traditions all transmitted the complete teaching of Buddha, but as the traditions spread, there developed slight differences of emphasis. On the basis of the dates when they first appeared, we speak of the earlier *(nyingma)* and later *(sarma)* traditions. These later traditions include several schools: the old Kadampas, Sakyapas, Kagyüpas, Jonangpas, and New Kadampas, who are also known as the Gelukpas. Each of these schools incorporates the complete teachings of the Basic Vehicle, Mahayana, and Vajrayana; they are all alike in combining the approaches of sutra and tantra; and they all follow the philosophical tradition of the Middle Way, or Madhyamaka.

Now the text that we are about to embark on, and make a connection with, belongs to the Nyingma ancient translation school. Originally, I had not intended to base my teaching on a text, as I thought it would be better to speak more generally about Dzogchen and Mahamudra. But after further thought, I decided that it might be better after all, and more complete, if I were to teach from a text. The one I have chosen was composed by the omniscient Longchen Rabjam. He was a prolific author, and his writings, such as *The Seven Treasuries,* range from the very detailed and elaborate to the markedly succinct. *Finding Comfort and Ease in Meditation,* which belongs to *The Trilogy of Finding Comfort and Ease,* is one of his more concise works.

My plan is to receive the transmissions for all of Longchen Rabjam's *Seven Treasuries* from Kyabjé Trulshik Rinpoche this winter, but at the moment I am receiving the transmission of *Finding Comfort and Ease in Meditation,* and I thought it might be appropriate to share with you an explanation of this text.

As I mentioned earlier, since learning is no guarantee of saintliness and being saintly no guarantee of learning, in all the Tibetan traditions—Sakya, Geluk, Kagyü, and Nyingma—it is held that a holy person should embody the three qualities of learning, discipline, and kindness.[34] Throughout Tibetan history, it was invariably the case that the greatest masters, saints, and scholars of all schools—those who made an outstanding contribution to the teachings—all combined within themselves both learning and accomplishment. If we take the Nyingma school, one example was Rongzom Chökyi Zangpo, a master who was unbelievably learned. He was an extraordinary scholar, who grew up around the time that Lord Atisha came to Tibet.[35] I received the transmission for his commentary to *The Secret Essence Tantra,* which is called *The Jewel Commentary.* He also wrote a famous text entitled *Entrance to the Way of the Mahayana.* Rongzom Chökyi Zangpo was one of the greatest of scholars, who was both exceptionally erudite and realized at one and the same time.

Likewise, the omniscient Longchen Rabjam, who lived before Tsongkhapa and at the same time as Butön Rinchen Drup,[36] was also exceedingly learned, as can be seen by looking at his *Seven Treasuries.* They betray a remarkable breadth of learning, encompassing every aspect of the teachings, from the sutrayana and ordinary fields of knowledge through to the highest levels of tantra. A few centuries later came the omniscient Jikmé Lingpa, who, it seems, may not have studied so much formally but naturally possessed many noble qualities and through his practice caused his innate wisdom and intelligence to burst out from within. He composed *The Treasury of Precious Qualities* and its two auto-commentaries, known as "the two chariots"—*The Chariot to Omniscience* and *The Chariot of the Two Truths,* which include numerous references to the classical scriptures.

There have been many learned masters in the Nyingma tradition, and in recent times particularly in eastern Tibet there appeared some truly outstanding teachers. Mipham Choklé Namgyal[37] is of course well known to everyone, but then the one whom I hold in especially high regard is Dodrup Jikmé Tenpé Nyima. I think his works are simply astounding. They really are incredible. They do not fill many volumes, but they are of such a high standard. To my mind, they are possibly even greater than the writings of the omniscient Mipham in the manner they explain the subtleties of the teachings and unravel the difficult points. Dodrup Jikmé Tenpé Nyima was simply amazing!

Among his students was a great teacher called Tulku Tsullo, or Tsultrim Zangpo, a fully ordained monk and a remarkable scholar. He wrote an extensive commentary on Ngari Panchen Pema Wangyal's *Ascertainment of the Three Vows,* which is quite exceptional, as well as instruction manuals on Dzogchen and a commentary on *The Aspiration Prayer of Kuntuzangpo.*[38] It seems that many of his writings were barely completed when the troubles began in Tibet, and although printing blocks were made, they were misplaced. Just recently, I received a copy of a set of his writings containing what has been recovered so far, all compiled together.[39] So the fact is that there were many extraordinarily learned practitioners in the Nyingma school of the early translations in Tibet.

BALANCING STUDY AND PRACTICE

Sometimes there is a feeling that the Kagyü practitioners of Mahamudra or the Nyingma practitioners of Dzogpachenpo have no need to study the great classical treatises. There is a notion that this is more the province of the Sakyapas and Gelukpas. People tend to think that the main practice for Mahamudra and Dzogchen practitioners is just to sit in meditation and look, as the Great Fifth Dalai Lama remarked, like a lifeless statue. But that is incorrect. It would be equally incorrect to think that the Sakya and Geluk approaches are about nothing but study. For study alone is not enough; it is essential to integrate whatever you have learned by applying it in practice. Otherwise, as I often joke, there is a danger of ending up like the geshe in the well-known story, who was very learned in debate but did not allow the teachings to penetrate his basic character. He ended up being reborn as a ghost with a donkey's head! So a scholastic approach on its own is not sufficient; we need to integrate the meaning of whatever we have learnt.

As Gungthang Tsang[40] said:

> Learned, due to studying many teachings and investigating them in great detail,
> Venerable, due to applying the meaning of what you learned to your mindstream,
> Kind-hearted, due to dedicating all this for the sake of the teachings and beings.

As this indicates, it is important to combine these three qualities—learning, discipline, and kind-heartedness. And Tsongkhapa writes:

> Bereft of the Dharma, even though you have heard many teachings—
> This is the mistake of not heeding the teachings as personal advice.[41]

As he points out, we need to apply ourselves diligently to the practice by taking all the teachings as personal advice, rather than simply leaving everything on the level of academic theory.

Of course, history tells us of great practitioners of the Mahamudra and Dzogchen teachings who did not study the classical texts at all and yet who, through devoting themselves to meditation practice with exceptional diligence and "raising the victory banner of spiritual practice," reached very high levels of realization. Such outstanding practitioners have indeed existed, masters such as the great lord of yogins, Milarepa. But they were individuals who had already trained in the past and whose karmic predispositions were then awakened. They were not like us, who have hardly done anything until now! If we tried to practice and make the same progress as them without, as they say, "lighting the lamp of study," I think it would be extremely difficult.

THE GENERAL AND INDIVIDUAL APPROACHES

Some scholars have drawn a distinction between the more general approach related to the teachings as a whole and the approach that is more specific to certain individuals. From the more general point of view, it is vitally important to gain some understanding of the teachings as a whole by studying the works of masters such as the Six Ornaments and Two Supreme Ones.[42] As an example of the teachings given for specific individuals, we can think of Milarepa and how he would teach his disciples, who had already reached a high level of realization, with an instruction in a very few words that would awaken their potential. For a master such as Milarepa, who possessed the ability to read others' minds, there is no need to present things in a more general way. Straightaway, he can give an instruction that is specifically tailored to a particular individual. Many of his songs of realization are like this; they encapsulate an instruction in just a few words and manage to convey the experience itself, directly, without the need for an elaborate explanation.

When such raw, naked advice is given according to a student's specific needs, it can easily bring about genuine experience and realization in his or her mind. Saraha and many of the great siddhas of India would teach in exactly this manner, through songs of realization, or *dohas.* These songs fall more into the category of teachings for specific individuals, whereas the works of Nagarjuna and Aryadeva, Asanga and Vasubandhu, Shantideva, Dignaga, Dharmakirti, and the like, represent more general presentations of the teachings in their entirety, intended to instill an overall understanding.

This same principle holds true for all four schools of Tibetan Buddhism. Each has a more general method of teaching, which presents the teachings as a whole, and the specific method catering to the individual. If we consider the Kadam school, for example, it has three traditions of teaching: the scriptural Kadam, the graduated path Kadam, and the pith instruction Kadam. I think it is possible to say that the pith instruction Kadam is more related to the specific approach for the individual, whereas the scriptural Kadam, which is based on instructions taken from the major classical texts, is more in keeping with the general approach to the teachings.

What I have just explained is an important point and one that we need to understand. Otherwise we might say things like, "I'm a Kagyüpa, I'm a Nyingmapa, I don't need to study books that much, I'll just concentrate on gaining the accomplishments of practice, the siddhis, right away". Of course, it is possible that someone could gain accomplishments with an attitude like this, but you need to take the greatest possible care. Otherwise, the danger is that you may have no idea how these accomplishments are going to come about.

On the other hand, we could study the great classical texts and get totally lost in the words, so that we don't really derive any benefit from them but instead become proud of ourselves and feel competitive toward others. But when we don't know much ourselves, it's hardly the time to start pitting ourselves against others or to feel self-important. It's only when we really know something for sure that we can afford to feel a little proud of ourselves! If not, there is no reason to be conceited. Still, this does occur: when people think they know something, they can get very full of themselves. This is known as "bringing gods down to the level of demons,"[43] or turning medicine into poison.

Going back to what we said earlier, learning is no guarantee of saintliness, just as being saintly is no guarantee of learning, and so our priority should be to combine all three qualities of learning, discipline, and kind-heartedness.

CHAPTER 7

THE UNIQUENESS OF THE GREAT PERFECTION

FINDING COMFORT AND EASE IN MEDITATION ON THE GREAT PERFECTION

Now we come to *Finding Comfort and Ease in Meditation on the Great Perfection,* by the omniscient Longchen Rabjam. Traditionally, we say that in Tibet there were three emanations of Manjushri, the buddha of wisdom: Longchen Rabjam, Sakya Pandita, and Tsongkhapa. In the early 1960s, at a time when only a few monasteries had been rebuilt in India, a small temple was constructed in Bylakuppe in South India by Drakyap Rinpoche.[44] He told me that inside the temple he had placed statues of these three emanations of Manjushri. I thought that this was wonderful, because Longchen Rabjam, Sakya Pandita, and Tsongkhapa are universally acknowledged as among the greatest scholars in the Tibetan tradition.

The title of this text is *Finding Comfort and Ease in Meditation on the Great Perfection.* The title is first given in Sanskrit: *Mahasandhi Dhyana Vishranta Nama.* This text does not originate in India; it was composed by Longchen Rabjam himself in Tibetan, but by providing the title in Sanskrit, he is indicating that the teaching has its origins in the sutras, tantras, and teachings of the great Indian masters of the past.

With regard to the title, *Finding Comfort and Ease in Meditation on the Great Perfection,* there are many ways to explain the Great Perfection, Dzogpachenpo. One of them, for example, is by means of the ground, path, and fruition of Dzogpachenpo. However, the most important way to understand the Great Perfection is in terms of "essence, nature, and compassionate energy," according to which the essence is primordial purity and the nature is spontaneous presence. Very simply, this refers to the fact that all the phenomena of samsara, nirvana, and the path are, by their very nature, the rigpa awareness that is the primordial buddha Samantabhadra, and they are never outside of the primordial expanse of buddhahood. This rigpa awareness, which is Samantabhadra, is the fundamental innate mind of clear light.

TAKING PRIMORDIAL WISDOM AS THE PATH

In the Nyingma tradition a sequence of nine vehicles is taught: the vehicles of (1) shravakas, (2) pratyekabuddhas, and (3) bodhisattvas; the three outer tantras of (4) kriya, (5) upa, and (6) yoga tantra; and the three inner tantras of (7) mahayoga, (8) anuyoga, and (9) atiyoga. The first eight vehicles, up to and including anuyoga, are systems based on the ordinary mind. It is said that they take the ordinary mind as the path. The ninth vehicle, atiyoga, which corresponds to Dzogpachenpo, takes primordial wisdom as the path.

There are many ways to interpret this term *primordial wisdom*. You could, for example, understand it to mean "the untainted wisdom of the aryas."[45] However, what we are referring to here when we say "taking primordial wisdom as the path" is the unchanging rigpa awareness, which is "just the same later as it was before."[46] This unchanging rigpa is Samantabhadra, the primordial buddha. Even while we remain in samsara, this ground, our fundamental nature, is never tainted by the transient stains of discursive thought. Neither the phenomena of samsara nor their causes, the karmic winds and ordinary thought patterns, have ever stained or defiled the purity of rigpa.

Although we might wish to attain enlightenment with our ordinary minds, if we think about this deeply and carefully, we will realize that the coarse level of our ordinary consciousness does not continue until buddhahood. Only the fundamental innate mind of clear light is present at the level of omniscience, and what is spoken of in Dzogchen as the rigpa awareness, the primordial buddha Samantabhadra, is in fact to be understood as this fundamental innate mind of clear light. It is the basis for the arising of all samsara and nirvana, and it has always been primordially free. This is the primordial wisdom that

Dzogpachenpo takes as the path. So the text of *Finding Comfort and Ease in Meditation on the Great Perfection* begins:

Homage to the glorious Samantabhadra!

Now, when we say that the first eight vehicles are systems based on the ordinary mind, the seventh and eighth vehicles—mahayoga and anuyoga—are in fact approaches that work with the fundamental innate mind of clear light. Nevertheless they do so indirectly, by using techniques in order to make this clear light manifest, such as the deity yoga of the generation phase or else the yoga of the channels, wind energies, and essences. For example, in the *Guhyasamaja Tantra,* which is followed in the new translation tradition, there are explanations of how to work mainly with the wind energy, or *prana,* as a method to bring about the arising of the fundamental innate mind of clear light. *The Kalachakra Tantra* teaches how to focus on vital points within the channels, wind energies, and essences in order to make manifest "the coemergent wisdom of unchanging great bliss." And the *Chakrasamvara Tantra* is similar. All the highest yoga tantras of the new translation tradition of tantra in fact follow this same principle. They are approaches that take the fundamental innate mind of clear light as the path, but they use techniques that are based on the ordinary coarse mind in order to make this fundamental innate mind of clear light manifest. Dzogpachenpo, by contrast, employs nothing but the fundamental innate mind of clear light, which is present up until buddhahood. It does not employ the ordinary coarse, adventitious mind at all.

Now, this ordinary coarse, adventitious mind lasts up until the three appearances of appearance, increase, and attainment dissolve. It does not continue until enlightenment. If we explain this using the terminology of the *Guhyasamaja,* at the point when one has realized the actual clear light, after having traversed the three appearances of the stages of dissolution and the three appearances of the reversal process, then the three appearances can never arise again. As the master Nagabodhi explains in his *Analysis of Action,*[47] until the three appearances are purified, no matter how much we might practice generosity, giving away even our limbs and our heads, or how much we might observe discipline or train in any other practice, we will not be able to attain enlightenment. But once these three are purified, there is no doubt that we will reach buddhahood. Upon cessation of the coarse adventitious states of mind—which continue for as long as these three appearances last—the wisdom of omniscience dawns. Therefore, the level of consciousness that continues until the level of omniscience can only be the fundamental innate mind of clear light.

Most paths operate on the basis of reversing the arising of these three appearances, but the uniqueness of Dzogchen is that it is based exclusively on the fundamental innate mind of clear light. This is the unique and profound feature of Dzogchen. The Dzogchen teachings are also very precise in talking about rigpa and categorizing it with many subtle distinctions. So they speak of "the essential rigpa," "rigpa of the ground," "rigpa of all-embracing spontaneous presence that is the ultimate state of freedom," and "the effulgent rigpa." A distinction is made between the ground of being and the appearances of that ground; the effulgent rigpa that is present in the appearances arising from the ground is not actually the same as the essential rigpa.[48] Nevertheless, these instances of rigpa are all alike in the sense that, in their essence, they are unstained by adventitious thoughts.

Therefore, the method for making manifest the fundamental innate mind of clear light is to arrive at the essential rigpa by means of the effulgent rigpa, which is the same in essence as the rigpa of the ground. This is based on the fact that all levels of consciousness, including the coarsest level of the ordinary confused mind, are permeated by an aspect of rigpa, or clear light, and that this can be pointed out to us by an experienced master in whom we have faith and devotion. When circumstances coincide like this in the right way and we actually recognize the nature of this rigpa, we can take rigpa, and rigpa alone, as the basis of our practice and use the ultimate rigpa of the ground as our path. This is what is meant by "taking primordial wisdom as the path."

So we are not confined to the level of the ordinary coarse, confused mind, nor is this a method that uses the ordinary mind in order to make manifest the fundamental innate mind of clear light. Rather, it is using the experience of an aspect of the fundamental innate mind of clear light *itself* in order to make the experience of the clear light of the ground progressively clearer. This is why it is more profound than the mahayoga and anuyoga approaches.

Whether we speak of the tantras of the new translation tradition or of mahayoga and anuyoga, the method for making the fundamental innate mind of clear light manifest is to cause ordinary thought patterns to cease. Then, for as long as the fundamental innate mind of clear light is experienced, the ordinary thoughts lie dormant. Conversely, as long as the ordinary thoughts are manifest, the fundamental innate mind of clear light remains dormant. But here, in Dzogchen, even though the rigpa of the ground may be similarly dormant, we can recognize the effulgent rigpa even in the midst of turbulent thoughts and emotions—if, that is, we have some experience and are therefore able to distinguish it correctly. There is a way to lay bare our rigpa, so that it does not get swept away by ordinary thoughts. In a nutshell, by staying unstained by clinging and not allowing awareness to chase after objects of thought, we can uncover or lay bare our rigpa and let it find its own stability. This is what is meant by "taking the primordial wisdom of rigpa as the path." And this is the special, profound feature of Dzogchen.

A PROFOUND CRUCIAL POINT OF DZOGPACHENPO

To put it simply, the basic space in which the three *kayas* or the four *kayas* of buddhahood[49] are accomplished is the fundamental innate mind of clear light. Like the other approaches, Dzogchen makes this fundamental innate mind of clear light manifest. However, the way it does so is not by using the ordinary coarse mind but by working with, and taking into experience, the aware aspect of the fundamental innate mind of clear light. This is the extraordinary, profound, and unique feature of Dzogchen.

The Great Fifth Dalai Lama, in his *Words of the Vidyadharas,*[50] says:

> The hollow assertions of some proud scholars,
> Who hope for buddhahood outside themselves,
> Are just like rituals in the west to exorcise demons
> to the east.

> Seeing this, the great secret of liberating the defiled aggregates into a body of light
> Is a special feature of the Ancient Tradition.[51]

The channels, wind energies, and essences of the body exist in coarse, subtle, and extremely subtle forms. It is by focusing on and penetrating the vital points of the extremely subtle channels, wind energies, and essences that we can cause the coarse physical body of flesh and blood to dissolve without leaving any physical remains behind.

This is not simply ancient history. Just two years ago, in the province of Nyarong in East Tibet, a great lama called Khenpo Achung achieved this. He had gone to Lhasa at an early age and spent several years studying at Sera monastery, where he may have received some teachings on Vajrayogini from Trijang Rinpoche. His main practice, however, was Dzogchen, which he practiced from a young age. He was also a practitioner of Vajrakilaya and was recognized as one of the custodians of Dudjom Rinpoche's Vajrakilaya teachings. Later, with the disturbances in Tibet, it seems he spent most of his time simply reciting mani mantras. Then, two years ago in Nyarong, he passed away at his residence. Before he passed away, he wrapped himself in his robes and instructed his followers not to touch his body until seven days after he had died. After the allotted time had passed, when they looked, all that remained were his robes. There was nothing else. Even his hair and nails had vanished. This definitely happened. One of his students came to see me in India and told me exactly what occurred. And his Dharma friend, whose name I think is Nyarong Lama Drimé Özer, also confirmed what had taken place.[52]

So this is not just ancient history, and these are not just tales. This is something people have actually seen with their own eyes. Yet it is not easily accomplished; it implies a lifetime entirely devoted to practice with concerted and single-pointed effort, having given up ordinary concerns and worldly affairs. You shouldn't ever imagine that attaining enlightenment in the rainbow body of the Great Perfection is something you can attain easily, just like that. It is extremely difficult.

The Fifth Dalai Lama continues:

> This is not an attempt to bring liberation by misleading others,
> Offering clever explanations invented after merely glancing through the texts,
> Like trying to pour from one empty vessel into another.
> For I have some measure of confidence and experience
> From applying the naked instructions directly to my mind.
> This was not composed with an afflicted mind out of mundane concerns,
> But with a noble intention, as pure as the autumn moon—
> The wish that these profound instructions may remain for as long as the Buddhadharma,
> In order to benefit the fortunate who have faith just as I do.[53]

I do really appreciate, and rejoice in, the extraordinary achievements of the Fifth Dalai Lama and likewise of all those great masters from all over Tibet, who upheld, preserved, and spread the teachings from different traditions, without any bias. Even though we might feel we are not able to continue their legacy, we can still consider that we are trying to follow in their footsteps and make every effort to do so.

In this text, he also speaks about primordial purity and spontaneous perfection. He says that *primordially pure* means never having been stained by faults, and *spontaneously perfect* means that the enlightened qualities have always been complete.[54]

There seem to be two ways of explaining primordial purity, which the Fifth Dalai Lama says has "never been stained by faults." The first is according to the view of the Middle Way that is common to both sutra and tantra, in which context it means freedom from all the conceptual constructs, such as the eight extremes.[55] The other explanation is that it refers to the purity of the fundamental innate mind of clear light, which is never stained by ordinary, adventitious thoughts.

When the text explains spontaneous perfection as meaning "the enlightened qualities have always been complete," it indicates that the potential for accomplishing the four kayas is complete within the fundamental innate mind of clear light, just as the potential for knowing objects is an inherent part of the ordinary mind "that is clear and knowing." That is just its nature. Rigpa will still be present when the four kayas are attained, once the ordinary habitual patterns of samsara associated with the three appearances have all ceased. And that is what is indicated by saying "the enlightened qualities have always been complete."

This means that the four kayas will actually manifest when the potential that is already there has been fully realized—that is to say, they do not have to be newly created. Yet this does not mean that the kayas are actually present within our minds right now. They are what we call qualities of basic space, as opposed to qualities of fruition. This potential for the four kayas, which is complete with the buddha nature, or sugatagarbha, corresponds to what is termed the qualities of basic space. When these qualities of basic space are perfected, they become the qualities of fruition. And so "the enlightened qualities have always been complete."

The Great Fifth Dalai Lama then goes on to say:

> Since all the phenomena of samsara and nirvana are perfect in this vehicle of naturally spontaneous perfection, it is called the *natural Great Perfection.* This natural condition, which has never been stained by the defilements of thoughts and emotions, is pointed out directly. A profound crucial point of the Great Perfection, a unique feature that is not to be found in the intrinsic emptiness or extrinsic emptiness traditions of Madhyamaka,[56] nor in the Mahamudra, and so on, is the secret terminology that draws clear and precise distinctions with regard to direct and naked realization and does not confuse the ordinary mind with rigpa. This is not just a profound crucial point; if you really understand it thoroughly, it is also none other than the ultimate intent of the new translation tantras.

What is implied here is that rigpa is the equivalent of the state that arises when, by following the new translation tantra tradition, one manages to arrest all the ordinary impure coarse, subtle, and extremely subtle karmic winds and thought states that are associated with the three appearances.

The Fifth Dalai Lama continues by quoting from the *Concise Kalachakra Tantra:*

> Pervading space, the vajra of space, devoid of object
> and feature,
> Also remains at the center of the body.

And then from the *Hevajra Tantra:*

> Supreme wisdom dwells in the body.
> Those who are obscured by the darkness of ignorance
> Hold that buddhahood lies somewhere apart from the body,
> But it dwells within the body, although not caused by
> the body.

EMPTINESS ENDOWED WITH ALL THE SUPREME ATTRIBUTES

The Fifth Dalai Lama's text mentions intrinsic emptiness, and this needs to be understood correctly. As I said earlier, when we talk about phenomena being empty, this does not mean that they are empty of something else, as in one thing being empty of another, but rather that they are empty of real existence by virtue of their very nature. In his writings, the glorious Chandrakirti quotes the following line from *The Heap of Jewels Sutra:*

> Emptiness does not make phenomena empty. Phenomena themselves are emptiness.[57]

So this is not a matter of one thing being empty of another but of things being empty by their very nature. In other words, it is not the absence of an object of negation that is separate from the basis for negation but the fact that the object of negation is not to be found within that very basis. If we consider it carefully, we can see that the genuine view of intrinsic emptiness, the view of the Middle Way, which is common to both sutra and tantra, is the direct antidote that removes the obscurations in both the Basic Vehicle and the Mahayana.

However, when we come to the actual attainment of omniscience, emptiness is explained as in this quotation from the *Kalachakra Tantra:*

> The aggregates, when analyzed, are found to be emptiness,
> Devoid of any substance, like a hollow plantain tree,
> But this form of emptiness is not like the emptiness
> That is endowed with all the supreme attributes.[58]

There are different ways of explaining the first two lines, but according to Khedrup Norzang Gyatso,[59] they refer to the process of analyzing the aggregates using the logical arguments, such as "neither one nor many" and recognizing the emptiness that is merely the negation of true existence. When we meditate on this, it functions as the antidote to the perception of things as real and can help us overcome this clinging to reality.

Yet meditation on just this emptiness alone cannot bring us the ultimate fruition of omniscience. To attain that, we need to cultivate "emptiness endowed with all the supreme attributes." In the teachings on the *Kalachakra Tantra,* this is explained as meaning that the mind that meditates on emptiness needs to be suffused with "unchanging bliss." Not only that, but we also need to meditate on "emptiness endowed with attributes." "Emptiness devoid of features" alone is not enough. We need to combine emptiness with features and emptiness without features in order to reach omniscience.

So when the text says "intrinsic emptiness," even the genuine view of intrinsic emptiness is not sufficient for reaching omniscience. Let's conclude by reviewing the words of the Fifth Dalai Lama:

> A profound crucial point of the Great Perfection, a unique feature that is not to be found in the intrinsic emptiness or extrinsic emptiness traditions of Madhyamaka, nor in the Mahamudra, and so on, is the secret terminology that draws clear and precise distinctions with regard to direct and naked realization and does not confuse the ordinary mind with rigpa.

HOMAGE TO THE PRIMORDIAL NATURE

In *Finding Comfort and Ease in Meditation on the Great Perfection* there now follows this verse of homage:

> **Homage to the primordial nature, sphere of purity, equal to space,**
> **Supreme Dharma, unfluctuating, utterly free of conceptual elaboration,**
> **The clear light nature of mind, essence of awakening,**
> **The perfect ground, beyond any transition or change!**

Here "primordial nature" signifies that the fundamental innate mind of clear light is not something that is newly created but our original nature. "Sphere of purity, equal to space" refers to the aspect of the empty essence, the basis for the arising of all the phenomena of samsara and nirvana. The comparison with space is made because space is the most fundamental of the elements, the one out of which all the other elements arise. First there is space, then wind, then fire, water, and earth. When the elements dissolve, they do so in the reverse order: earth, water, fire, wind, and finally space. So I think the analogy here is that just as space is the basis for the arising of all the other elements, this is the basis for the arising of all the phenomena of samsara and nirvana. It is called the "sphere of purity" since, even though impure phenomena may arise, its essence is never stained by these impurities.

"Unfluctuating" means that it is beyond change. This is not quite the same as being permanent, however. The fundamental innate mind of clear light is sometimes said to be "uncompounded." When we say *uncompounded clear light,* Dodrupchen Jikmé Tenpé Nyima and many other scholars agree this means that it is not something newly created by the coming together of causes and conditions. It is uncompounded not in the sense of being permanent and static but in not being newly created by causes and conditions. And yet it is permanent in the sense of being a permanent continuity that has always been there primordially, from time without beginning. This is also why we use the term *permanent* for the enlightened activity of the buddhas, because they exhibit this everlasting continuity.[60]

The phrase "utterly free of conceptual elaboration" can refer firstly to the freedom from the conceptual elaborations that are to be negated. When we say the *union of awareness and emptiness,* this means that the wisdom of rigpa is empty by its very nature. Since it is empty by its very nature, it is beyond all the conceptual elaborations and mental imputations that are to be negated. Alternatively, we could say that when the fundamental innate mind of clear light is realized, as the rigpa of the ground manifests, all the conceptual elaborations of "the appearances from the ground" are naturally pacified.

That clear light is the nature of mind, its essence untouched by any stain. To sum up, as all the conceptual elaborations of the appearances of the ground subside, the ground itself comes to the fore and is evident. And when, like this, the alaya[61] is completely purified, the two truths are understood in a single instant and the states of meditation and postmeditation merge.

As the verse says, this is what we call "clear light," and it is "the nature of mind," since it is the basic nature that underlies all the adventitious states of mind. It is called "the essence of awakening" because ultimately "awakening" refers to the fundamental innate mind of clear light. It is "the perfect ground, beyond any transition or change."

THE WISDOM OF ONE'S OWN SELF-KNOWING AWARENESS

Following the homage comes a verse expressing the intention of the author and his reason for writing the text.

> **In order that you might realize the wisdom of your own self-knowing awareness,**
> **The exceedingly wondrous wisdom mind of all the victorious ones,**
> **I have gathered the quintessence of tantras, oral transmissions, and pith instructions**
> **And offer this explanation according to the way it is practiced. So listen well!**

The term *wisdom of one's own self-knowing awareness* is found in both the sutras and the tantras, but there seem to be slight differences as to how it should be understood in the various texts. The meaning common to both sutra and tantra is the enlightened mind of the buddhas, the wisdom in which the nature of reality is ascertained directly. This is described as "the exceedingly wondrous wisdom mind of all the victorious ones." The uncommon understanding of *wisdom of one's own self-knowing awareness,* which is specific to the inner tantras, is that it refers to the ultimate state of Dzogpachenpo, the wisdom of the fundamental innate mind of clear light. Longchenpa says that in order for us to realize this wisdom of our own self-knowing awareness, he has gathered the quintessence of the tantras, oral transmissions, and pith instructions, meaning that he has brought together the essential points respectively from the mahayoga, anuyoga, and atiyoga. He explains that he has not done this as a theoretical exercise but so that it can be put into practice. In this verse he not only states his intention to compose the text but also encourages the appropriate students to study these teachings.

The wisdom of our own self-knowing awareness, as it is explained in the interpretation that is common to both sutra and tantra, could be said to refer to the transcendent perfection of wisdom, *prajnaparamita,* which is the "mother" who gives birth to the four types of "sublime" offspring—the shravakas, pratyekabuddhas, bodhisattvas, and buddhas—as mentioned in the homage from *The Ornament of Clear Realization:*

> Homage to you, the mother of the buddhas and all the hearers and bodhisattvas.

Even to realize the awakening of a shravaka or a pratyekabuddha, it is necessary to have the view of emptiness and to recognize the wisdom of one's own self-knowing awareness. If we take the state of liberation, it is the freedom from the bonds of the disturbing emotions. The root of the disturbing emotions is the delusion of clinging to things as real. And the direct antidote to this is to arouse within one's mind the wisdom that realizes emptiness. When the wisdom directly realizing emptiness becomes fully developed, it functions as an antidote to all forms of self-clinging.

This is the authentic view of the Middle Way from the point of view of sutra and tantra. But this alone is not able to counteract the subtlemost cognitive obscurations. From the point of view of the highest yoga tantra teachings, even the wisdom that realizes emptiness endowed with all the supreme attributes, the skillful means of the six transcendent perfections motivated by bodhichitta, is still not able to function as an antidote to the subtlest cognitive obscurations. In order to overcome these subtlest of cognitive obscurations, or the habitual tendencies of the transference of the three appearances, there needs to be the realization of the fundamental innate mind of clear light, which is beyond the three appearances. This clear light is the only antidote to the subtlest forms of cognitive obscuration. Therefore, in order to attain the wisdom of omniscience, we need to make manifest the rigpa that is Samantabhadra, the fundamental innate mind of clear light. This seems to be the way it is explained in all the old and new traditions of tantra.

Longchenpa continues:

On mountaintops, in secluded forests, and on islands, and the like,
Places that are agreeable to the mind and well suited to the season,
Cultivate tranquil samadhi, which is single-pointed and unwavering—
Clear light, which is free from the slightest conceptual elaboration.

This is achieved naturally when three pure factors come together:
The ideal location, individual, and Dharma to be practiced.

These are the three main divisions of *Finding Comfort and Ease in Meditation on the Great Perfection:*

- the place where the practice is carried out,
- the individual who does the practice,
- and the actual Dharma that is practiced.

CHAPTER 8

THE ENVIRONMENT AND PLACES CONDUCIVE TO MEDITATION

WHEN WE FIRST BEGIN to meditate, our outer circumstances, such as our location and our companions, can have a significant influence and help or hinder us in our practice. It is when we become more familiar with the practice and gain some measure of stability and assurance that outer conditions will no longer affect us. It is because the environment for practice is so important for beginners that it is explained here in quite some detail.

Longchenpa begins, then, by explaining the locations for practice:

First of all, the location must be one that is secluded and agreeable,
Somewhere conducive to spiritual practice in the different seasons.

First, he describes the ideal locations in terms of the four seasons:

In *summer*, meditate in cooler dwellings and cooler locations,
In places near to glaciers, or on mountaintops, and the like,
In simple dwellings made out of reeds, bamboo, or straw.

In the *autumn,* adjust your diet, your clothing, and your conduct,
And stay in a region and dwelling of moderate temperature,
Such as a forest, or a mountainside, or a building made of stone.

In *winter,* stay somewhere warmer at a lower altitude,
Such as a forest, a rocky cave, or a hollow in the earth,
And adjust your diet, clothing, bedding, and the rest.

In the *spring,* stay in the mountains or on the edges of a forest,
On a deserted island or in buildings with mild and even temperature,
With diet, clothing, and conduct all suitably attuned—this is crucially important.

Next, he explains the reasons that there is a benefit to certain *particular* locations.

There is an important interconnection between outer and inner,
So keep to inspiring and secluded places that you find uplifting.

This brings to mind a more general maxim: "A good place, with good companions…" That is, you need a place that is attractive and pleasing to you, where you are away from distraction and where your surroundings make you feel comfortable and at ease.

High among the mountains the mind grows clear and expansive,
The perfect place to bring freshness when dull and to practice the generation phase.

Indeed, it is said that when we practice in places that are high up, like mountaintops, our mind becomes clear and expansive. We can see this for ourselves when we go to places that have vast panoramic views; they definitely make our minds more expansive, open, and lucid. Of course, when we advise practicing on top of mountains, you should not go too high, or you might just end up with a headache or altitude sickness!

Such places, it says, are particularly good for avoiding mental dullness. This means a lack of brightness and enthusiasm. There are, of course, different degrees of dullness, gross and subtle. Sometimes it is the equivalent of feeling discouraged. It can take the form of a lack of enthusiasm and inspiration, a listless and lethargic state in which there is no freshness or alertness. Mountainous places are said to be good for clearing away such states of dullness.

The text then continues:

Snowclad regions help make samadhi clear and awareness bright
and lucid,
Ideal for cultivating vipashyana and where obstacles are few.

Forests bring stillness of mind and help us develop mental stability,
So they are ideal places for cultivating shamatha with a sense of ease.
Below rocky cliffs a vivid sense of impermanence and disenchantment dawns,
Clear and inspired, helping us to achieve the union of shamatha
and vipashyana.

On the banks of a river, our attention becomes well focused,
And the wish to escape samsara comes rapid and afresh.

Charnel grounds are powerful places for swift accomplishment,
Ideal for the generation or completion phases, it is said.

Charnel grounds and cemeteries are powerful because they cause us to feel apprehension and fear, and we can make use of this experience of fear to understand better the nature of mind. It becomes a kind of catalyst for progress in our practice.

Villages, markets, empty houses, solitary trees, and the like,
Which are frequented by humans and nonhuman demons,[62]
Are distracting for beginners and can bring many obstacles,
But for stable practitioners, they are a support, regarded as supreme.

For beginners, crowded and eerie places such as these are a source of distraction and so cause obstacles. But for someone who has reached a level of stability in their practice, such locations can provide a challenge and stir things up, which can help to deepen experience and realization.

Temples and shrines, inhabited by *gyalpo* and *gongpo* spirits,
Can disturb the mind and incite thoughts of anger and aversion.

Caverns in the earth and such places, haunted by the *senmo* demonesses,
Cause passionate desire to arise and bring excessive dullness and agitation.

Solitary trees and other places, which are inhabited by *mamos* and *dakinis,*
As well as boulders and mountain spurs, where *mutsen* and *theu'rang* reside,
Contribute, it is believed, to mental turmoil and bring all manner of obstacles.

The lands of outcasts, *nagas, nyen,* and local spirits,
By the lakeside, or in meadows, forests, and such places,
Adorned with beautiful flowers, plants, and trees,
Are pleasant enough at first but later prove disruptive.

In short, all the areas and dwelling places that seem agreeable at first
But not so once you come to know them are sites of lesser accomplishment.
Whereas those that seem frightening and unpleasant at first
But prove agreeable once you have grown accustomed to them
Are powerfully transformative, bringing great accomplishments without obstacle.
And everywhere else in between is neutral, neither beneficial nor harmful.

As our minds are affected by the places in which we stay,
This can make our practice grow stronger or make it weaker,
So it is said that to examine locations is of crucial importance.

This is the main reason that we go on pilgrimages, for example. Places where our kind teacher, the Buddha, carried out his enlightened deeds, or places where the great realized, learned, and accomplished masters of the past have set foot and practiced, have all been blessed and made holy. In this regard, *The Ornament of Clear Realization* says:

Awakening and sites worthy of veneration.[63]

This means that anywhere inhabited by the bodhisattvas who have reached the stage of the path of meditation becomes a sacred place. This is known as "an individual transmitting blessings to a place," and yet places can also transmit blessings to individuals. First, a place is made holy by a spiritually realized being who transmits his or her blessings there. Then, at some later date, when beginners like ourselves go to that place, we can receive the blessings from it. And because of the power with which the place has been imbued, any virtuous actions we perform there become more powerful.

Moreover, there are four types of place based on the four activities:
***Peaceful* places, where mind naturally becomes focused and still,**
***Expansive* places, delighting the mind, which are awesome and inspiring,**
***Magnetizing* places, where mind feels captivated and develops attachment,**
And *wrathful* places, where mind is disturbed by feelings of fear and dread.

This refers to when we need to perform a specific type of activity: peaceful, expansive, magnetizing, or wrathful. If we perform that activity in the corresponding location, it is more likely to be accomplished.

Further divisions can be made, countless and beyond measure,
But in this context, for samadhi, peaceful places are the best,
And so, fearing an excess of words, I will elaborate no further.

Now the text addresses the type of *dwelling place,* or meditation hut, in which you should stay.

In such a peaceful place, the meditation dwelling should be isolated,
As this will suit the development of concentration in the mind.
The ideal dwelling is one that is open at the sides and has a clear view.

Here a distinction is made between daytime and nighttime practice; the latter can also refer to a retreat done in total darkness.

> For nighttime yoga, practice inside a circular "dark house,"
> In a high place, and in the middle of the central chamber,
> With your pillow to the north, lying down in the posture of nirvana.

This kind of dark meditation room is also mentioned in the teachings on the six yogas related to the *Kalachakra Tantra*. The light should be blocked out completely, but it is important that the place is well ventilated, or there could be a risk to your health. The verse also describes the walls of the house and finally gives the posture for the yoga of sleep.

> The location for practicing the yoga of light during the daytime
> Should be mild in temperature and should have an entrance
> With a broad, unobstructed view onto glaciers, waterfalls, forests, or valleys,
> And the vast and open sky, so that mind becomes clear and bright.
>
> When cultivating shamatha, a solitary hut surrounded by a fence
> Is the ideal place for stillness of mind naturally to arise.
> For vipashyana, it is important to have a clear, inspiring view
> And to be constantly cheerful and well attuned to the seasons.
>
> Low-lying and shaded areas, such as forests and ravines,
> Are ideal for practicing shamatha, whereas higher regions,
> Such as among snowy mountains, are ideal for vipashyana—
> It is important that you know these different specifications.
>
> To put it simply, any region or retreat house,
> Where renunciation and disenchantment arise, attention is well focused,
> And samadhi grows in strength—any such place of virtuous activity—
> Is said to be the equal of the place where the essence of enlightenment was attained.

Whereas any place in which virtues decline, mental afflictions
increase,
And one is overcome by distractions and the affairs of this life,
Is a demonic haunt of evil actions, only to be avoided by the wise.

Since these points were taught by Padmasambhava,
They should be learned by all who wish for liberation.

This concludes the first section, being an explanation of the locations for cultivating samadhi, from Finding Comfort and Ease in Meditation on the Great Perfection.

Of course, in our case we should practice meditation wherever we happen to live, and there is no real need for us to go to some separate "meditation house" in order to practice. But for those who are "raising the victory banner of practice" these considerations are very important. For the rest of us, we have to stay in a certain place on account of our work and other commitments, and there is not much else we can do. Frankly, I think that it is best if we can stay within our community and find a vocation that is in keeping with the Dharma—one that is not connected with negative, harmful actions. And if we can find a way to earn our living by actually serving the community that would be wonderful, especially by working as a teacher or in the health sector, but there are also many other roles in which we can be of service to the community. These are ways of helping others directly. If we can live our lives this way, always conducting ourselves ethically and keeping the Dharma in our minds, then our lives will really contribute to the good of society. I feel this is so important.

With the Dharma, as with any other worthy project, if we can do it in the best possible way, then that is wonderful. But if we find we are not able to do it in the best way possible, we should not just give up and do nothing. Of course, it is ideal if we are able to devote our whole lives to practicing the Dharma. If this is a possibility, we should do just that. But if this is not possible because of our current situation, we should not just give up completely and do nothing—that would be a mistake. Whatever it is we might be trying to achieve, if we can do it one hundred per cent, that is first rate. But if we cannot manage that, then even to do one per cent is still some progress in the right direction.

In certain rare cases, when all the right causes, such as karma and prayers of aspiration, come together, it is possible for people to make sudden progress along the paths and stages. But for everyone else, this is a gradual process, in which the ten stages and the five paths are traversed gradually, step by step. This shows that we need to eliminate the obscurations in stages, beginning with the coarsest, and equally we need to generate the states of mind that will counteract these obscurations, developing them bit by bit from lesser states at first, until they become stronger and more powerful.

So in order for us to practice the Dharma, it is not necessary for us to change our outer appearance. As it says in the *lojong* teachings, "Change your attitude, but remain natural."[64] This is important. We need to develop and strengthen the power of our minds, day by day, but it is better if we just keep to our usual dress and outer appearance; if we start radically altering the way we look, there is a danger we might become overly concerned with the eight worldly preoccupations.[65] We are always thinking of these eight worldly concerns, so as long as we are caught up in that kind of predicament, it is not a good idea to keep changing the way we look. It is much better to go along with common customs and convention and put our effort into transforming our minds little by little over the months and years, so that we become increasingly positive, happy, and at ease.

We need to do this throughout our whole lives and especially in our later years. When we reach the age of retirement, we should not just be sitting around waiting to die. It would be much better to spend our time focusing on practice. I know many people who, when they have reached old age, act as if their whole lives are behind them, and there is nothing more left to do. I think that this is a little foolish, because they may have retired, but they are not dead yet! They have only reached the first retirement, not the second one, which is the big retirement when it really is too late. That's what you might call a permanent retirement! But between the first and second retirements, there is a real opportunity to practice, because, as I mentioned earlier, although the body might grow old, if we have developed the faculty of the mind, then its clarity and wisdom will continue, giving us the opportunity to practice in a vast and profound way.

CHAPTER 9

THE INDIVIDUAL PRACTITIONER

THE SECOND SECTION of Longchenpa's text concerns the meditator, or practitioner. It begins by explaining that we have to purify our minds by following the stages of the common path:

> **Secondly, as an individual who takes up the practice,**
> **You must have faith, perseverance, renunciation, and a sense of disenchantment.**

Faith and perseverance are key qualities. Renunciation springs from recognizing that as long as we are in the grip of afflictions, we can never hope to achieve anything that is meaningful or positive in any true sense. When we realize just how hollow such a life can be, and we are filled with an urgent longing to escape from this meaningless state and emerge from it definitively, once and for all—this is what is meant by renunciation. Once we have this determination to be free, then no matter how comfortable the circumstances of our life and how attractive or plentiful or luxurious our resources, we will always be aware that, eventually, they will run out and come to an end. What's more, we'll know they are not the key to genuine happiness because they are all governed by karma and afflictions. Thinking about this will evoke a natural sense of weariness and the sadness of disenchantment.

To sum up then, we need to possess faith, renunciation, and this sense of disillusion:

You must be saddened and wearied by samsara and strive for freedom.
Renouncing the concerns of this life and seeking eventual enlightenment,
You must leave distractions and busyness far behind, and have few mental afflictions,

When we have a real eagerness to strive, lifetime after lifetime, for the ultimate goal of liberation and omniscience, we will feel inspired to avoid outer distractions and busyness and to leave them far behind. At the same time, we will no longer indulge the mental afflictions. When they do arise because we lack the antidotes, we won't allow ourselves to pander to them or get caught up in them. We will be weary of them and try to turn away from them. The more we can remind ourselves of how disturbing emotions or afflictions lie at the root of all our suffering, the more it will give us the strength of mind not to give in to them. If we refuse to surrender to them, then even if we do encounter the causes that usually provoke them, the disturbing emotions will no longer arise so easily. And when they do arise, they will be less powerful. This is why the text advises "have few mental afflictions."

Be easygoing and tolerant, and have pure perception and great devotion,

Then we will naturally become more easygoing and relaxed, because we will have an extremely long-term perspective. We will not be thinking about the temporary joys and sorrows of just this single lifetime but looking ahead and in the longer term. This automatically makes a person more broad-minded and discerning. Recognizing that as long as we are subject to karma and disturbing emotions we cannot find real happiness, we set our sights on the state of freedom. And not just that—we look even further, to the attainment of complete enlightenment and the welfare of all sentient beings who are as infinite as space. When we begin to think along these lines, it naturally brings a sense of courage and a feeling of joy.

If every day we give thought to bringing about the welfare of others, it will imbue our lives with meaning. Our lives are made useful, and we are of service to others. In time our thoughts turn naturally toward benefiting others. As it is said:

> In general, meditate on the kindness of all beings.
> In particular, train in pure perception of all who practice the Dharma.[66]

If we cherish all the infinite beings throughout the universe and think of them as dear and precious, it seems to me that we will quite naturally have pure perception and devotion.

The next verse says:

> **As well as stability of mind, and deep respect toward the teachings—**
> **Practitioners such as this will accomplish the supreme liberation!**

As practitioners of meditation, we need these qualities as a basis or foundation, but it is not enough simply to possess them. We need to work hard to develop them. The Buddha, our kind teacher, as well as all the great masters of India and Tibet who were his followers, all worked extremely hard. They followed their teachers and applied themselves with enormous effort and perseverance. That is how they consistently deepened their understanding and realization and traversed the paths and levels. And we must do the same. We may not have any great capacity right now, but if we know what to adopt and abandon for the long term, then even though our practice right now might be quite weak, we will still have set our sights on a clear, *long-term* objective, and so we know where we are going and how to get there. Our practice now in the *short term* is about assembling all the right causes and conditions for achieving that long-term goal.

So this is how we identify the individual who is a suitable "support" for the practice.

HOW TO FOLLOW A SPIRITUAL TEACHER

You must serve, in the best possible way, a noble teacher

At the very heart of the path to enlightenment is the matter of knowing how to follow a spiritual teacher. In any kind of education system, even when we are learning the skills we need for just a single lifetime, studying with a teacher is the key principle. The teacher guides us, we have to put effort into our studies, and that is how we learn. In the same way, when we are following the path to liberation and omniscience, we must have a teacher who can show us the way; on our own side, we need to show interest, and we need to apply ourselves. So by saying "You must serve, in the best possible way, a noble teacher," the text is acknowledging how much we rely upon the teacher, and by describing the teacher as "noble," it indicates that he or she must be completely qualified.

The *Ornament of Mahayana Sutras* states that a master should have ten qualities:

> One should follow a spiritual teacher who is disciplined, peaceful, serene,
> Endowed with special qualities, diligent, rich in scriptural learning,
> Highly realized concerning the nature of reality, skilled in speaking,
> The embodiment of love, and indefatigable.[67]

When Tsongkhapa explains this verse in the *Great Treatise on the Stages of the Path*,[68] he says that those who have not brought their own minds under control cannot guide others. So those who wish to guide others must begin by disciplining their own minds. When it comes to disciplining one's own mind, he says, it is not sufficient just to gain one or two good qualities and label them genuine qualities of realization. Instead, we must discipline the mind in a way that is in keeping with the general teachings of the Buddha. The approach that accords with the general teachings of the Buddha is the practice of the three higher trainings: discipline, meditation, and wisdom. They are referred to in the quotation by describing the teacher as, respectively, "disciplined, peaceful, and serene."[69]

Yet simply to have practiced the threefold training is not in itself sufficient qualification for guiding others. A genuine teacher must also have a good understanding of all the various categories of the teachings. Therefore it says "rich in scriptural learning," which means to have studied many teachings.

A teacher should be loving toward others and have a real concern for their welfare. Unless a teacher has a caring, loving attitude, it does not matter how erudite he or she might be or how profoundly he or she might be able to expound upon the teachings. Unless the teacher is motivated by compassion and a deep altruistic urge, it will be difficult to make any impact on others' minds or have much effect at all. So compassion is vital. Of course, this compassion needs to be accompanied by wisdom. We are not talking about a simple-minded compassion: this needs to be compassion that is coupled with a direct insight into the nature of reality or at the very least a good intellectual understanding of it. The generation of compassion on the basis of genuine understanding is extremely powerful for attaining either liberation or omniscience. This is why the text says the teacher must be realized and compassionate. He should also be "skilled in speaking" and "indefatigable," meaning that he has the forbearance to keep teaching without growing weary or frustrated. A true spiritual teacher must possess all these qualities.

The Buddha regarded the person who teaches us what we need to abandon and what we need to adopt as extremely important, and he therefore specified the qualifications of a teacher in great detail. He gave very complete descriptions, from the basic teachings on the qualities of a teacher contained in the monastic code, or Vinaya, through to the Vajrayana teachings on the qualifications that a vajra master must possess in order to grant an empowerment. It is because of the central importance of the teacher that the Buddha spoke so explicitly in both the sutra and the tantra teachings.

So it is essential that we follow a teacher who possesses all the right qualifications. It is up to us to examine the teacher and see whether or not he has these qualities. We should not immediately consider someone to be our teacher and then start receiving instructions; we need to begin by examining the individual concerned. Also, we need to know a little about the Buddha's teachings, so that we are able judge for ourselves what the qualities of an authentic teacher are. Then, if we do wish to follow a particular person as our teacher, we should investigate and see whether or not he or she does in fact possess these qualities.

I sometimes jokingly say that we need to spy on the teacher. We need to look from the front, from the back, from above and below. It really is a mistake not to do this. Otherwise it's possible that at the beginning we might have a lot of faith, but at some point later on, when something goes awry, we lose all our faith and think, "Oh no! I was wrong." In fact, the teacher has not changed. If he was ordinary to begin with, he has just remained ordinary. We were the ones who made the mistake because we failed to do any research. We need to check whether or not a teacher is following an approach that accords with the general teachings of the Buddha. If we have carried out that examination, thought about it for ourselves, and decided that the teacher is genuine, then we should follow him.

However, to begin with, we can just consider the teacher as our Dharma friend and listen to the teachings. There is no problem with that. Then later on, if we decide to part company from a spiritual friend, it is not quite so serious. But if we decide straightaway that someone is our teacher and subsequently we lose faith, that is not so good. So right from the start, we need to ensure that this does not happen.

In the teachings on following a spiritual master, it says that it is important to follow a teacher with devotion and to see everything he does as positive. This is talking about a genuine spiritual relationship between an authentic teacher and a student who also has the qualities of an authentic disciple. This is crucial on the Vajrayana path of secret mantra, when the practice of guru yoga takes on special importance. Single-minded devotion toward our teacher plays a vital role in the practices of Dzogchen and Mahamudra, where it is essential for gaining realization and for taking the fundamental innate mind of clear light into our experience. Devotion to the teacher at that point becomes all-important. Of course, it is wonderful if we can practice this even as beginners, but it is not essential that we do so.

From the Vinaya onward, all the levels of the Buddha's teachings describe how to follow a teacher. In the Vinaya it says that if a teacher instructs us to do something that does not accord with the Dharma, we should refuse.[70] Even once we have taken someone as our teacher, if he says something that contradicts the teachings, we should reject it. Note that it does not say that we should see everything the teacher does in a positive light. In the Mahayana sutras, too, it says that we must follow what the teacher says as long as it is virtuous, and we must not follow what the teacher says if it is unwholesome. If the teacher who is guiding us along the path says something that accords with the general teachings, we should put it into practice. But if he says something that does not accord with the general teachings, we should not put it into practice. We should follow whatever virtuous things the teacher tells us to do but not if he instructs us to do something that seems strange or nonvirtuous. Even with regard to the highest yoga tantras it is said:

> If you cannot reasonably do as the guru has instructed
> Excuse yourself with polite and respectful words.[71]

In any case, we need to discern for ourselves what is right and wrong. You should not think that there is no room for making your own independent assessments as to what is right or wrong, by using your intelligence and discernment. I am emphasizing this because I think it is an important point for you to understand.

In the past there were legendary masters and disciples like Tilopa and Naropa or Marpa and Milarepa, and some of their deeds were a little unconventional, but they were masters with exceptionally high levels of realization. Their disciples had all the qualities of a genuine student. I personally think it is very difficult to compare the gurus and students of today with the great masters and students of the past.

This is the reason, then, that the Buddha taught on this topic in such precise and careful detail. To sum up, at the outset we need to examine to see whether or not a teacher possesses all the necessary qualifications. Then, even once we have taken someone as our teacher, we should still check to see if anything is in conflict with the general teachings of the Buddha, and if it is, we should consider it an error.

Our text continues:

You must serve, in the best possible way, a noble teacher

There are three main ways of serving and pleasing a qualified teacher. The first is to make material offerings, the second is to serve the teacher and carry out tasks for him, and the third is to put his instructions into practice. Of these, the most important is to put the teachings into practice. This means that we must rely on an authentic teacher, who has all the qualities of the three higher trainings and has already attained omniscience or else is significantly advanced along the path leading to omniscience and buddhahood. When such a master instructs us not to allow ourselves to get caught up in the afflictions but to focus our minds on liberation and omniscience, if we can put this into practice diligently and wholeheartedly, that is the best way to please the teacher. That is the best offering that we can make to the buddhas and the bodhisattvas. There can be no better way of accumulating merit and purifying obscurations and no better practice for this and future lives.

MEDITATION: THE POWER OF FAMILIARITY

And purify your mind through study, reflection, and meditation.

When we say meditation in the context of "study, reflection, and meditation," as in the verse here, it carries the sense of familiarization. We need to develop some familiarity with the training and become accustomed to it. At the moment we are at the mercy of the ordinary mind, and the ordinary mind is at the command of the afflictions. In our minds we want to be happy, but we don't do what will bring us happiness. We don't want suffering, but the very causes of suffering, the afflictions, just take us over and control our minds. We must find a way to take charge of our minds for ourselves.

Now, we might see only too well that afflictions are disastrous, but still, at the same time, we fall prey to them. We might know that something is not right, but still we act, speak, or think inappropriately. So we need to find a way to bring our minds under control. Of course there are many different techniques for this. But whichever one we choose, we need to prevent the mind from following the wrong course and make it follow the right one. In order to do this we need to increase the tendency for virtue in the mind—which might be very weak right now—and the only way we can achieve this is by training our minds so that the tendency toward virtue becomes increasingly familiar. That is the only approach; there is no other way. As it is said, "Getting used to something is the way to become skilled in it."

The more familiar something is, the greater its strength. The reason that the afflictions come to our minds so readily at the moment, and with such vigor, is that we are already so accustomed to them. By the same token, the only way to increase the strength of the antidotes to these disturbing emotions is to keep familiarizing our minds with the antidotes, so that we grow more and more accustomed to them.

So *meditation* really means making our minds more familiar with something positive, in order to effect a transformation, and so achieve our temporary or long-term goal. For this to happen effectively, as I said earlier, we must begin by thinking about whatever our target is and come to a firm decision for ourselves that this is something really valuable and worthwhile. That means we need to go through a process of *reflection* and contemplation. Even before we can do this, however, we need to have a clear idea of what is, or is not, involved, what the benefits and drawbacks might be, and so on, which means we need to have *studied*. Therefore it is clear that the three kinds of wisdom—the wisdom born of study, the wisdom born of reflection, and the wisdom born of meditation—must be developed in the right order.

The text says that we should "purify our minds" through study, reflection, and meditation. Sometimes we use this same term *purify* to talk about purifying impurities or negativity and obscurations. In those contexts, it means to clear away or to eliminate something altogether and render it nonexistent. But here we are not talking about eliminating the mind! Rather, it means that we must train the mind and purify it, so that it goes from being undisciplined and out of our control to being disciplined and under control. Sometimes we also talk about "purifying or refining the intrinsic nature of reality itself," in which case it means that we make evident what was not evident before.

The text goes on to say:

In particular, you should spend your days and nights
Diligently applying yourself to the essential instructions of the oral lineage.

As we saw, we need to purify the mind by means of study, reflection, and meditation. The ultimate purification of the mind in this context comes about through study, reflection, and meditation on the essential pith instructions of the oral lineage; by training ourselves, we develop strong familiarity with them. This refers to the practice of Dzogpachenpo, where we have made a clear separation between ordinary mind and rigpa.

Without becoming distracted for a moment by ordinary concerns,
Diligently apply yourself to the profound innermost meaning.

"Ordinary concerns" could refer to many things: the concerns of this life, the concerns of the next life, thinking exclusively of our own welfare, clinging to things as real, and more. It has a slightly different meaning depending on whether it is used in the context of the sutras or the tantras. But in any case, this verse indicates that we have to concentrate entirely on the practice, without allowing our minds to be distracted by ordinary, mundane concerns for even an instant.

INTEGRATING THE COMPLETE TEACHING OF BUDDHA

Then, in our practice we need to know how to draw together and integrate the different levels of the teachings:

Never transgressing the precepts of shravakas, bodhisattvas, and vidyadharas,
With your own mind under control, help others in any way you can,
And take whatever you experience onto the path to liberation.

This is such an important point. In a very concise way, this verse points out that our practice should integrate all aspects and levels of Buddha's teachings. The precepts of the shravakas are the pratimoksha vows, the vows of individual liberation. We should uphold these vows, as well as the bodhisattva vows and the Vajrayana vows of the vidyadharas. To put it simply, we should be what is called a *vidyadhara with the three levels of commitment.*

When we talk about the nine successive vehicles, they are not just some abstract description of the teachings. They are something we need to understand for ourselves and then apply in practice. This is how it is explained in some of the instruction manuals—that we have to find a way to practice all these nine successive vehicles for ourselves. In other words, there is a way for a single individual to practice all nine yanas together at the same time. These manuals do not say that we have to practice the shravaka vehicle first, then move on to the pratyekabuddha vehicle, and so on. Rather, they say that we need to follow an approach that shares certain features with the shravaka path and with the pratyekabuddha path. For instance, when it is said that we must practice the common features of the shravaka path, this refers to the four noble truths and their sixteen aspects such as impermanence, as well as the thirty-seven aspects of enlightenment. The practice that is common to the pratyekabuddha path is the contemplation of the twelve links of dependent origination, both in progressive and reverse order.[72] Then we must also practice what is taught in the Bodhisattva Vehicle—bodhichitta, which has as its root loving-kindness and compassion, as well as the six transcendent perfections. Included within them, in connection with the practice of the transcendent perfection of wisdom, there is the view of *shunyata,* or emptiness. It is the same with the practices of the lower tantras: we don't practice each one individually. We take elements of each, all the crucial points, and integrate them into our practice.

In the practice of Dzogchen we take wisdom as the path; it is effortless and transcends the approaches based on the ordinary mind. However, all the crucial points of these lower approaches must still be complete and fully integrated within the Dzogchen approach. All the key points from the different levels of the teachings need to be complete in Dzogchen, and when they are, this is the special feature of Dzogchen, which makes it so profound and so powerful.

Needless to say, if we are to practice all the levels of the teachings like this, we must have some knowledge and understanding of these various levels.

> **As a beginner, it is most important that you secure your own well-being,**
> **Guarding your mind in solitude, abandoning distractions and busyness,**
> **Avoiding unfavorable situations, and subduing the mental afflictions with appropriate antidotes.**
> **Ensuring that your view and conduct are in harmony, enthusiastically devote yourself to meditation.**
> **Whenever any of the ordinary five poisons arise, in that very moment,**
> **Catch them with mindfulness and, without distraction, apply the antidotes.**

Although we always generate the motivation of bodhichitta and pledge to work for the well-being of all sentient beings throughout the entire universe, yet as beginners, in our own practice we need to focus on *ourselves* first and put all our effort into refining the conduct of our body, speech, and mind and into making our minds more peaceful and controlled.

This is why we need to take care not to get caught up in distractions and busyness and to distance ourselves from adverse conditions, as we set about "subduing the mental afflictions." We try to avoid those circumstances that provoke afflictions, and even if we do encounter them, we have to make sure the afflictions do not sweep us away.

As the text says, our view and conduct must be in harmony. We could describe the view as the view of the Middle Way that is common to both sutra and tantra or as the view of the union of pure awareness and emptiness. In either case, from the absolute point of view, appearances in all their profusion and variety are explained as causing us neither benefit nor harm. Nevertheless, we should still take great care and be very meticulous in our actions. Our view should enhance our conduct. If we really understand the crucial points of the view of the Middle Way that is common to both sutra and tantra, as I already mentioned, it is very closely connected with dependent origination. Emptiness implies causality. So our understanding of the view should only make us more careful and meticulous about our conduct.

The text mentions the arising of the "ordinary five poisons," which means our ordinary ignorance, attachment, anger, pride, and jealousy.[73] When we apply the view or the practice of deity yoga, we can transform a disturbing emotion into wisdom. But when an emotion has not been transformed like that, it is called *ordinary*.

A disturbing emotion or mental affliction is a state of mind that disturbs and afflicts the mind and undermines our experience of inner peace. It weakens and wears us out; it creates misery and dissatisfaction. This is the general definition of afflictions. When they arise, they cause us to lose all peace of mind.

Then there are particular types of affliction, such as the five mental poisons. The text says that as soon as one of the five poisons arises in our minds, we should react as if an enemy had invaded our mind and without the slightest hesitation, without allowing any time to elapse, apply some antidote or countermeasure.

The Dzogchen explanation of how the five poisons arise as wisdom is perhaps the clearest explanation of all. Usually this subject is quite tough and difficult to understand. However, it is like this: The nature of the five poisons is pervaded by an aspect of awareness, or clear light. Therefore if there is no grasping or clinging and, through this aware aspect of clear light, we can recognize the nature of an emotion—its ultimate, intrinsic nature—it will dawn as wisdom. There is a lot to think about here.

MINDFULNESS, VIGILANCE, AND CONSCIENTIOUSNESS

With conscientiousness, introspective vigilance, self-restraint, and a sense of dignity, bring your own mind under control.

As we try to ensure that the conduct of our body, speech, and mind does not degenerate and is properly disciplined and controlled, the main instruments we need to employ are mindfulness and introspective vigilance. And as a basis for these two, we need conscientiousness. For without being conscientious, we will never be able to develop either mindfulness or vigilance.

Take the example of a good monk. Even in his dreams he will have the idea, "I am a monk," and if he has the *conscientiousness* that comes with that thought, whenever something inappropriate comes up, he will think, "Oh, that's not right," and catch himself with *mindfulness*. He will then ensure that it does not recur by standing guard over himself with *vigilance*. Conscientiousness, therefore, is of utmost importance.

It is vigilance that checks and stands guard to see whether the actions of our body, speech, or mind are virtuous or nonvirtuous. Then, imagine we are about to do something inappropriate. Suddenly we become aware that it is wrong and we choose not to act, out of our own sense of personal ethics. That is known as *self-restraint*. On the other hand, if we recognize something as wrong, and we refrain from it out of a consideration for others, then that is termed *a sense of moral dignity*. By practicing with these two, self-restraint and moral dignity, over a long period of time—months and years—we can learn to discipline ourselves and bring our minds under control.

THE EIGHT WORLDLY CONCERNS

See the equality of praise and blame, approval and disapproval, good and bad reputation,
For they are just like illusions or dreams and have no true existence.

This verse refers to the eight worldly concerns: wanting to be praised and not wanting to be criticized, wanting happiness and not wanting suffering, wanting gain and not wanting loss, and wanting fame and approval and not wanting rejection and disgrace. We all experience these, don't we? Even animals probably have them in some slight measure.

I think all of us are concerned in particular about maintaining a good reputation. For example, when I am up here on this throne teaching, from time to time, somewhere in the back of my mind, there appears the thought: "How am I doing? How are people going to react to this? Are they going to praise me? Maybe not...Oh! That did not go well. Will people criticize me?" Whenever this happens I need to catch myself and say, "Look, now that I am here on this throne transmitting the Dharma teachings, I should not allow myself to be affected like this by the eight worldly concerns."

However, we will find that hopes, fears, and discursive thoughts of every description will come into our minds. Even very pure monks might sometimes harbor a concern in the back of their mind about whether or not people give them a few words of praise. Even worse, they might start trying to impress others in order to receive offerings or be invited to perform rituals. Thoughts like these are really dreadful. The eight worldly concerns can creep up on us, quite stealthily and sneakily, and even when we do something virtuous, they will try to find a way to slip in.

As it says in *The Way of the Bodhisattva,* praise and a good reputation do nothing to increase our longevity or good health.[74] Maybe if lots of people praised us we might get a bit richer! But apart from that, praise does not make us live longer or in better health or help us in any other way. If people criticize us, it does not make us sick or unhealthy, nor does it shorten our lives. It does not affect us in any substantial way at all.

If we really stop to think about praise and criticism, we will see they do not have the least importance. Whether we receive praise or criticism is of no account. The only important thing is that we have a pure motivation, and let the law of cause and effect be our witness. If we are really honest, we can see that it makes no difference whether we receive praise and acclaim. The whole world might sing our praises, but if we have done something wrong, then we will still have to suffer the consequences for ourselves, and we cannot escape them. If we act only out of a pure motivation, all the beings of the three realms can criticize and rebuke us, but none of them will be able to cause us to suffer. According to the law of karma, each and every one of us must answer individually for our actions.

This is how we can put a stop to these kinds of thoughts altogether, by seeing how they are completely insubstantial, like dreams or magical illusions. When people praise us and we glow with delight, it is because we think that being praised is beneficial. But that is like thinking that there is some substance to a rainbow or a dream. However much benefit appears to accrue from praise and acclaim, actually there's none at all. However convincing it seems, it is as unreal as a magician's illusion. And so Longchenpa advises:

Learn to bear them patiently, as if they were mere echoes,

In exactly the same way, when somebody says something unpleasant or hurtful to us, we need to learn to be patient and forbearing and remind ourselves that their words are like the sounds of an echo, and just as insubstantial and unreal.

CHAPTER 10

SELF AND SELFLESSNESS

GETTING TO THE ROOT OF ATTACHMENT AND AVERSION

The following verse says:

And sever at its root the mind that clings to an "I" or a self.

We need to cut through our clinging to the belief in a self or an "I," and here the profound view of emptiness becomes extremely important. As I mentioned earlier, the root of all the afflictions and the problems that arise from them is the clinging to an "I" or a self. As Chandrakirti says in *The Introduction to the Middle Way:*

Seeing that all afflictions and faults
Arise from the view of the transitory collection,
And that the self is the object of this view,
The yogin sets out to disprove the self.[75]

All our faults come about as a result of our clinging to the reality of a self. Let's take a look at the process whereby attachment or aversion develops. In the case of attachment, we focus on something pleasant, and we wish to possess it and never lose it. With aversion, it is a matter of something unpleasant that we wish to be rid of. Now, whenever we feel attachment or aversion, we attribute it to certain properties in the objects themselves, and we never consider the role of our own perception. We think that the objects of our attachment or aversion are inherently good or inherently bad. This fosters a belief that there is no possibility for them to change their status. If, for example, we see someone or something as really bad today but as good the very next day, we can hardly believe it. We think it is impossible. This is because, when we had our initial reaction of attachment or aversion, we believed we were reacting to inherent properties existing independently of anything else. A truly autonomous property could never change. If something was good, it would have to remain good and never change. If something was bad, it would always be that way. This is how we tend to view things, and this causes us to feel attachment for what we think of as good and aversion for what we regard as bad.

In addition to this belief that the objects of our attachment and aversion are inherently good or bad, if we also think that something is good because it will benefit *me,* or something is bad because it will harm *me,* then that is even worse. In those cases, the sense of a self who is benefited by what we consider good or harmed by what we consider bad is extremely strong.

So not only do we believe that the object of our attachment or aversion is real and inherently good or bad but also we believe that the self, the one who feels attachment and aversion and who is either benefited or harmed, is real as well. This leads us to make a separation between "self" and "other," and then to feel attachment toward ourselves and all that we perceive as being on our side, and aversion toward what we perceive as "other," or opposed to us and our interests.

Therefore, in order to reduce our attachment and aversion, we can consider the unpleasant features of the objects of our desire or the positive qualities of the objects of our hatred. Or we can consider the drawbacks of anger and aversion and how they actually harm us and use this as an inspiration to cultivate patience and forbearance. These are the kinds of technique we can use in order to lessen our attachment or aversion; but, if we think about it, what really underlies this tendency to feel attachment or aversion is the belief that the objects themselves are actually the way we perceive them to be and that there is a real self who is being benefited or harmed by them. It is this strong belief—that both things and the self are real—which is triggering the responses of attachment and aversion.

THE SENSE OF SELF

However, if we think deeply about the objects that provoke our attachment and aversion, we will come to see that they are not real in the way we first thought they were. Similarly, if we think deeply about the one who is supposedly being benefited or harmed by these objects, we will discover that we cannot find any such self. Then, when these two—the objects and the self—no longer seem as real and solid to us, there will no longer be any grounds for our attachment and aversion. What originally seemed such a solid and stable basis will begin to crumble and look insubstantial and false.

This is something we should really take time to reflect on. We should think about what goes through our minds when we feel attachment or aversion. The first thing we will discover is that there is a strong sense of our own self, a sense that "I exist." And not just a sense that "I exist," but that this "I" is independent from anything else.

In the general philosophical tradition of the Buddhadharma, we speak of the "four seals that are the hallmark of Buddha's teachings." They are:

All compounded phenomena are impermanent.
All that is contaminated is suffering.
All phenomena are empty and devoid of self.
Nirvana is true peace.

- As we saw earlier, things are impermanent because they are dependent on causes. The aggregates, like all conditioned phenomena, depend on certain causes, and this means they, too, are impermanent.

- Then, the main cause of the aggregates is ignorance. The fact that they are caused by ignorance means that they are all, by nature, suffering. Everything that comes about as a result of ignorance is said to be "contaminated" and is by its very nature suffering.

- The third of the four seals is: "All phenomena are empty and devoid of self." We just noted that everything that is contaminated is suffering, but it is possible to become free from this suffering. The reason is as follows. It is because we are subject to ignorance that we suffer, but this ignorance that causes us to suffer is basically just a misperception of things. We take things to be real when in fact they are not real. In fact, all phenomena are empty and devoid of self. If we stick to the general presentation that is accepted by all Buddhist schools, then "devoid of self" refers mainly to the absence of any concrete personal identity. The sense of "I" and the sense of "mine" that we impute upon phenomena are actually absent from phenomena themselves. This means that the ignorance that lies at the root of our afflictions can be eliminated.
- And when we have eliminated it, the peace that will ensue is genuine and lasting happiness. This is what is meant by "nirvana is true peace."

All the various schools of Buddhism accept this notion of selflessness. They agree that the root cause of all our suffering and afflictions is the strong clinging to a sense of "I." To put it simply, they assert that there is no self or individual that exists apart from, and independently of, the aggregates. If we think about this deeply, after a while it can gradually undermine and reduce our strong clinging to such a self, a self that exists independently of the aggregates and controls them. The simple understanding that there is no such independent self can counteract our tendency to believe in it.

When we classify the philosophical schools of ancient India and delineate between Buddhists and non-Buddhists, those who subscribe to a belief in this kind of a self are categorized as non-Buddhists, while those who seek to refute this belief in a self are considered to be Buddhists. In the teachings it says, in fact: "The assertion or refutation of the basis for the view of self is what separates followers of the Buddha from others."[76]

DESIRE OR ATTACHMENT

Let's take an everyday example to look at desire or attachment. Imagine we go shopping and see something we want to buy. What happens next takes place in two stages. First, as soon as we see the object, we simply perceive it as something good. At that point there is not yet any attachment. There is still the sense that the object is real, but there is no clinging. Then, *in the next moment,* we start to think about the object. We say to ourselves, "Mmm, this is nice! I need something like this. It really suits me, too." At that moment, it is as if our mind becomes absorbed into the object. It feels like the mind is almost sucked in. This is what we call attachment. Then, impelled by this desire and attachment, we buy the object. Once we own it, our new possession seems even more attractive. It is the same object, but because we are now treating it as something connected with ourselves, something we own, it seems much more precious and desirable.

But then imagine you go into a shop and see some beautiful object, and somehow, suddenly it falls onto the floor and smashes. You are slightly startled and disappointed, but you are hardly likely to be too upset. On the other hand, if you have actually paid for the item and bought it, and then it drops on the floor and breaks, you feel a sudden jolt, almost like a blow to the heart. It is when we start relating to something as being closely connected with ourselves and with our sense of self that we feel much more tightly attached to it.

If you think about this, it is quite clear. In the beginning the mind evaluates things in terms of good and bad, but as soon as we start relating to them in terms of our sense of self, then attachment and aversion crop up. Once we feel attachment, it is easy to feel aversion or aggression to an identical degree of intensity. Because with desire comes anger. When we feel attached to ourselves and our own self-interests, we will feel the same degree of aversion or hostility as soon as we suspect those interests are in jeopardy or actually being harmed.

THE HARM INFLICTED BY ANGER AND HATRED

Yet the one who really does us harm is our anger. The real damage, the real violence, is inflicted on us by anger itself. The moment we feel angry, our minds become agitated and completely ill at ease. The discomfort anger causes in our minds even transforms our entire physical appearance. Our face changes and looks ferocious and ugly. Our breathing becomes uneven and wild. Our whole manner of speaking changes, and we bark out harsh and spiteful things. This is the real violence, and it is something that anger is doing to us. Then, at the same time as we feel miserable ourselves, we lash out and cause harm to others. But the perpetrator of all this harm is our anger.

Compared to anger, desire seems quite gentle and pleasant, friendly even, but it is actually desire that causes us to feel anger and aversion.

It goes without saying that desire and aggression are not just problems from a spiritual point of view. They cause all kinds of trouble for us as individuals and for society as a whole. It does not make any difference where people are, whether they live in a tiny village or a huge city, in the West or in the East, or if they are rich or poor. If you take someone who is constantly plagued by attachment and aversion and compare him or her with someone who has less desire and aggression, the one who has less will definitely be happier and more at ease, there is no question. The person who is prey to strong attachment and aversion will never really feel settled and happy. You can see the effects on family life at home. With someone who is more relaxed, the whole family is more serene as well, and there are not so many arguments and disagreements. But with someone who is temperamental and riven by strong feelings of craving and hostility, every other member of the family will be affected, and there will be never-ending problems and quarrels. This is something we can observe for ourselves from our own experience of living in society.

Think about it carefully, and you can see that it is actually impossible to fulfill all the desires that come from our strong feelings of attachment and aversion. They are insatiable. Look at anger. When we fly into a rage, we cannot destroy every single thing and every single person who is irritating us. If some insect is annoying us, we might swat it and make ourselves feel better or give ourselves some tiny sense of triumph, but there are just so many things that feed our irritation and make us angry. We cannot destroy the whole world! In fact, there is nobody in the history of the world who has ever succeeded in satisfying all the impulses excited by attachment and aversion.

As long as you are dominated by inordinate attachment and aversion, it is absolutely impossible to be happy. But, apart from joy and well-being, there is another meaning to the word *happiness* and that is contentment. It is when we are content that we can relax and feel at ease. As long as we are dissatisfied, happiness will elude us. And what prevents us from finding that contentment is attachment and aversion. The more prominently they figure in our lives, the harder it will be for us to find satisfaction. So you can see that on a personal level, it is attachment and aversion that really cause us the most harm. If we look at others, too, we can see that it is really desire and hatred that are the source of every conflict and every quarrel; it is not the people themselves. So it is crucial that we distinguish between the individuals and their attachment and aversion.

As we have already observed, the afflictions agitate and disturb our minds, which then has its effect on a physiological level, making us much more susceptible to health problems. The evidence for this is very clear. I often mention the psychological research that showed how people who use the words "I," "me," and "mine" most frequently in their conversation—and who are, in other words, intensely preoccupied with themselves—face a greater risk than others from heart disease.[77] This is quite a significant finding.

Whenever we are driven by desire and hatred, it really does torment our minds. Imagine, for example, we finish work one day and go back home. When we get there, we simply relax and take a break from it all. This is our chance to refresh ourselves. Yet we can be sitting comfortably at home on our own, with no one else around to bother us, but if our mind is unsettled, we will find it impossible to rest and relax. At night we will toss and turn in bed, and we cannot sleep. If we get desperate, we resort to pills or tranquillizers. Then, as despair sets in, we become self-destructive and turn to alcohol or drugs, even though we know them to be harmful. When the mind is ravaged by attachment and aversion, it can make our lives a misery.

There is a story that I tell, half-jokingly but half-seriously. Let us imagine that we have a next-door neighbor who for some reason or other does not like us and who is always trying to pick a quarrel or get the better of us. If we let him goad us into feeling resentment and animosity, those feelings will not have the slightest harmful effect on him. But on us they will have an immediate effect: they will rob us of our peace of mind. After a while we can think of nothing else. We lose our appetite. Or if we do feel like eating, our food is devoid of any flavor. We have trouble sleeping. If a friend comes over to visit, we cannot shake off our mood, and all we can say to ourselves is: "Why does he have to come and bother me?" Word gets around to our other friends; they are surprised to hear about the change in our character, and that we are no longer good company. People stop coming round, one after another, and soon we have no more visitors. Finally, we are left alone to brood over our gloomy thoughts. We cannot even go out and enjoy the flowers in our garden. Stuck indoors by ourselves, seething with angry, resentful thoughts, disheartened and depressed, our hair starts to turn grey, and we begin to grow old before our time.

If this is what happens, our neighbor will be thrilled. This is exactly what he wanted. He wanted to harm us. When he sees how lonely, sad, and depressed we have become, he will applaud and think, "I've done it!"

But what if, when our neighbor does his best to spite us, we remain completely serene and at ease, we eat and sleep well, we go on seeing all our friends, and we enjoy all the pleasures of life? He is going to be exasperated. Not only do we stay in good health, but our neighbor's desire to harm us is thwarted.

The only thing then that anger ever achieves is to disturb our mind, and it can never hurt our adversary.

What is more, it is totally ineffective to get angry. There's an example I have that is quite comical. Imagine you have a stick in your hand. You have lost your temper; you are so worked up, you want to hit someone, and you just lash out indiscriminately in all directions. You might land a blow on anything at all; you even risk whacking yourself on the leg. On the other hand, if you are very composed, with a winning smile on your face and take careful aim, you can be sure to hit the target and not to bungle it!

ATTACHMENT AND AVERSION: THE WIDER IMPLICATIONS

Attachment and animosity are definitely *solely* harmful and nothing else. And yet some people believe that these very powerful emotions of desire and hatred are what make life exciting and give it color. Without them, they think, our lives would be bland, colorless, and drained of any vitality. Sometimes we do have the tendency to admire people with a lot of desire and aggression, imagining they are strong and capable individuals who really know how to take care of their loved ones and confront their enemies. But if we really think about this carefully, it is just as Nagarjuna says:

> There is some pleasure to be had by scratching an itch,
> But it is even more pleasurable to have no itches at all.
> Likewise there are pleasures to be had from worldly desires,
> But with freedom from desire comes pleasure greater still.[78]

This is really true, and it is not necessarily anything to do with religion. It is just a fact of life. The afflictions, and particularly attachment and aversion, make our lives miserable. They upset us, and they are responsible for all manner of problems.

In modern society we all accept that a lack of knowledge is detrimental, and so we do our best to remedy this by providing education for our children. Everybody agrees that it is vital for children to go to school, and today in the developed countries of the world people who are illiterate find themselves excluded from all kinds of opportunity. To be illiterate or uneducated makes it hard to survive—lack of knowledge and education is a root cause of poverty and destitution. This is why we put effort and resources into education. Yet when attachment and aversion cause us just as many problems in life, why don't we take a stand against them and try to reduce them, in the same way that we seek to eradicate ignorance through education? I think this really merits serious thought.

Of course, we might say that desire and hatred are simply natural and that they are just traits we are born with. But then so is ignorance; we are not born educated. So there is no difference. Other species have remained more or less the same for millions of years, but humanity has come to see ignorance as a fault, and we have worked hard to educate ourselves. In some ways, this has made our lives much more complicated and given us much more to think about, so it has been a mixed blessing, but the fact that we all see ignorance as a fault is definitely correct. We do need to eliminate lack of knowledge and poor education. But just as ignorance can cause us many problems in life, these other negative states of mind like attachment and aversion are also responsible for immense suffering, and so as a society we must find ways of dealing with them. I am not talking about religion or spirituality here, because this is a concern for society at large.

TRUE PATIENCE AND FORBEARANCE

When we get angry with people, it is usually because of the harm that they have done us. But what really helps in this kind of situation is to make a clear distinction between the actions committed and the person who commits them; this is related to the development of patience or forbearance. Far and away the most important quality that can prevent us getting angry or resentful toward someone who is harming us is patience.

Now, patience should not be construed as just passively accepting mistreatment from others without confronting it. We need to understand this properly—as I said earlier, many of us believe that the people who show strong emotions of attachment and aggression are the strong and capable ones, because they stand up for themselves. You might mistakenly think that being free from desire and anger, cultivating compassion, and practicing patience mean simply putting up with verbal and physical abuse from others. But this is not the case. We should not accept mistreatment by anyone but face up to it and take action to stop it. At the same time, however, we should not feel any anger or malice toward the person who is the cause of harm.

There are particular reasons to feel compassion for that person. This is something we may need to reflect on a little. Whenever we ourselves do something wrong, and later on we feel remorse and apologize for what we have done, we distinguish between the mistake and ourselves as the ones who made it. However, when it is others who are harming us, we don't make that separation between the action and the perpetrator quite so readily. We use the harmful action as an excuse to get angry with the person who did it. Instead, we should draw a distinction, just as we do in our own case.

Then again, just as we would see our own wrongdoing as a mistake, we should understand that, as the victim of disturbing emotions like desire and anger, the other person is also making a mistake. This is why we ought to feel compassion. From our own experience we know just what it is like, just how terrible it feels, to be overwhelmed by compulsive feelings of attachment and animosity. If we remember that this is what the other person is going through, naturally we will feel compassion for this individual who is harming us. That is true patience and forbearance. Meanwhile, if his or her actions are unjust and unwarranted, we should face up to them, tackle them, and try to stop them.

PERSONAL SELFLESSNESS: THE EMPTINESS OF "I" AND "MINE"

In the teaching of Buddha, the way to prevent attachment and aversion is not simply to see their faults and avert them temporarily but to get to their very root: grasping or clinging to the sense of a self or an "I." There are different types of clinging, but in this case it means grasping at the notion of some substantially existent self that is somehow autonomous or independent of the psychophysical aggregates and yet in control of them. This is how the self seems to be, and the belief that it actually is the way that it seems is what we call *self-grasping.*

So we start by establishing that this autonomous basis for our self-grasping does not exist. Then we become progressively more used to this fact by reflecting and thinking about it deeply, over and over again. At some stage, even though that notion of the self still arises very stubbornly because of our strong habituation, we reach the point where we can see for ourselves that when we search for this "I" or self we cannot find it at all anywhere, from the top of our head down to the soles of our feet. If there really were some autonomous self in control of the aggregates we should be able to find it somewhere, either in the body or in the mind, somewhere amid the different states of consciousness, coarse and subtle. But it is too difficult for us to find. When we see that there is no such independent self as there appears to be, then this has an impact on our self-grasping, undermining and reducing it.

Among the schools of Buddhist philosophy, the Vaibhashikas and the Sautrantikas understand selflessness only in terms of personal selflessness, or the emptiness of "I" and "mine." They do not speak about the selflessness of all phenomena. As I said earlier, this view of the selflessness of the individual helps to reduce the clinging to the notion of "I," and it also diminishes the attachment and aversion that are connected with the sense of self—the result of viewing things as "mine" and seeing them as good or bad. Yet this does not undermine attachment and aversion by establishing the absence of any inherent identity in the *objects* of attachment and aversion *themselves.*

SELFLESSNESS OF PHENOMENA: THE MIND ONLY VIEW

In addition to the selflessness of the individual, the higher philosophical views of the Mind Only and Middle Way schools speak of the selflessness of phenomena. They establish that even the phenomena of our experience, such as the aggregates, are not real and solid in the way that they appear to be. There are many stages and layers to this process. The approach of the Mind Only school is to analyze the phenomena of our everyday existence, such as the psychophysical aggregates, break them down into their component parts, down to the smallest particle, and show that, in all of it, there is nothing to be found. This makes us question our everyday assumption that things are real, solid, and substantial. In other words, we begin to challenge the assumption that external things and events have an intrinsic reality of their own, from their own side, independent of our subjective projections. This process leads us to the conclusion that these phenomena are of the same nature, the same substance, as the mind that perceives them.

How this helps us overcome attachment and aversion is by undermining the assumption that things have their own real, intrinsic qualities of good or bad, somehow independent of the projecting mind. Then the question arises: If these phenomena are not real intrinsically, and from their own side, in what way do they exist? The answer is that they arise as a result of habitual tendencies implanted in our consciousness. This is a little difficult to understand.

There are said to be four types of habitual tendencies: those of expression, similar type, the view of self, and the links of conditioned existence.[79]

Let us relate these four to our perception of this flower here in front of me. When we analyze the flower, we find that there is nothing intrinsic to it. So then we may wonder what it actually is. According to this presentation, the mind that perceives the flower and the flower that the mind perceives both arise from habitual tendencies planted in the all-ground consciousness. We have had the perception of similar flowers in the past, and when those perceptions ceased they became habitual tendencies planted within the all-ground consciousness. When they meet the right conditions, these habitual tendencies are activated—they arise partly as the aspect of the perceived object and partly as the aspect of the perceiving mind. Both the perceived object and the perceiving mind are of the same substance. They both arise from the same perpetuating cause or seed. It is because the subjective and objective aspects of the perception both come from the same seed that we say they are of the same identity. That is how the perception comes about through the awakening of *the habitual tendency of similar type.*

Then the basis for labeling it as a flower is the imprint of *the habitual tendency of expression*. It becomes slightly complicated here, because that basis for labeling is said to exist according to its own characteristics; in any case, there is some basis for the labeling yet not something that exists from its own side, which is how it seems to us. Our clinging to it as being the way it appears is *the habitual tendency of the view of self,* and also *the habitual tendency of the branches of conditioned existence,* but mainly the habitual tendency of the view of self. This is how it is explained, so that even a single cognition involves various different imprints from different types of habitual tendencies.

For example, the fact that this flower appears as a flower is based on the habitual tendency of similar type. Our labeling of this flower as a flower is based on the habitual tendency of expression. The impression that this basis to which we apply the label "flower" exists from its own side comes from the habitual tendency of the view of self. This impression is false; it is what is being negated, in other words, what we need to disprove.

In any case, if we refute the existence of outer objects, we need to come up with an alternative explanation for all the phenomena of samsara and nirvana. So, according to the explanation offered by the Mind Only school, these appearances are aspects of consciousness that arise due to the activation of habitual tendencies. It gets complicated when we explain the process in detail, but the point is that these appearances are simply the self-perceiving mind and its perceptions. This is how they explain the selflessness of phenomena. And this explanation is helpful, because when we see that these objects that cause us to feel attachment and aversion do not exist independently of our perception, that will help to reduce our attachment and aversion. Still, as proponents of true existence, the followers of Mind Only make a distinction between the outer objects that do not truly exist and the inner perceiving mind that does really exist from its own side, inherently.

SELFLESSNESS OF PHENOMENA: THE MIDDLE WAY VIEW

To look at this more profoundly, according to the texts of the Middle Way, there is not this separation of knowable phenomena into the categories of outer and inner, and both perceived outer objects and perceiving mind are found to lack any true or inherent existence. Attachment and aversion are states of mind, and all states of mind are shown to be lacking in true reality.

So through the meditation on the selflessness of the individual, the clinging to "I" is reduced, and then through meditating on the selflessness of phenomena and realizing that all the phenomena of our experience are not truly existent, we begin to see things as more like illusions. We begin to lose our habitual impression that things are so solid and fixed and, along with it, the idea that what is good is only ever good and what is bad is only ever bad. That is how the realization of selflessness cuts through the clinging to self at its root.

CHAPTER 11

LIFE, DEATH, AND PRACTICE

LET US RETURN now to Longchenpa's text:

> **In short, by never transgressing the Dharma in all that you do,**
> **Bring your mind under control, do no harm to others,**

The way to avoid "transgressing the Dharma in all that we do" with our body, speech, and mind, is, as we noted earlier, to cultivate mindfulness, introspective vigilance, and conscientiousness, so that we do not harm others in any way.

> **And without succumbing, even for an instant, to the mental afflictions,**
> **Devote your days and nights to virtue—this is crucial!**
>
> **Nowadays, when people are so unruly,**
> **It is vital that you first achieve your own well-being in solitude.**

There are many awkward and disruptive people these days, Longchenpa points out, and it can be difficult to bring about the benefit of others. So it is more important for us to accomplish our own well-being in seclusion and solitude. To illustrate this, he says:

> **Just as a bird cannot fly without both wings,**
> **The welfare of others cannot be accomplished without the higher faculties of perception,**

So strive diligently for your own well-being, while mentally considering the welfare of others.

Without letting your mind be deceived by the devious maras of distraction and busyness,
It is vital that you apply yourself to the practice—

If our efforts to benefit others are superficial, and we are tricked and carried away by the obstructive forces of distraction, we may presume to be practicing the Dharma or achieving something of benefit to others, although we are not. However noble it all might seem, in actual fact we are not accomplishing anything relevant. Longchenpa refers to this as being "deceived by the devious maras of distraction and busyness."

THE MESSAGE OF IMPERMANENCE AND DEATH

Do not cause yourself to suffer regrets at the time of death!

In the course of our lifetime, we may try to impress others by boasting of our achievements and qualities and by covering up our failings. It may work to some extent, and we might get away with it. But when death comes, there is no room for this kind of deception. None of our power or strength can put things right, none of our wealth and resources can pay anyone off; there's nothing at all in fact that we can do. As death draws near each one of us has to think hard and deep and look into our minds without any pretense. We need to ask ourselves: What have I made of my life? Now that I am about to die, what real confidence do I have? And what sense of fulfillment? If there is nothing we can point to, then we have been quite foolish. In Longchenpa's words, "Do not cause yourself to suffer regret at the time of death!"

Therefore, inspect your mind, make it ready now,

The Tibetan expression that is used here conveys the sense of preparing the mind by making it ready and workable, like a field that has been prepared so that it is ready for seeds to be planted and grow.

And consider this: Were you to die now, what would become of you?
Without any assurance as to where you'd go or what might happen,[80]
To spend your days and nights in the grips of confusion and distraction,
Is to squander and make meaningless the freedoms and advantages.
Meditate therefore on the essential meaning, alone and in solitude.
For it is now that a long-term strategy is really needed.

In other words, we need to start practicing now, so that we can really accomplish the ultimate, long-term goal.

How can you be sure where you will go in future?
You must diligently apply yourself this very day!

We need to appreciate the extraordinary opportunity to practice the Dharma afforded by this precious human birth and the freedom that it gives us to devote ourselves to what is truly meaningful. What helps us make the best use of this opportunity is meditation on impermanence.

There are two levels to impermanence—the subtle impermanence of momentary change and the more obvious form of impermanence of change. This verse is talking about the second, more apparent, form of impermanence.

Death will certainly come to us all. Once we are born, death is bound to follow. And when death strikes, all our wealth and possessions, relatives and friends, fame and reputation, whatever we have, will not be of the slightest help. That is abundantly clear. Once we have died, we do not simply cease to be, like a flower that withers away. As we saw earlier, consciousness continues. You might not accept with complete certainty that there are future lives, but I think it is also very difficult to completely rule out the possibility. What reasons can you give for denying rebirth? The fact that it is not universally accepted? Or that you have not seen direct evidence for yourself? Maybe these are the only reasons. But if you don't accept the possibility of future lives, you cannot accept the possibility of past lives either, and yet there are clear testimonies from people who remember their previous lives. There are also some who can predict their future lives. Somehow you would need to account for these phenomena.

So there are some grounds for belief in past lives, but there is little we can provide as grounds for completely discounting the possibility, other than the fact that we have no direct experience ourselves—which is only a reason for doubt and not a reason for excluding the possibility altogether. I believe we can say that there is more evidence to support the reality of past lives than to disprove it. Besides, there is no specific evidence that might oblige us to rule out the possibility. I think, too, that if we refuse to accept past and future lives we are required to accept the notion of "causeless production."[81] We will need to say that the universe is created spontaneously without any cause, and then there will be many questions to which we cannot provide an answer.

However, if there are past and future lives, it is only the virtuous habitual tendencies we create now within our mindstream that will be of any benefit to us in future, because it is the stream of consciousness that continues. Anything connected with us on the level of our physical body, no matter how helpful it might be in this lifetime, will not be of benefit to us in future. That much is clear.

In any case, whether we accept the existence of past and future lives or not, death is something we all fear and something that none of us wants. Yet even though we do not want it, it is certain to happen. The fact that something we do not want is going to happen makes us anxious and afraid. But since we know it is going to happen, it would be better to accept it and come to terms with it in advance. We should accept that it is just a natural fact of life that we are going to die. It is a fact, as well, that we are going to grow old. If we refuse to accept the facts, and we choose not even to think about death because it is too unpleasant, one day, when we actually come to die, we will experience a lot of panic and fear. On the other hand, if we do think about death—what it is like, what the process of dying involves, and what kind of thoughts we should have as we die—all of this will only help us prepare for the moment of death and reduce our unnecessary fears and anxiety.

So whether or not we accept past and future lives, it can only be beneficial to accept the fact of death and to think about it in advance. Not to think about it at all is only setting ourselves up for a great deal of fear and suffering at the end.

Death is certain, but the time of our death is uncertain. So we need to think about what might happen to us after death, and we need to prepare for dying by doing whatever will help us. This is the way to reflect on death and dying.

The text continues:

> **These delusory appearances of samsara are like treacherous pathways.**
> **Keep this in mind: You must find the methods to free yourself.**
> **For if you remain deluded now, you'll wander in delusion forever.**

Now that we have obtained this wonderful opportunity of a human existence with all its freedoms and advantages, and we can work toward securing our ultimate goal, if we do not make full use of this opportunity our time will be squandered, this chance of ours wasted, and "we will wander in delusion forever."

> **So arouse perseverance and keep this in your heart.**

> **The ocean of mental afflictions and the sea of self-grasping are difficult to cross,**
> **But now that you have the vessel of the freedoms and advantages, use it to reach the distant shore!**

Now we have to release ourselves from this ocean of samsara with its churning waves of mental afflictions, and from the vast sea—so difficult to cross—of the self-clinging that is the source of these afflictions. We have the opportunity offered by the freedoms and advantages of this human life; so we must put all our effort into making the crossing.

> **Now, when through the force of your merit, you have gained this opportunity—**
> **Access to the paths of liberation and enlightenment, so rare to find—**

Strive from the depths of your heart to bring about benefit and happiness!

At the moment we have this wonderful opportunity to travel toward liberation and omniscience, which is the result of merit we have accumulated in many lifetimes in the past. So now, when we have the chance to secure our happiness in many lifetimes to come, we should arouse perseverance, enthusiasm, and diligence from the very depths of our heart and then accomplish our ultimate well-being and happiness.

Life is impermanent and changes from one moment to the next,
And we expertly deceive ourselves with distractions, postponing virtuous practice.

While we spend our time busy with preoccupations that seem so important but are devoid of meaning, our lives rush by, very quickly indeed. Distractions are always enticing and ingenious at deceiving us. And all the while, day after day, we constantly postpone virtuous activity. As our lives go by, we spend more and more time trying to earn a living and building our careers, while the time spent on spiritual practice keeps dwindling. We think that we should devote more time to our work, so we get up earlier in the morning and work later in the evenings, and the one thing we reduce to make up for this extra time is spiritual practice. Gradually, we come to neglect spiritual practice and give it little importance. This can happen, can't it?

When we have long become accustomed to delusion,

Fundamentally, the causes of delusion are clinging to true existence and self-cherishing. These two are as hard and unchanging as a diamond, and we all have them in our hearts. Until now, in fact, we have taken them as our refuge. There is not a single living being, even a tiny insect, that does not want to be happy, but with clinging to true existence and self-cherishing as our sources of refuge and trust, such happiness will never come.

At this point, however, we can see the flaw in such self-cherishing.

We have been introduced to the fact that this attitude—the grasping at an existing self where no self exists—is mistaken. We have been introduced to the fact that self-cherishing lies at the root of all the various fears of samsara. We can see how we have put our trust in clinging to true existence and self-cherishing, and all that we have ever done is surrender ourselves to them completely, body and soul. What we need now is a new kind of attitude altogether.

In each moment we're naturally drawn into the mental afflictions,

Up until now, we have stayed so entrenched in our habits that negative actions, afflictions, and lack of control over our own minds have all become instinctive, almost second nature.

And even if we apply ourselves to merit and virtue,
We find they do not easily arise.

Putting into practice the antidotes to negativity, the virtuous actions that will bring about our temporary and ultimate happiness, can seem a struggle, like trying to swim upstream. Whereas negative actions, because they feel so completely natural to us, seem more like letting ourselves float downstream.

Strive, therefore, to avert the miseries brought about by your own actions!

It is right now that we need to apply ourselves, with effort, in order to secure lasting happiness.

There is not the slightest joy to be found within the states of samsara.
The sufferings of conditioned existence, if you think of them, are impossible to bear.
Therefore apply yourself, right now, to the means for gaining freedom.

Both the roots and the rulers of our afflictions are our deluded clinging to true existence and self-cherishing. As long as we remain under their domination, we will continue to experience one form of suffering after another, until the very end of the universe. This we can see from our own experience, right up until today.

> If you do not earnestly devote yourself to the essential meaning,
> The state of leisure and intermittent Dharma will bring no benefit.

We have to seize this opportunity and persevere. It is highly unlikely that practicing the Dharma occasionally for a few months, or even doing a three-year retreat, will be enough to lead us to complete enlightenment. We will need to continue for eon after eon to reach the final goal, liberation and omniscience.

> So develop a strong sense of weariness for all that is impermanent,
> And, without being distracted even for an instant, generate enthusiasm for the practice!
>
> If you realize this at the very outset,
> You will swiftly achieve the state of a sublime one!
> Accomplishing your own welfare, the welfare of others will come naturally,
> And you will find the supreme path of liberation from the states of samsara.
> When everything that you do is in accordance with the Dharma,
> Then you are one who has the basis for attaining enlightenment.

This concludes the second section, being an explanation of the individual practitioner, the meditator, from Finding Comfort and Ease in Meditation on the Great Perfection.

CHAPTER 12

THE DHARMA TO BE PRACTICED: THE PRELIMINARIES

THE THIRD SECTION of *Finding Comfort and Ease in Meditation on the Great Perfection* concerns the Dharma to be practiced.

In this section there are three parts: (A) the preliminary practices, (B) the main practice, and (C) the concluding practices.

A. THE PRELIMINARY PRACTICES

THE GENERAL AND SPECIFIC PRELIMINARIES

> **Reflection on impermanence and feeling disenchanted are the general preliminaries**

Meditating on impermanence, reflecting on the suffering of samsara, and contemplating the effects of karma, cause, and effect—these are general preliminary practices. They are what give us the motivation to seek liberation. As we saw earlier, we need to have some understanding of why nirvana, "passing beyond suffering," is the key feature of the Buddha's teachings, and such understanding can come from these general preliminaries.

> **That radically counteract our attachment to the things of this life.**

Since our motivation in these preliminaries is not merely the thought of gaining higher states of rebirth but the wish to find liberation, so we let go of our attachment to the things of this life and of future lives as well. This corresponds to the paths of those with lesser and middling spiritual capacity.[82] While these general preliminaries outlined here can lead us to higher rebirths and the definitive goodness of liberation, the specific preliminary of generating bodhichitta, which is mentioned next, is the cause for us to attain the ultimate level of omniscience. We will look at bodhichitta in greater depth presently. The text continues:

> **And compassion and bodhichitta are the specific preliminaries**
> **That transform all spiritual practice into the path of Mahayana.**

The sequence here is that first of all we have to put a stop to our attachment to samsara and begin to practice the Dharma with the wish to attain liberation. Then we have to generate bodhichitta, with love and compassion at its root, and practice the teachings of the Mahayana.

> **Train therefore at the outset in both these preliminaries.**

THE SPECIAL SUPREME PRELIMINARIES

> **Afterward, there are the special, supreme preliminary practices.**
> **Having received all the empowerments, there are two aspects to the generation stage:**

1. PURE PERCEPTION OF THE DEITY

> **Imagining your own body as the deity and the surrounding environment and sentient beings also as the deity**
> **Counteracts attachment to our ordinary perception.**

Once you have completed the general preliminaries, the extraordinary, or "special, supreme preliminaries," involve: receiving empowerment, maintaining your discipline and samaya pledges correctly, and training in the generation stage practice. In the generation stage you visualize the clear appearance of the deity in order to counteract your fixed perception of the universe as ordinary. Then, as Longchenpa says, you embark on the practice of guru yoga, which is the source of all blessings:

2. GURU YOGA

> By practicing the profound path of guru yoga,
> Blessings beyond measure arise through the force of realization,
> All obstacles are dispelled and the two types of siddhi are achieved.
> Therefore, after the general and specific preliminaries, practice the two supreme preliminaries.[83]

> Boundless qualities arise as a result of these four preliminaries:
> Your mind enters the unerring path,
> You reach the supreme path of liberation,
> Realization of the natural condition swiftly arises,
> It becomes easy to train in the main practices, with no obstacles,
> Accomplishments are readily achieved, and so on.
> Therefore it is crucial to train in these preliminaries.

CHAPTER 13

BODHICHITTA, THE HEART OF THE AWAKENED MIND

THE VAST SCOPE OF THE MOTIVATION

At this point let us turn to bodhichitta, the altruistic intention to attain enlightenment for the benefit of all beings. Whether your practice can truly be counted as a Mahayana practice depends on whether or not you have developed this bodhichitta and regard the welfare of others as more important than your own.

Whenever we set out on a course of action, we always begin with some kind of objective, which is what motivates us to think: I am going to do this, for such and such a purpose. This is our normal way of going about things. Here, in this instance, we are following the path that will lead us to liberation. Simply to recognize what liberation is will inspire us to think: I'm going to attain liberation. When we understand the value of attaining liberation and the drawbacks of not doing so, we will feel determined to achieve it. This, in turn, will give us the incentive to take up the three higher trainings of discipline, meditation, and wisdom, which become the actual cause for us to attain liberation.

In exactly the same way, if our objective is the state of omniscience, we have to possess a deep wish to pursue the realization of omniscience. But for attaining omniscience there is a second, additional requirement, which is a "vast gathering of accumulations." And this means that our whole attitude needs to be really quite special.

If we think about ordinary events in the world, there are some instances when individuals act for their own benefit and others when they act for the benefit of many people. In terms of their intention to produce happiness, the impulse is just the same. One person's sole aim is personal happiness, while another is intent on securing happiness for others. It is interesting though that when someone is motivated purely by self-interest, nobody sees it as particularly remarkable, do they? However, when someone is motivated to help many other sentient beings, as a rule this will be regarded as admirable. I am not speaking in a spiritual context but from a perfectly ordinary point of view. People are automatically impressed. They rejoice in the fact that somebody is acting for the benefit of others. For us, this is a natural response.

Let's look at this from a spiritual point of view. As long as we are motivated by our own interests, thinking only: "How can *I* acquire the qualities that come from freeing *myself* from all the flaws that I have to remove?" our motivation is very narrow in scope. Consequently, we might have the wisdom that realizes emptiness or practice generosity and maintain discipline perfectly, but it does not really matter what practice we do, because our focus is only on ourselves and that automatically diminishes the power of our actions.

Suppose our focus is not exclusively on ourselves but on all sentient beings, limitless in number, who have been our mother in one lifetime or another and who want only to be happy and avoid suffering, just like us. That altruistic aspiration to take upon ourselves the responsibility for the welfare of others makes the scope of our *attitude* much, much *vaster.* Our *objective* is also much *vaster,* because we are focusing on countless living beings.

As for the ultimate goal we are seeking to accomplish, it is nothing less than eliminating all flaws and acquiring all qualities. When we set about this, we summon a courage and determination that disregard the duration or difficulty entailed. And because of this attitude, whatever practice we do, whether maintaining perfect discipline, cultivating generosity, or developing the wisdom that realizes emptiness, all our *efforts* possess *vast* power and scope.

For it to lead us to omniscience, this attitude must be combined with a vast accumulation of *merit*. For when our accumulation of merit is held, and infused with, this bodhichitta—which places others' welfare ahead of our own—it enables the accumulations to be perfected much more quickly. Therefore, we can see that bodhichitta is a practice imbued with enormous power.

THE ROOTS OF COMPASSION

Whether or not we can arouse bodhichitta—and how powerful it will be—fundamentally depends upon our compassion. All of us have compassion to a certain extent. For example, whenever we think of someone suffering, we are naturally moved by a feeling of compassion and wish for that person to be free from pain or anguish. This seems to be a fundamental experience. But now we take this compassion that we already possess and expand it, until it is without any bias or restriction and becomes a courageous sort of compassion—infused with "an extraordinary altruistic resolve" that you yourself *can* and *will* free all beings from suffering and guide them toward enlightenment. That is what is meant by *great compassion.* It is the source and the root of bodhichitta.

And so we are actually taking our natural capacity for empathy—that love and affection we all feel for one another—combining it with wisdom, and progressively increasing it. However, before we can develop the compassionate desire to free others from suffering, first we need to identify what suffering is, from our own perspective. Then, by extension, we can feel empathy for others who are going through suffering, whatever it might be. These two steps are essential.

Earlier we discussed human life with its freedoms and advantages, death and impermanence, the sufferings of samsara, and karma, the cause and effects of our actions. Contemplations such as these show us clearly that the very nature of our current experience is one of suffering. The root of our suffering lies in the way we fall under the domination of our negative emotions. You might think, Well, that's due to external circumstances, isn't it? But the cause of the trouble is not outside us, it is within. The afflictions—the disturbing emotions—in our own minds are our true enemies, and they must be recognized as such. We have to understand just how dangerous these negative emotions are and how imperative it is that we free ourselves from their grip.

There are said to be two ways to develop a deep sense of empathy toward a person who is suffering. The *first* depends upon seeing all sentient beings as extremely close and dear. We think about the individuals who have been the kindest to us in this life—it could be our parents or very possibly our mother. We appreciate the depths of kindness this person has shown us and then consider that all limitless sentient beings are as kind as this one person. On the basis of seeing everyone as dear and close to us, empathy is developed, to the extent that we cannot bear others to suffer.

The *second* way to develop this empathy is to reflect on and compare the damaging effects of a constantly self-centered view with the benefits of continually having the welfare of others at heart, even cherishing them more than ourselves.

COMPARING A SELF-CENTERED AND AN ALTRUISTIC VIEW

This point is made concisely in *The Way of the Bodhisattva*[84] in the well-known verse:

> Whatever happiness there is in this world
> All comes from desiring others to be happy.
> And whatever suffering there is in this world
> All comes from desiring oneself to be happy.

In our world anything that is beneficial by nature—that is, anything positive that contributes to happiness in the short-term or to the long-term good—comes about fundamentally as a result of an attitude of cherishing others. That is what it comes down to. Anything in our world that is inauspicious, that produces unhappiness in the short-term and suffering in the long run, stems from the attitude of being concerned only with oneself.

Now as long as we are concerned solely with ourselves and with the short term, thinking, "How can I get ahead? What do I need? What should I have...?" our scope remains very narrow. We find ourselves imprisoned in a cramped and claustrophobic state of mind, unable to bear even the slightest misfortune or discomfort. On top of that, we will tend to shirk our responsibilities and blame others, announcing: Oh, so-and-so didn't do what he or she should have done, or Look what so-and-so is doing to me. And the tiniest difficulty is multiplied into many problems, until there is no end to them.

Say we reject that attitude, however, and think instead of countless beings, who have all been extremely close and dear to us in lifetime after lifetime. Perhaps right now we cannot quite conceive of "limitless beings." Suppose, then, we just consider those who are close to us or with whom we are often in contact and try to understand how we are all the same: just like us, all they wish for is to be happy and avoid suffering. Even with a slight effort to think like this, we find our minds automatically expand and become more spacious. Our perspective opens up and no longer are we so obsessed with our own suffering and misfortune. We see that *we are simply one among many,* all of whom are suffering, and that our suffering is relatively minor by comparison. The feeling that our own suffering is so overwhelming and unbearable fades away. It really does make a difference.

We will find that if we are solely concerned about ourselves, day in, day out, all kinds of misfortunes occur and our unhappiness only increases. But when we think of the welfare of others, our mind *automatically* becomes more spacious and excitement and sorrow will affect us less intensely. So if we think about this carefully, it will be apparent that when our motivation is to benefit others, *our own welfare is taken care of as a matter of course.* We will observe, too, that when we think of ourselves alone and neglect or discount others, we do not end up happy as a result. In fact, nothing is accomplished that is of benefit to anyone else and happiness still eludes us. This is strikingly clear.

THE LONG-TERM AND SHORT-TERM OUTCOMES

In our hearts we all want happiness. Yet we need to use our intelligence in order to discern what will really bring about happiness in the long run. Take the case of someone who is beside himself with anger; he becomes so enraged that he loses all sense of restraint and seeks to hurt, or even kill someone. If he uses his intelligence, he will realize that to surrender to anger and harm another person will most likely mean arrest and punishment, possibly imprisonment. In the worst case it may even mean a death sentence. So it would be a very grave mistake. In the heat of the moment, in the grip of that emotion, there is an impulsive desire to act, fired by anger. But that desire is a deluded one, and so it needs to be stopped.

At the moment when they fly into a rage, people imagine that they will derive some kind of satisfaction from harming someone else. This is senseless, because all they are doing, in the long term, is bringing ruin onto themselves. Even as a general rule, everyone agrees that what is important is that which brings lasting benefit. That is why our customs and laws reflect the fact that our short-term, selfish desires and urges have to be restrained, because they only cause long-term problems and ruin.

Concern for the welfare of others benefits us in the long term, and it actually helps us in the short term as well. Once we realize this, we can see the extraordinary value of an attitude that brings nothing but benefit to others and to ourselves. At the same time we will see the need to reduce its opposite, that attitude of cherishing only ourselves, which not only does not benefit others but does not even benefit us.

When we say that concern for ourselves is a flaw that we have to get rid of, it could be misunderstood as implying that you ought not to have any love for yourself. Nothing could be a greater mistake. On the contrary, love *must* begin with you. You have to love yourself, and then you will be able to expand the love you feel for yourself to embrace others. People who have no love for themselves will find it very difficult to love others.

First and foremost, then, we need to begin by loving ourselves. Through understanding how others are just like us and how similar we all are, we can extend that love to others, appreciating on an ever-deeper level that they, too, wish to be happy and avoid suffering.

Let me summarize all this by quoting once again from *The Way of the Bodhisattva:*[85]

What need is there to say a whole lot more?
The childish work for their own benefit,
The buddhas work for the benefit of others:
Just look at the difference between them!

THE LEGACY OF COMPASSION

We might ask ourselves: Our teacher, the Lord of Sages, the Buddha Shakyamuni, was such an embodiment of skillful means and compassion. What were the causes and the conditions that allowed him to possess such wisdom, love, and spiritual power? The answer lies in the Buddha's lack of concern for his own welfare and his emphasis on concern for the welfare of others. At a time when it had not yet arisen in his mind, he gave rise to that altruistic attitude; he maintained it once it had arisen; and then he made it flourish, all the while supporting it with the wisdom that he was steadily developing. By following such a path with unwavering courage, he finally became "free from all flaws and endowed with all qualities."

Up until now our constant strategy has been to try to gain happiness for ourselves with our self-centeredness, and yet this has failed to bring us the happiness we have been seeking. As we saw earlier, not only have we cherished ourselves, but also we have clung to the belief in things as real. These two types of grasping have blocked us from achieving our wish to be happy, but still we naïvely place our complete trust in them and remain continuously in their clutches.

Yet when we contrast the qualities of our teacher, Lord Buddha, and the flaws of ordinary beings such as ourselves, we should always keep in mind that at one point the Buddha was as ordinary as we are now. The fact that the Buddha became "free from all flaws and endowed with all qualities" is because he understood the importance of cherishing others, and he put it into practice. He realized the shortcomings of clinging to things as real, and so he countered it with antidotes. And if we think about it, this is the reason that the Buddha was able to speak about the virtues of cherishing others and the faults of being excessively concerned with oneself.

This is why Nagarjuna, too, states in his text of Middle Way philosophy entitled *The Precious Garland:*[86]

> Just like earth, water, fire, and air,
> Medicine, and wild forests,
> May I always be of service to all beings,
> Without impediment and according to their wish.

The characteristic of the elements—earth, water, fire, and air—is that they are freely available to all living beings. They are completely in the public domain, for there is no one who can claim ownership over them. We aspire to be like them and to be of service to all sentient beings, who are equal in their number to the vastness of space. Nagarjuna is pointing out that this is the kind of intention that ought to motivate our practice. The same idea, in fact, is expressed in the following verse from *The Way of the Bodhisattva:*[87]

Like the earth and other great elements,
And like space itself, may I remain forever,
To support the lives of boundless beings,
By providing all that they might need.

Further on in *The Way of the Bodhisattva* we find:

For as long as space exists
And sentient beings endure,
May I too remain,
To dispel the misery of the world.[88]

To recite prayers of aspiration like these has an extraordinarily powerful effect on our minds. When we look at these quotations from the masters such as Nagarjuna and Shantideva, we can see how they downplayed any concern for their own welfare, while being able to devote themselves wholly to the well-being of others. Altruism was both their aspiration and their practice.

This, then, is the legacy of our kind and compassionate teacher, Lord Buddha, as it was passed down by the Indian masters such as Nagarjuna and Aryadeva, Asanga, his brother Vasubandhu, and others and then by the authentic masters who upheld the Buddha's teachings in Tibet, belonging to all four major schools—Sakya, Geluk, Kagyü, and Nyingma—down to our own lamas of the present day. These masters practiced what the Buddha himself practiced, and they followed the training he taught: the training in bodhichitta, in which others are considered more important than ourselves. In this way they brought enormous benefit not only to themselves but also to others; not only to the teachings but also to living beings. And while we are in no way their equals, yet we seek to emulate their example.

THE IMPORTANCE OF BODHICHITTA

This bodhichitta is of extraordinary and crucial importance. Don't you find it truly moving, the more you think about it? We should say to ourselves:

> While I live, I will meditate on bodhichitta;
> This is what will give meaning to my life.
> At the moment of death, I will meditate on bodhichitta;
> It will help me to continue onward, on my way toward enlightenment.
> When I am thriving and happy, I will meditate on bodhichitta;
> It will enable me to use my prosperity to serve others and avoid the pitfalls of pride, envy, and lack of respect.
> When I face failure and sadness, I will meditate on bodhichitta;
> It will prevent me from losing heart and losing hope.
> So, all the time and in any situation:
> In life, when death is near, in success or failure, in joy or sorrow,
> Bodhichitta is something I cannot be without.

I would like to make it clear at this point that I do not have bodhichitta in my heart to any extent at all. It may seem as though I do, because of my familiarity with the subject, but I do not. I certainly try to have bodhichitta, I hope to have it, and that hope is not an entirely empty one. Yet it is still just a hope. I hope that I may become able to arouse true bodhichitta, but I do not experience it now. Nevertheless, even to have the inspiration to develop bodhichitta changes your mind, doesn't it?

COURAGE: THE GIFT OF COMPASSION

There is something that I often mention, which I would like to bring up at this point. The Tibetan term *nyingjé* is usually translated into English by the word "compassion." If this is understood to mean not thinking of oneself but thinking solely of others, then I think the translation is a useful one. When we speak of the loving or caring element in compassion and we say "great loving compassion," it means that love must begin with oneself and then be extended to others. Yet some people may get the wrong impression and think that compassion is exclusively directed outwardly toward others and does not concern us at all.

There is another aspect to this. Many people think that it is wonderful to hold love in such esteem and to cultivate compassion, because of the benefit and help it brings *others*. But compassion, they feel, does not bring *us* any benefit at all; in fact it is more like a tax being levied on us or a heavy burden loaded onto our backs that is going to overwhelm us. This seems to be quite a common feeling.

It is a complete mistake. Think about it carefully. Look at your own experience. Once you get used to feeling compassion in your heart, as each day goes by you will naturally feel a growing courage and determination. For when you think about the welfare of others, it makes your mind broader and more expansive. Also, when you have discovered that kind of courage, you can shoulder responsibility for the welfare of others. In no way then does it seem like a tax or something that Buddha is imposing on you because you can see and feel the benefits of altruism, here and now. You can see the shortcomings of self-centeredness too, and this has given you a deep, heartfelt conviction, confidence, and inspiration—the source of your courage. You feel, I *can* do it. I *will* free all beings from their suffering. I *will* bring them all to the ultimate state of enlightenment. Isn't this incredibly courageous? You are saying you can do it yourself. You are not saying that you will sit by and let the Buddha do it for us. This is unbelievably courageous. It is courage with a purpose, authentic courage, courage that is pure and faultless. And once it becomes part of you, your mind will be happy and at ease, and you can accept and deal with anything that comes along.

Whether such an attitude helps others or not is uncertain. If the circumstances are right, then another person can surely benefit from your having this attitude toward him or her. However, it could happen that the whole time that you are feeling compassion for someone, he or she does not appreciate it at all and even complains about you! There is no guarantee that your compassion can be communicated directly to someone else. So it is uncertain whether your compassion benefits others directly. But you, however, benefit immediately. So never make the error of thinking: Others benefit from our cultivating compassion, but we do not.

BODHICHITTA WITHIN THE TEACHING OF BUDDHA

The fundamental reason that we are able to attain omniscience lies in bodhichitta, which itself is rooted in compassion. If bodhichitta is present, the state of omniscience—and buddhahood—is possible; without it, buddhahood can never be attained. Everything then depends upon whether we have bodhichitta.

Our kind teacher Lord Buddha, on the basis of his own experience, taught that the principal training for us to follow is that of bodhichitta. We could think of the Basic Vehicle as a foundation or preliminary to bodhichitta and all the teachings given on bodhichitta itself in the Mahayana as the main body of the path. This includes the six transcendent perfections, and it is within the practice of concentration and wisdom that the cycle of the Vajrayana teachings and practices fall. They constitute a training in bodhichitta. So I feel that all the 84,000 teachings of Buddha—the Basic Vehicle, Mahayana, and Vajrayana—are rooted in bodhichitta. You can say that within the scope of preliminaries to bodhichitta, training in bodhichitta, or conduct associated with bodhichitta, the meaning of all these 84,000 teachings is completely contained.

This bodhichitta, which carries such benefits and advantages, will need to be cultivated, perhaps for many years. Some of us might need to cultivate it eon after eon before it is truly aroused in our mindstreams. With others, it might happen in a few years. In any case, we have to train in the principles of bodhichitta, gathering the accumulations and purifying our obscurations as we do so.

This is where the view of emptiness is of vital importance. Our quest is to bring true benefit to others and to gain enlightenment. In order to seek enlightenment, first of all we need to identify exactly what "enlightenment" might be. Then, if we seek to benefit others, we need to understand what those words "benefit for others" mean, or indeed what that "benefit" could be. We must understand that the ultimate benefit is nirvana. So, without identifying what nirvana is, it will be very difficult for us to appreciate what both "benefit for others" and "enlightenment" could mean. Such an appreciation depends on the view of emptiness—at the beginning, in the interim, and in the long term. This explains why training our minds in this view and familiarizing ourselves with it are so very important.

CHAPTER 14

TAKING THE BODHISATTVA VOW

THE VISUALIZATION: INVITING THE FIELD OF MERIT

Today we are making the aspiration to arouse and cultivate bodhichitta, this attitude that is the source of such extraordinary goodness and benefits. In order to formulate this aspiration to develop bodhichitta, we need to feel that we are actually in the presence of our teacher, the Lord of Sages, the Buddha Shakyamuni. Imagine, then, the Buddha surrounded by the sixteen great arhats who uphold, preserve, and spread the teachings, the seven patriarchs who succeeded him, as well as all of those training on the path—the hosts of bodhisattvas, such as Maitreya and Manjushri, and in particular the great masters of the Buddhist tradition of India: Nagarjuna, Aryadeva, Buddhapalita, Bhavaviveka, Chandrakirti, Shantideva, Asanga, his brother Vasubandhu, Vimuktisena, Gunaprabha, Shakyaprabha, Dignaga, and Dharmakirti. Through their works, which we can still study, they have ensured that the teachings of the Buddha have lasted for over two thousand years. All these superb followers of the Buddha, including the "six ornaments" and "two sublime ones," who composed these wonderful treatises, we consider are actually present, here with us.

In addition, we include the original masters of our Tibetan Buddhist tradition—the gracious Dharma king Trisong Detsen, the great scholar Shantarakshita, Guru Padmasambhava, and his twenty-five close disciples. We include the masters of the earliest of the newer schools, the older Kadam tradition, such as Atisha, his students Ngok Lekpé Sherap and Dromtön Gyalwé Jungné, and the three spiritual brothers of the Kadam tradition: Potowa Rinchen Sal, Chengawa

Tsultrim Bar, and Phuchungwa Zhönu Gyaltsen, and others; the masters of the Kagyü school of Mahamudra practice, including Marpa, Milarepa, Gampopa, and their followers; the masters of the Sakya school, including the "three white-clad ones,"[89] Sachen Künga Nyingpo, Sönam Tsemo, and Jetsün Drakpa Gyaltsen and the rest of the "five founding fathers," Sakya Pandita and Chögyal Phakpa, as well as the other gurus in the lineage of Lamdré teachings; and the masters of the newer Kadam, Ganden, or Geluk tradition, including Lord Tsongkhapa, his students Khedrup Jé and Gyaltsap Jé, and the other gurus of this lineage. All of them we imagine are actually here, present with us.

We imagine, too, that all around us are all other sentient beings, who are equal to space in their extent. Just like us, all these countless living beings wish only to be happy and to avoid suffering. We focus our minds clearly on all of them as well.

Imagine the victorious ones and their spiritual heirs, the buddhas and bodhisattvas, perceive the qualities of their enlightened form, speech, and mind, and allow a feeling of faith to arise. Moved and inspired, ask yourself, "What if I were to have such qualities? What if all beings, who have been my mothers, were to possess these qualities? If only they could, wouldn't that be wonderful?" Feel that joy and inspiration intensely. And thinking of all beings and their suffering, let love and compassion arise. Visualize all of this as clearly as you can.

THE SEVEN-BRANCH PRAYER

Keeping all this in mind, we recite the seven-branch prayer, as a means of gathering accumulations and purifying ourselves of obscurations, before arousing the aspiration to develop bodhichitta. To request this transmission of the bodhisattva vow, we begin by offering the mandala of the universe and reciting its four-line verse. As for the seven-branch prayer, the *first* branch is homage, by which we show our respect and devotion for the sources of refuge with our body, speech, and mind.

The *second* branch is to make offerings—material offerings, which can be our personal possessions, or things we see around us that do not belong to anyone, and visualized offerings, which we create with our imagination.

The *third* branch is to confess the effects of harmful actions and wrongdoing that we have committed through countless lifetimes from time without beginning, confessing them with an awareness of the harm they cause us. Here, I think it would be appropriate to consider all the ways we have succumbed to our self-cherishing and disregarded others. Let alone the actual harm we have done to others, it is good to acknowledge and confess as well the mistakes we have made in neglecting and turning our backs on them.

The *fourth* branch is rejoicing. For example, we definitely rejoice when we think of the immeasurable qualities of the buddhas. When we think of the physical, verbal, and mental actions of the bodhisattvas who have attained high levels of realization, it arouses in us a sense of admiration and joy. When we think of bodhisattvas who have not yet reached the bodhisattva stages, we recognize how amazing it is that, while they are still subject to self-cherishing and the effects of their mental afflictions, they nevertheless have given rise to an altruistic motivation to bring happiness and benefit to all sentient beings, who are equal to space in their extent, and we rejoice. When we consider the arhats, the sublime ones of the shravaka path, who have developed the wisdom that realizes the absence of the personal self, who aspire to liberation, and who practice accordingly, we appreciate their qualities, and we are moved with admiration. When we think even of those who have not entered the path, who are ordinary human individuals but who are practicing as virtuously as they can, again we are moved in admiration. In short, we rejoice in anything that anyone has accomplished that will lead to some positive result.

We rejoice in whatever others have achieved, without any sense of jealousy, envy, or competitiveness. In a similar vein, whenever we contemplate anyone endeavoring to do something as best they can, we should rejoice and think, What they are doing is really good. What a wonderful person. Likewise, for the virtuous deeds we have done ourselves, we should not feel any trace of doubt or hesitation nor harbor any regrets but rejoice from the depths of our heart and the core of our being.

The *fifth* branch is requesting the wheel of Dharma to be turned, a request that is directed to the supreme nirmanakaya, who displays the twelve deeds such as being born into this world and passing from it into nirvana.[90] We request the supreme nirmanakaya to turn the wheel of Dharma.

The *sixth* branch is to request the supreme nirmanakaya not to pass into final nirvana but to continue to remain here, accessible to us all.

The *seventh* branch is dedication, in which we take into consideration all the virtue we have gathered, aspiring that it does not ripen into any lesser result but becomes a source of benefit and happiness for all countless sentient beings. In brief, may this merit become the cause for us and all others to reach the level of buddhahood.

The Seven-Branch Prayer from "Samantabhadra's Aspiration for Good Actions"

PROSTRATION

To all the buddhas, the lions of the human race,
In all directions of the universe, through past and present and future:
To every single one of you, I bow in homage;
Devotion fills my body, speech, and mind.

Through the power of this prayer, aspiring to good action,
All the victorious ones appear, vivid here before my mind,
And I multiply my body as many times as atoms in the universe,
Each one bowing in prostration to all the buddhas.

OFFERING

In every atom preside as many buddhas as there are atoms
And around them, all their bodhisattva heirs:
And so I imagine them filling
Completely the entire space of reality.

Saluting them with an endless ocean of praise,
With the sounds of an ocean of different melodies,
I sing of the buddhas' noble qualities
And praise all those who have gone to perfect bliss.

To every buddha, I make offerings:
Of the loveliest flowers, of beautiful garlands,
Of music and perfumed ointments, the best of parasols,
The brightest lamps, and finest incense.

To every buddha, I make offerings:
Exquisite garments and the most fragrant scents,
Powdered incense, heaped as high as Mount Meru,
Arranged in perfect symmetry.

Then, offerings vast and unsurpassable
I imagine I give to all the buddhas, and moved
By the power of my faith in Samantabhadra's good actions—
I prostrate and make offering to all you victorious ones.

CONFESSION

Whatever negative acts I have committed,
While driven by desire, hatred, and ignorance,
With my body, my speech, and also with my mind,
Before you, I acknowledge and purify each and every one.

REJOICING

With a heart full of delight, I rejoice at all the merits
Of buddhas and bodhisattvas, pratyekabuddhas,
Those in training, and the arhats beyond training,
And every living being, throughout the entire universe.

IMPLORING THE BUDDHAS TO TURN THE WHEEL OF DHARMA

You who are like beacons of light shining through the worlds,
Who passed through the stages of enlightenment to attain buddhahood, freedom from all attachment,
I urge you: all of you protectors,
Turn the unsurpassable wheel of Dharma.

REQUESTING THE BUDDHAS NOT TO ENTER NIRVANA

Joining my palms together, I pray
To you who intend to pass into nirvana—
Remain, for eons as many as the atoms in this world,
And bring well-being and happiness to all living beings.

DEDICATION

What little virtue I have gathered through my homage,
Through offering, confession, and rejoicing,
Through exhortation and prayer—all of it
I dedicate to the enlightenment of all beings!

AROUSING THE BODHICHITTA IN ASPIRATION

Keeping in mind the visualization for generating bodhichitta, as I just described it, you focus on all sentient beings and think, "I will lead them all to the state of enlightenment, which is entirely free from suffering and its causes. In order to achieve this, may I myself reach the state of omniscient buddhahood!"

Now we will recite three verses. The first establishes the motivation, as we vow to take refuge in the Buddha, Dharma, and Sangha, from now until we attain enlightenment. This is the uncommon refuge of the Mahayana.

With a wish to free all beings,
I will always go for refuge
To the Buddha, Dharma, and Sangha,
Until I reach full enlightenment.

The second verse is inspired by wisdom and compassion. We take the buddhas and bodhisattvas as our witness and in their presence we arouse bodhichitta for the sake of all infinite sentient beings.

Filled with wisdom and compassion,
Today, in the Buddha's presence,

I generate the mind set upon perfect awakening,
For the benefit of all sentient beings.

This is the main part of the practice for generating the bodhichitta of aspiration.

Then we reinforce that bodhichitta and pray that it develops further and further, by reciting this third verse, which comes from *The Way of the Bodhisattva:*

For as long as space exists
And sentient beings endure,
May I too remain,
To dispel the misery of the world.[91]

So we recite these three verses together twice and during the third recitation, when we come to the words "I generate the mind set upon perfect awakening," we must make a promise, saying to ourselves: In all circumstances, until the end of time, I will maintain this bodhichitta, without ever allowing it to fail or decline. If we do, then our bodhichitta in aspiration is secured by our determined pledge. It becomes an active promise. Otherwise it remains at the level of a simple aspiration. Finally, after this third recitation, consider that we have aroused bodhichitta in aspiration, held with this strong and determined resolve. At this point we will take the bodhisattva vow.

TAKING THE BODHISATTVA VOW

There are several ways to confer the bodhisattva vow. One occurs during a Vajrayana empowerment, when we generate bodhichitta in connection with the ritual for entering the mandala. There is also a brief way to transmit the vow, based on Shantideva's *The Way of the Bodhisattva*. Another way, which is more elaborate, comes from Shantideva's *The Compendium of Training.* Today I will give this transmission from the chapter on discipline in Asanga's *Bodhisattva Stages.*

To begin, you should repeat after me the following lines of request, to indicate that you wish to receive the bodhisattva vow, and you therefore request the teacher to grant it:[92]

> *"Teacher, please grant me your attention. I, the son or daughter of an enlightened family, request that you grant me the transmission of the bodhisattvas' vows of discipline. If this will not cause me any harm, it is right that you kindly listen to me and grant me this request."*

This is normally recited three times. Then, before taking the vow itself, the master poses a series of questions, to which the disciples generally answer by saying "*Dö la,*" which means "Yes, I have the wish."

So the teacher asks: "Are you taking the bodhisattva vow in order to free those sentient beings who are not yet freed from their cognitive obscurations?" To which you reply, "Yes, I have the wish."

> *"Listen, son or daughter of an enlightened family. Do you have the wish to liberate beings who have not yet gone beyond?"*
>
> *"Yes, I have the wish."*

The following question concerns whether you wish to free those sentient beings who are not yet freed from their emotional obscurations.

> *"Do you have the wish to liberate beings who are not yet free?"*
>
> *"Yes, I have the wish."*

Then the teacher asks whether you have the wish to free those sentient beings who are now suffering in the lower realms and to relieve them of their torment by guiding them to the higher states of existence.

> *"Do you have the wish to bring relief to those who are tormented?"*
>
> *"Yes, I have the wish."*

In brief, the next question asks: Do you have the hope and the wish to lead all beings to buddhahood?

"Do you have the wish to lead beyond sorrow those who have not yet passed beyond sorrow?"
"Yes, I have the wish."

The following question is: Do you wish to ensure the continuity of the buddhas' lineage?

"Do you have the wish to continue the line of the buddhas?"
"Yes, I have the wish."

Then the teacher enquires whether you are taking the bodhisattva vow out of a sense of rivalry and competition with others. To this you should answer "*Ma yin la,*" which means "no."

"Are you taking this vow in order to vie with others?"
"No."

The next question is whether you are taking the vow under duress, because you have been coerced into doing so by the Dalai Lama. So kindly answer no!

"Are you taking this vow against your will?"
"No."

Once we have taken the bodhisattva vow, we need to observe the precepts of the training. So you should know what these precepts are before you take the vow. They are explained in the teachings of the bodhisattva *pitaka,* in the *Avatamsaka Sutra,* for example, and in the *Bodhisattva Stages,* in particular its chapter on discipline. In any case, the questions that follow are whether you have heard these teachings belonging to the bodhisattva pitaka, whether you are familiar with them, whether you have faith in them, and whether you will be able to maintain them. Let's go through them, one at a time. The first question is whether you have heard these instructions, and you can answer that you have heard a little.

"Have you heard the teachings of the bodhisattva pitaka?" [93]

"Yes, I have."

When I ask if you know the meaning of these teachings, you should answer "a little" or "I know, but I have already forgotten them!"

"Do you know the teachings of the bodhisattva pitaka?"

"Yes, I do."

The next question is: Do you have faith in these teachings? Your answer could be something like: "When I feel good, I have faith in them."

"Do you have faith in the teachings of the bodhisattva pitaka?"

"Yes, I do."

Then the teacher asks: Do you think you can maintain the precepts? And your answer could be: "I'll try my best."

"Do you have the capacity to observe the bodhisattvas' precepts?"

"Yes, I do."

"Now let your bodhichitta and your commitment remain firm and stable."

The next stage is the accumulation of merit through the seven branches, which you do not need to recite aloud, but simply bring the meaning to mind.

What little virtue I have gathered through my homage,
Through offering, confession, and rejoicing,
Through exhortation and prayer—all of it
I dedicate to the enlightenment of all beings![94]

Now there comes a plea to the master, requesting him to grant us the vow swiftly. Here, the teacher is referred to as "venerable one," which indicates that he is a monk who is more senior than the students.[95] Repeat after me:

"Teacher, please grant me your attention. Venerable one, please grant me swiftly the vows of the bodhisattvas' discipline."

The subsequent question is: "Are you a bodhisattva?" The meaning of this is: Has the potential of the family[96] of the bodhisattvas awakened in you? Whether or not the potential has awakened comes down to whether or not you have generated great compassion. Some of you may well be bodhisattvas, and you may have already developed this great compassion. For most of us this is not yet the case; however, if we reflect on what has been said previously about its many benefits, we can at least develop a strong and single-minded aspiration to generate bodhichitta. So you should answer the question by thinking of how you will be able to awaken this potential before too long, and say "yes."

Then the next question will be: "Have you made the aspiration toward enlightenment?" We are being asked whether or not our aspiration is stable. Even though we may not have actually developed the aspiration, we should still answer yes, because we have the wish to do so. To sum up, the questions are: "Do you have great compassion? Do you have a stable aspiration?"

"Sons and daughters of an enlightened family, Dharma brothers and sisters, led by the great holder of the Vinaya, Ngawang Chökyi Lodrö (Kyabjé Trulshik Rinpoche), are you bodhisattvas? Have you made the aspiration to enlightenment?"*

"Yes, it is well done."

Although it has now been established that you are able to take the bodhisattva vow, there is no reason that you should necessarily take it from me. So the next question is: "Are you sure that you want to take it from me?" The answer here is: "Yes, we do."

"Do you wish to receive the bases for the trainings of all the bodhisattvas and the discipline of the bodhisattvas from me?"

"Yes, we do.

*His Holiness includes here the name of the seniormost member of the assembly.

THE MAIN PART OF THE TRANSMISSION OF THE BODHISATTVA VOW

Now we come to the main part of the transmission of the bodhisattva vow. For this, we need to call upon the buddhas and bodhisattvas as our witnesses, considering that they have perfect knowledge from which nothing is hidden. As it says in *The Way of the Bodhisattva:*

> The buddhas and the bodhisattvas
> Possess unobstructed vision.
> Everything lies before their gaze,
> And I am always in their presence.[97]

Then the question will be asked: "Do you wish to receive from me the vows of discipline of the bodhisattvas, the discipline followed by the buddhas and bodhisattvas of the past, the buddhas and bodhisattvas of the future, and the buddhas and bodhisattvas of the present? In short, do you wish to receive the vows of the three kinds of discipline—the discipline of avoiding negative actions, the discipline of cultivating virtue, and the discipline of benefiting others?" Each time you should answer, "Yes, I wish to receive it."

We will recite this three times; on the third repetition, you should consider that you have received the pure bodhisattva vow, and that, from now on, it is present in your mind. Those of you who have already received the bodhisattva vow should consider that it is strengthened even further. Those of you who are Buddhist practitioners and would like to receive the bodhisattva vow today, please kneel on your right knee.

As we go through the ceremony, try to cultivate deep compassion for living beings, clear faith and devotion for the buddhas, a sincere desire to receive the bodhisattva vow, and a resolute wish to train in the bodhisattvas' actions. Pray as fervently as you can.

> *"Sons and daughters of an enlightened family, led by the great and learned holder of the Vinaya, Ngawang Chökyi Lodrö, do you wish to receive from me the vows that are the discipline and basis of training*

for all the bodhisattvas of the past, the discipline and basis of training for all the bodhisattvas of the future, the discipline and basis of training for all the bodhisattvas of the present throughout the ten directions, the basis of training and the discipline that was followed by all the bodhisattvas of the past, that will be followed by all the bodhisattvas of the future, and that is now being followed by all the bodhisattvas of the present throughout the ten directions, all the bases for the bodhisattvas' training, and all the disciplines of the bodhisattvas—the discipline of avoiding negative actions, the discipline of cultivating virtue, and the discipline of benefiting others, which include all the disciplines of the bodhisattvas?"

"Yes, we do."

The question and response are repeated a second time.

Now, when we come to the third repetition, as you listen, bring to mind especially faith and compassion, feel an inspired and enthusiastic longing to receive the bodhisattva vow and aspire to follow the training of the bodhisattvas. As you do so, pray with real fervor. Say to yourselves that you will do your best to follow the Buddha and do just as he did.

The question and response are repeated a third time.

You can take your seats again. Now that we have received the bodhisattva vow and it has taken root in our minds, the benefits of this are unimaginable. There is no greater offering that we could make to please the buddhas and bodhisattvas. We have given meaning to our lives and the freedom they afford us, and we have put them to good use. If now we try to observe the precepts and follow the training to the best of our ability, we will go from one state of happiness to the next, until before long we arrive at the ultimate state of buddhahood. Of that, we can be utterly certain.

By encouraging you to do something as virtuous as this, I, as the teacher, have accomplished something meaningful, too; I will now prostrate to the buddhas and bodhisattvas of the three times and ten directions and request that they consider all of you who have taken this vow. At this point the teacher should prostrate to each of the four cardinal directions and, if there is time, to the four intermediate directions and then to the zenith and nadir, making ten in all. But since there is not much time, I will prostrate to the four directions and consider that the four intermediate directions are included; then I will prostrate to the east once again, considering it as the zenith, and to the west, considering it the nadir. Having offered prostrations, I will bring to mind the buddhas of those directions and offer flowers. At this point you should also make prayers of aspiration but not ordinary prayers that your lives may be long, your health good, and your careers successful, and the like. They should be prayers that, just as you have pledged in taking this vow, you may swiftly attain the level of omniscient buddhahood and bring about your own and others' ultimate welfare.

At this point[98] I will call upon the buddhas and bodhisattvas as witness and state that you have all now become bodhisattvas, having received the bodhisattva vow from me, Tenzin Gyatso, a monk who has some devotion to the bodhisattva path, and that you will maintain the discipline and precepts.

> *"Buddhas and bodhisattvas residing throughout the ten directions, grant us your attention! These bodhisattvas, such as the learned holder of the Vinaya, the incomparable Ngawang Chökyi Lodrö, have hereby received the vows of the bodhisattvas' training from me, the monk Tenzin Gyatso, who holds the name of bodhisattva. May you, the sublime ones, to whose wisdom minds nothing throughout the entire infinity of the universe lies hidden, bear witness to this!"*

CONCLUSION: UPLIFTING ONE'S OWN AND OTHERS' MINDS

Now we uplift and inspire ourselves, by bringing to mind and celebrating the benefits of having taken the bodhisattva vow. The text says that as soon as the ritual of taking the vow is complete and we consider that we have fully received the vows of the bodhisattvas, all the buddhas throughout the worlds of the ten directions and all the bodhisattvas who have reached the ten stages will become aware of what has happened. They will use their wisdom minds to discover the place and circumstances in which the vow was transmitted. In this case, they will come to know that the vow was transmitted to an assembly of fortunate people from various nationalities and races, from various lineages of Dharma including the Sakya, Geluk, Kagyü, and Nyingma, all of whom share the same unwavering devotion and spiritual commitment, led by the bodhisattva who is like the crowning jewel of the Ngagyur Nyingma tradition, the learned holder of the Vinaya, Ngawang Chökyi Lodrö Rinpoche. They will come to know that all those present aroused in their minds the bodhichitta wish for supreme enlightenment. They will come to know that this took place in this world of ours, in the country of France, in the newly created center of Dharma of Lerab Ling, and that the vow was transmitted by one who has devotion to the bodhisattva teachings, a monk from Amdo called Tenzin Gyatso. Henceforth, they will all regard us with their love and compassion, and the buddhas will consider us as their child, the bodhisattvas will consider us as their brothers and sisters, and they will all have the positive wish that our intentions may be fulfilled without any obstacle. Through this, our virtue will increase enormously and will not diminish. What we have done here today in taking this vow has been the greatest possible offering we could make to the buddhas and bodhisattvas.

As it says in *The Way of the Bodhisattva:*

Today, my birth has been fruitful,
I have well obtained a human existence.
Today I am born into the family of the buddhas;
I have become a son or daughter of the buddhas.

From now on, at all costs, I will perform
The actions befitting to my family.
I will not be a stain
On this faultless noble family.

Now we have entered the faultless and noble family of the bodhisattvas and will do nothing to bring any stain upon this family.

The text advises us against making any imprudent proclamations, which means that from now on we should avoid boasting about having received the bodhisattva vow. You don't need to start wearing it emblazoned on your chest. And when you get on a bus or train, you should not say, "Stand aside! Here comes someone who has received the bodhisattva vow!" You need to keep it to yourselves and not talk about it to others. Why? Because we should always take the lowest place, and we should aspire to be the servant of all sentient beings, who are as infinite as space.

Some of you might feel that because you have aroused bodhichitta and received the bodhisattva vow today, you are now bodhisattvas. But that is not what you should think. It is much better to consider that you have taken the first step toward becoming a bodhisattva and that you have simply planted the seed. If we take care to nurture this seed, it will grow and eventually ripen.

Finally, we will express our gratitude for having received the bodhisattva vow. Normally at this point we would recite the seven-branch prayer, but today we will simply remind ourselves of its meaning and once again recite the single verse:

What little virtue I have gathered through my homage,
Through offering, confession, and rejoicing,
Through exhortation and prayer—all of it
I dedicate to the enlightenment of all beings!

CONCLUDING PRAYERS

O sublime and precious bodhichitta,
May it arise in those in whom it has not arisen;
May it never decline where it has arisen
But go on increasing further and further!

May all sentient beings, our very own parents, be happy.
May all the lower realms be forever empty.
May the aspirations of all the bodhisattvas
Of the various bhumis be fulfilled!

May all those vast prayers of aspiration
Made by the Lord Avalokiteshvara for the land of Tibet
Before the buddhas and their bodhisattva heirs,
Quickly bring their positive results, here and now!

Through the profound interdependence of appearance and emptiness,
Through the power of the compassionate Three Jewels and these words of truth,
And through the strength of the infallible law of cause and effect,
May this, our prayer of truth, be swiftly accomplished, without any hindrance![99]

CHAPTER 15

THE EMPOWERMENT OF PADMASAMBHAVA AND HIS EIGHT MANIFESTATIONS

THE EMPOWERMENT TODAY is for the mind sadhana of *The Union of All the Innermost Essences.* It belongs to the cycle of pure visions of the Great Fifth Dalai Lama, called Sangwa Gyachen, *Bearing the Seal of Secrecy.* In the Nyingma tradition there are three forms of transmission: the long oral transmission of the *kama* or canonical teachings, the shorter transmission of *terma* or revealed treasures, and the profound transmission through *dak nang* or pure visions. There are different kinds of pure vision, it seems: some arise as meditative experiences, some arise purely on the level of the mind, and some arise to the sense consciousnesses. This particular cycle arose from pure visions in which the Great Fifth Dalai Lama experienced meeting the deities as clearly as if it were an ordinary human encounter. The text I will be using on this occasion was arranged by Jamyang Khyentse Wangpo.[100]

I myself received this transmission at the age of around twelve or thirteen, when I received the entire cycle of Sangwa Gyachen from Tadrak Rinpoche.[101]

The empowerment text explains:

> The great master from Oddiyana, Padmasambhava, embodies the indestructible primordial wisdom of the body, speech, and mind of all the buddhas of past, present, and future. On more than one occasion, with his unmistaken vajra words, he declared that the continuing manifestation of King Trisong Detsen, who was the emanation of Manjushri, and of his

> inexhaustible enlightened activity of the ultimate fruition, is primordially the protector of Tibet, the victorious, great, all-knowing, and all-seeing sovereign lord of speech, Dorjé Thokmé Tsal. Within the twenty-five sections of the revelations *Bearing the Seal of Extreme Secrecy* that appeared to him in pure wisdom visions is to be found the profound practice under the vajra seal that is the mind sadhana of the guru, *The Union of All the Innermost Essences.*[102]

After the time of the Great Fifth Dalai Lama, this cycle of Sangwa Gyachen became one of the main teachings entrusted to the successive Dalai Lamas. It seems that the thirteenth Dalai Lama practiced the Sangwa Gyachen regularly. During that period the revealer of terma teachings destined for that time, Lerab Lingpa, came to Lhasa, and it was then that the Dalai Lama received from him the Vajrakilaya cycle of Yang Nying Pudri.[103]

In Lhasa there was a set of texts for the whole Sangwa Gyachen cycle, which had been handwritten and compiled at the time of the Great Fifth. They were wonderfully well made and beautiful, and I had them in my room, but at that time, when I had the texts, I had no interest in the teachings. Later, when I became interested in the teachings, I no longer had the texts! When I came to India, I read the biographies of the previous Dalai Lamas; I thought about them, and for this and other reasons too, I became much more interested in the life of the Great Fifth and consequently in the Sangwa Gyachen cycle. Then slowly, as a result of karma and aspiration prayers, I gradually acquired the texts.

Every tenth day of the waxing moon, the thirteenth Dalai Lama would perform in his private quarters the tsok feast offering practice of Avalokiteshvara from the Sangwa Gyachen cycle, known as *Nine Deities of the Great Compassionate One, Lord of the World.*[104] And on every twenty-fifth day of the month, he would practice the Hayagriva tsok feast offering from this cycle, known as *Prevailing Over the Three Worlds.*[105] When I arrived in India, I wanted to reestablish the tradition of doing these practices from the Sangwa Gyachen cycle on the tenth days of the waxing and waning moon, and so I sought out and gradually acquired the texts. I did a recitation retreat for the Kagyé practice from the Sangwa Gyachen, and I had the opportunity to ask Dudjom Rinpoche about the details of how to practice the recitation. When I did the practice, there were some positive signs, including a few remarkable dreams. In fact, even when I first received the Sangwa Gyachen cycle, although I was quite young and did not have much interest at the time, there were still certain signs that appeared. So I believe that I do have some special connection with these teachings.

The Union of All the Innermost Essences is a brief sadhana. It is a guru yoga focusing on Guru Rinpoche. It carries a lot of blessings, and yet it is very short. I practice it regularly and have recited it many times.

SKILLFUL MEANS AND WISDOM

This morning we all took the bodhisattva vow, and, from the moment you received the vow, you pledged to attain the level of complete and perfect enlightenment. In order to attain that level we need an infallible method. The wisdom of omniscience is a conditioned phenomenon, meaning that it arises based on causes and conditions. It is inconceivably good and completely transcends all our ordinary thoughts and activity, but still, since it arises on the basis of this stream of consciousness we have now, it is a compounded or conditioned phenomenon, which comes about as a result of certain causes and conditions. We need therefore to assemble the correct causes and conditions, all complete and in the right sequence. These causes were mentioned by Nagarjuna in his famous dedication prayer:

> Through this merit, may all beings
> Complete the accumulations of merit and wisdom,
> And so attain the dharmakaya and rupakaya
> That come from merit and wisdom.[106]

As he says, the causes are twofold—"the accumulations of merit and wisdom"—through which we attain the results of the dharmakaya for our own benefit and the rupakaya for the benefit of others. The accumulation of merit corresponds to the aspect of skillful means and is the principal cause of the rupakaya.[107] The accumulation of wisdom refers to the wisdom that realizes emptiness, which enables us to attain the wisdom dharmakaya. When we gather these accumulations, which will result in the sublime rupakaya for others' benefit and the sublime dharmakaya for our own benefit, we should accumulate them both together at the same time. This is to say, we should bring together these two aspects of skillful means and wisdom. Uniting skillful means and wisdom is the general approach of the Mahayana.

Since it is so vital to unify means and wisdom, if we can bring the two together into a single entity, where the key points of both are complete within one consciousness, that unity of skillful means and wisdom becomes so much more powerful and profound.[108] In the sutra system and the vehicle of transcendent perfections, the practice is such that the two aspects of skillful means and wisdom support and complement one another but remain distinct. It is in the practice of Vajrayana, according to all four levels of tantra—kriya, charya, yoga, and anuttarayoga tantra—that there is a method of uniting both of these factors of skillful means and wisdom indivisibly, so that they become a single entity. The most refined and ultimate form of this indivisible unity is elicited in the highest yoga tantra.

In Dzogchen, if we are able to actualize in practice the naturally arising rigpa that is Samantabhadra, our own ultimate innate primordial wisdom, then that is the most profound form of the indivisible unity of means and wisdom. Therefore, in order to bring about "the fruition that is all-embracing spontaneous presence"—which is the inseparability of the kayas and wisdom mind—we need to bring together all the right causes, with nothing missing, while we are on the path. That is why the path should unite the practice of primordial purity related to the dharmakaya of inward radiance and the practice of spontaneous perfection related to the sambhogakaya of outward radiance. In other words, we need to practice *trekchö* and *tögal* as the causes for accomplishing the kayas and wisdom mind. In order for the practice of tögal to be truly effective, we need the practice of trekchö.

As a preliminary, we need to take the practice of guru yoga, or the practice that focuses on the guru,[109] as the life force of our path. In fact, all the different lineages of Dharma within Tibet and all the schools of

Tibetan Buddhism have spoken of the need to hold guru yoga as the most vital practice on the path. In the practice of trekchö, devotion is an extremely important factor in bringing about a direct experience of the all-penetrating pure awareness of rigpa. The empowerment of *The Union of All the Innermost Essences,* which you are about to receive, is a practice of guru yoga related to Guru Rinpoche.

CHAPTER 16

THE CLEAR LIGHT

B. THE MAIN PRACTICE

Having explained the preliminaries of *Finding Comfort and Ease in Meditation on the Great Perfection,* now we come to the main practice. Longchenpa says:

> **The main practice is the recognition of the natural condition,**
> **Through meditation involving bliss, clarity, and nonconceptuality.**
> **The clear light primordial wisdom free of conceptual elaboration,**
> **Arises as the fundamental innate mind.**

The main practice then is meditating on the fundamental innate clear light. This clear light can be considered from the point of view of the object and from the point of view of the subject. The objective clear light represents emptiness, which is the freedom from all conceptual elaborations. As we saw earlier, this is the absolute truth, the actual nature of all phenomena. And we observed that conventional appearances, when we do not investigate or analyze them, are the relative truth.

For example, the *Guhyasamaja Tantra* in the new translation school of tantra speaks of five stages of the completion stage, where the clear light is called the absolute and the illusory body is called the relative. The most important factor then is the direct realization of the subjective aspect of clear light.

THE HIGHER TWO TRUTHS

In the same manner, the *Guhyagarbha Tantra* of the Nyingmapa tradition speaks of the higher two truths: the higher absolute and higher relative. The higher absolute truth is described in terms of what are known as "the seven bountiful attributes of absolute truth."[110] Dodrupchen Jikmé Tenpé Nyima, in his overview commentary on the *Guhyagarbha Tantra,* explains the higher absolute truth in the following way:

> Although there are many ways to explain the two truths, here we are concerned with the two truths according to the extraordinary approach of the Secret Magical Net, or the *higher two truths.* You might wonder what is meant by the higher absolute truth. The higher absolute truth refers to the *natural absolute of basic space* that is free from any conceptual elaboration.[111]

"Basic space" here refers to the subjective aspect of clear light, the fundamental innate mind of clear light, which is Samantabhadra, the primordial buddha. As I said earlier, there are two aspects to primordial purity, two ways to understand what it means. The first kind of primordial purity is pure emptiness, in the sense of the absence of the property that is being negated. The second is when the fundamental innate mind of clear light, or rigpa, is divided into primordial purity and spontaneous perfection. Here the quotation seems to be referring to this second interpretation, the aspect of rigpa, or pure awareness.

So we speak of "the natural absolute of basic space that is free from any conceptual elaboration." Now the term *natural* here is not necessarily referring to the nature of things, which is emptiness. It is natural more in the sense of being fundamental and innate, as when we say "natural innate kaya"; in the new translation schools of tantra this is one of the four kayas of the fruitional state of buddhahood, the compounded *svabhavikakaya.* So when we speak of the natural, the innate, or the primordial, that is the natural absolute. Then, as Dodrupchen Jikmé Tenpé Nyima says, the natural absolute is understood in terms of "basic space that is free from any conceptual elaboration." He continues:

> And to the *wisdom absolute,* which is inherent luminosity free from obscuring veils.

The term *wisdom absolute* refers to that fact that this basic space, which is devoid of any conceptual elaboration, is free from any obscuring veils. Dodrup Jikmé Tenpé Nyima concludes:

> And to the *resultant absolute,* the presence of the treasure of the five resultant factors—enlightened body, speech, mind, qualities, and activity—within this very [unity of basic space and wisdom]. Since the latter is divided into five, these are then known collectively as the *seven bountiful attributes of the absolute.*

This further subdivision into the five aspects of enlightened body, speech, mind, qualities, and activity gives us the "seven bountiful attributes of absolute truth."

The subjective aspect of clear light, then, is being referred to as the absolute. The reason for this is that the fundamental innate mind of clear light is empty of any adventitious property. For example, the terminology of the *Guhyasamaja Tantra* of the new translation schools speaks of the *four empties.*[112] *Empty* here means one thing being empty of something else. The first kind of emptiness is the emptiness of the eighty indicative conceptions together with the wind energies that serve as their mounts, which is *appearance.* That which is empty of appearance and the wind energy that serves as its mount is *increase.* That which is empty of increase and the wind energy that serves as its mount is *near-attainment.* That which is empty of all three experiences together with the wind energies that serve as their mounts is *clear light.* This emptiness is a form of extrinsic or *other emptiness.*

As Jikmé Tenpé Nyima says, when the absolute truth is discussed for the purpose of teaching, it is mainly spoken of in terms of a non-implicative negation. But when it comes to meditation on emptiness, it is best considered as an affirming negation. When we cultivate the aspect of rigpa awareness in meditation, we meditate on appearances, which lack true reality. The focus of the main practice is nothing other than sustaining the recognition of our own rigpa, which is the primordial buddha Samantabhadra, forever and always pure.

Yet, before this, we need to accomplish certain preliminary practices for purifying the body, speech, and mind. As part of the purification of mind, we investigate where mind comes from, where it remains, and where it goes; that is the point when we need to establish the subtle view of emptiness according to the Middle Way Prasangika[113] approach. When practitioners who have already arrived at some certainty in understanding this subtle emptiness are then introduced to, and recognize, the pure awareness of rigpa in the rigpa itself, they can rest in one-pointed meditation sustaining that recognition. With the certainty and understanding of subtle emptiness they acquired earlier, as they maintain their focus on rigpa's pure awareness, they are in fact meditating on the unity of appearance and emptiness, and so, it seems to me, they are indeed meditating on emptiness as an affirming negation.

The fundamental innate mind of clear light is where the depth of highest yoga tantra becomes evident. This is also where the exceptionally profound quality of Dzogpachenpo is highlighted and likewise that of Mahamudra. When the glorious Sakya tradition of Lamdré speaks of the view of the inseparability of samsara and nirvana in the context of the "triple tantra," or "three continuums,"[114] this is also what it comes down to. If we consider the view of the Geluk school—although this does not correspond to the basic view of the Middle Way—in connection with the inseparable unity of coemergent bliss and emptiness, then that again has exactly the same connotation. So it is fair to say that they are all speaking of the same ultimate point.

The Sakyapas call this clear light the *alaya,* the ground of all. In the Sakya tradition of *lamdré lopshé*, one of Tsarchen Losal Gyatso's students, Mangtö Ludrup Gyatso,[115] said that the clear light is the absolute truth. However, another of Tsarchen Losal Gyatso's students, Jamyang Khyentse Wangchuk, says in his writings that, of the two truths, the clear light belongs to the relative truth; of conditioned and unconditioned, it is conditioned; and of the three categories of the conditioned, that is, form, consciousness, and nonassociated formations, it is consciousness. So there are different viewpoints. When Mangtö Ludrup

Gyatso says it is the absolute truth, that is without making any distinction in terms of subjective or objective aspects, and yet it does seem to be in accordance with what is taught in connection with the completion stage, where the absolute corresponds to clear light.[116]

Still, as we find in *Distinguishing the Middle from Extremes,* where it speaks of the absolute meaning, absolute practice, and absolute result, there are many references for the term *absolute.*[117]

All in all, whether we say it is absolute truth or relative truth does not make that much difference, as the basic point is that all these approaches emphasize the fundamental innate mind of clear light and take it as the path.

Now, turning to the higher relative truth, Jikmé Tenpé Nyima says:

> As for the higher relative truth, although it is said to be the appearance of the energy of the absolute, I think it is preferable to describe it as the magical manifestation, because as Deshek Zurchungwa said, "Regarding all phenomena, their appearance as the magical manifestation of rigpa is the approach of Maha, their appearance as the energy of rigpa is the approach of Anu, and their appearance as rigpa itself is the approach of Ati."[118]

This is a little complicated, but the gist of what I am saying is this: Earlier, we concluded that these different approaches all emphasize the fundamental innate mind of clear light, and in each approach there is a special way of presenting the two truths. Here, in this case, they are referred to as the higher two truths.

The higher absolute truth is the fundamental innate mind of clear light. What is called fundamental innate mind of clear light in the terminology of the new translation traditions of tantra is the rigpa awareness that is *rigpa Samantabhadra,* the ground dharmakaya, or the primordial buddha.

Dodrupchen Jikmé Tenpé Nyima explains:

> The coarse states of mind that arise from the habitual tendencies of the transference of the three appearances are not present at the level of the fruition, and so not even their emptiness

is present. Therefore, the suchness that goes on to become the "reality kaya"[119] of the buddhas must be the basic space of this fundamental wisdom. This is precisely the ultimate intent of the teachings on the buddha nature, the *sugatagarbha,* found in the sutras of the final turning of the wheel of Dharma.[120]

The fact that this is also the fundamental innate mind of clear light spoken of in the texts of the new translation schools of tantra is clear from Longchenpa's *Treasury of Philosophical Tenets.* In the teachings on the nature of the ground, he says:[121]

> The primordial ground, self-arising wisdom, which is beyond limitation in scope or magnitude, is empty in essence like the sky, clear by nature like the sun or moon, and pervasive in its compassion like rays of light. These three properties, indivisible in essence, abide within the basic space that has always been beyond any transition and change, and they have the nature of the wisdom of the three kayas. The empty essence is the dharmakaya, the clear nature is the sambhogakaya, and the pervasive compassion is the nirmanakaya.

WHERE THE CLEAR LIGHT RESIDES

The essence is primordial purity, the nature is spontaneous presence, and the unceasing radiance is compassion. Where do these abide? Longchenpa says:

> While we remain deluded among the six classes of beings, these three appear to our deluded perception as the ordinary body, speech, and mind. Yet even though the wisdom of the enlightened body, speech, and mind does not appear, that does not mean it is not there. The channels depend on the physical body, the wind energy and elements depend on the channels, and at the subtle level, in the center of the center of the four chakras, there is the palace of self-arisen wisdom.[122]

There are four chakras, one of them, for example, being the chakra of great bliss at the crown of the head. What is called "the palace of self-arising wisdom" is located in their center, in the middle of the central channel at the dharma chakra at the heart. As we saw earlier, there are different degrees of subtlety to the channels, wind energies, and essences, and here we are talking about the extremely subtle. In the unique terminology of Dzogchen, this is spoken of as "the *kati* crystal channel." Longchenpa continues:

> In the palace of dharma at the heart, the essence, the self-arisen luminous primordial wisdom, is firmly present, together with infinite attributes of wisdom. As it says in *The Fine Array of Jewels:*
>
> > The great self-arising wisdom
> > In the jewel palace of the heart.[123]

So here the principal location of the fundamental innate mind of clear light is identified as the center of the dharma chakra at the heart. Longchenpa then says:

> The clear light resides there in four extraordinary channels; the great golden kati channel comes through the center of the central channel and connects with the center of the heart, and so it is filled with *tiklés* of the ground, Samantabhadra.[124]

This then describes the principal place where clear light resides.

THE CLEAR LIGHT AS BUDDHA NATURE

The fact that the fundamental innate mind of clear light is the same as the buddha nature is mentioned even in the sutras, for example in *The Sutra of the Wisdom of Passing Beyond,* one of the root sources for Maitreya's *Sublime Continuum.*

In *The Wish-Fulfilling Treasury* and the chapter entitled "How samsara originates from the ground," Longchenpa discusses the ground for delusion:

> The original clear light, the very essence of blissful buddhahood,
> The ultimate ground of all is naturally uncompounded,
> Utterly pure from the very beginning, like the sunlit sky,
> Yet clouded by habitual tendencies based on ignorance,
> And this is why sentient beings are deluded.[125]

In commenting upon these lines, he says:

> The ground, like space, has always been free from any basis or support that depends upon samsara, and it is selfless by its very essence. It is clear and luminous like the sun or moon and spontaneously perfect. It has been present timelessly, without any beginning, and so it is beyond any transition or change.[126]

This is why the fundamental innate mind of clear light is portrayed as "uncompounded," which, as Dodrup Jikmé Tenpé Nyima points out, means that it is continuously present and not newly created by transient causes and conditions. Longchenpa explains:

> Since it is beyond all the limitations of fixed ideas, it is naturally luminous. Since it abides within the basic space in which the kayas and wisdoms are united inseparably, it is the sugatagarbha.

In other words, the full potential for the three kayas is present.

> Since it supports all the phenomena of samsara and nirvana, it is called "the natural state that is the ultimate ground of all." It is uncompounded and has always been entirely pure.

As long as we have not yet removed the adventitious stains, the fundamental innate mind of clear light is referred to as the *sugatagarbha,* and the potential for the three kayas that is inherently present is referred to as *the qualities of basic space.* When the adventitious stains that cloud our true nature are removed, the potential for these kayas, which has always been present within the fundamental innate mind of clear light, is activated or made manifest and becomes "the qualities of fruition." Therefore the kayas and buddhahood are both intrinsic to the fundamental innate mind of clear light.

ANALYTICAL MEDITATION AND THE MIDDLE WAY VIEW

When we say that the essence is primordially pure or empty, the understanding of emptiness here is mainly according to the Prasangika view. As Longchenpa says in *The Wish-Fulfilling Treasury:*

> Now when it comes to the presentation of the Prasangika tradition, which is the pinnacle of the Mahayana vehicle of characteristics within Buddhism...[127]

In his detailed commentary, there is one section on how the Prasangikas eliminate conceptual elaboration, since there can be no assertions with regard to the actual absolute nature in itself; another section discusses how the Prasangikas present relative, conventional reality without refuting how things appear. In the latter section, he says:

> Here, in the section presenting relative reality without refuting how things appear, there are three parts: the ground of the Middle Way, the two truths; the path of the Middle Way, the two accumulations; and the fruition of the Middle Way, the two kayas.[128]

The main point is that this is presented principally from the Prasangika point of view. As for "the empty essence," in both sutra and the common tantras, certainty has to be reached about the nature of emptiness. Highest yoga tantra has its own special understanding of emptiness. Then in the texts of Dzogpachenpo in particular we find mention of different modes of liberation, such as primordial liberation, self-liberation, naked liberation, complete liberation, and liberation from extremes, each of which presents different nuances and has its own distinctive character. All of them involve recognition of the same empty essence.

The fact that the meditation on subtle emptiness according to the Prasangika approach takes place in the context of the investigation of where mind comes from, where it remains, and where it goes is explained by Dodrup Jikmé Tenpé Nyima as follows:[129]

> Although many different vehicles have been taught as means to gain realization,
> There is only one way to the essence that must be realized.

He is saying that there is only one path to buddhahood, one door that leads to peace.

> The basic nature of one's own mind beyond arising, dwelling, and ceasing—

If we examine where mind comes from, we cannot find any origin or basis for its arising. If we examine where mind stays, we cannot find any basis for its abiding. If we examine where mind goes, we cannot find any such location. So the basic nature of mind is beyond arising, dwelling, and ceasing. Dodrup Jikmé Tenpé Nyima continues:

> It is here that the eyes of intelligence are first opened wide.

In other words, you must begin by investigating the mind and searching for where it comes from, where it stays, and where it goes. But then he cautions:

> But simply not seeing the three locations—the origin, dwelling place, and destination—
> Is not in itself sufficient for finding the natural state.

Searching for where mind comes from, where it remains, and where it goes and then finding nothing at all is not enough to find the natural state.

> It is not just, as in the well-known saying, "beyond any basis or origin,"
> Or just "merely words"; it needs to be investigated further.

Now the term *beyond any basis or origin* has the same connotation as *merely words and labels.* The latter is stated from the point of view of how something appears, whereas *beyond any basis or origin* is expressed from the point of view of its emptiness. We should not just leave the investigation there, saying mind is beyond basis or origin or that mind is merely a label. We need to go further and come to a real understanding of the meaning of the Middle Way that eliminates the two extremes.

> Even though one might not be focusing on true reality, to even the slightest degree,
> This will not put an end to false appearance and perception.

This is the same point that Nagarjuna makes in the *The Precious Garland of the Middle Way:*

> A person is not earth, not water,
> Not fire, not wind, not space,
> Not consciousness, and not all of them.
> What person is there other than these?[130]

When we search for the basis on which the label *person* is applied, and we cannot find it, we don't immediately say that the person does not exist. The fact that we cannot find a basis for the labeling when we search for it eliminates the extreme of eternalism. But the elimination of just one extreme, that of eternalism, does not count as a complete understanding of the Middle Way. In itself, this cannot eliminate the two extremes, which is why Nagarjuna continues:

> Since the person is a composite of the six elements...[131]

In other words, the person is a label we apply to the gathering of the six elements. So there is actually a person, although not a real and truly existent person. This eliminates the extreme of nihilism. In this way, both extremes are eliminated.

The same principle applies here. Investigating where mind comes from, where it stays, and where it goes, and then not finding anything called *mind,* is not yet the true view of the Middle Way. If mind truly existed, we should be able to find some basis for it when we investigate its origin, dwelling place, and destination, but we don't find any such basis. This is a sign that mind does not *truly* exist, but we cannot conclude that mind does not exist at all. When we understand that mind is a dependent imputation, something that exists dependently, this is enough to counter the idea of mind as something independent. This is the genuine conclusion that we arrive at through the view of the Prasangika Middle Way concerning "the essence," that is, primordial purity. Dodrupchen continues:

> So, until you are satisfied about this profound and crucial point,
> Investigate thoroughly, relying upon the works of the learned and accomplished.[132]

The point here is that in order to arrive at the definitive view of the Middle Way, it is necessary to practice analytical meditation. But there is no place for analytical meditation when we are practicing the inseparable unity of awareness and emptiness. That is exclusively a form of settling meditation. So the context for analytical meditation is during the Dzogchen preliminaries. It is then that we have to come to a decisive understanding about the view.

There is a connection here with a profound crucial point in highest yoga tantra, which is that when we meditate on emptiness, the phenomenon on which we are meditating is mind. For example, when the *Guhyasamaja Tantra* speaks of "body isolation," "speech isolation," and "mind isolation,"[133] mind isolation involves meditating on emptiness but specifically the emptiness of the mind. So this is referred to quite often in the texts of highest yoga tantra as a "superior phenomenon."

In general, emptiness depends on an object or a particular phenomenon. If the object is transient or adventitious, then its emptiness, although it is not conditioned, will cease to be when the object ceases to be. To put it another way, if the phenomenon ceases, its empty nature also ceases. One reason therefore why we practice deity yoga and visualize the "permanent form" of a deity, is that within our imagination that deity then continues and does not perish. So if we take the *pure* form of the deity as the basis and realize its empty nature, that emptiness will become the *svabhavikakaya,* the "essential nature body" of a buddha. Otherwise, if we take some *impure* phenomenon as the basis for realizing emptiness, although the emptiness is the same, the phenomenon does not continue until buddhahood so neither will its emptiness. This is why we talk about emptiness in terms of pure phenomena; in summary, the whole basis for meditation on emptiness is the mind.

CHAPTER 17

A REVIEW OF THE TEACHING

I HAVE BEEN TOLD that there are some people who have arrived today, and so for their benefit, I will review the essence of what we have discussed so far. This will also serve as a kind of revision session for those who have been here all along.

HAPPINESS, THE PURPOSE OF LIFE

What is the purpose of this life of ours? What is the heart of being human? These are questions that I often wonder about. I think you can say that the purpose of our life is to be happy. If people practice a religion or a spiritual path of some kind, it is in order to be happy; there's no other reason. Buddhist practitioners, for example, strive to attain buddhahood with the aim of finding happiness and bliss. However, it is not for themselves alone, because they are aspiring to reach that level of buddhahood so that limitless sentient beings can all enjoy ultimate happiness and bliss. This is what they are working toward. Achieving happiness, in fact, is a fundamental right that belongs to each and every one of us, and it is a perfectly reasonable aspiration, too.

If you look at this happiness we strive so hard for and the suffering we try to avoid, there are various kinds. Take the developing countries of the world, where people face all kinds of hardship because of poverty, poor education, disease, and hunger. On top of the shortage of food, water, and clothing, they have to undergo the difficulties inflicted on them by their environment as well. That is one kind of suffering. In the more economically advanced countries, people are generally more affluent and better educated, and greater care is taken over the environment. But still people are unhappy, because of another kind of suffering.

So I think we can discern a pattern that in countries facing economic difficulties most forms of suffering are related to the five senses and the domain of the body. In the richer countries, problems and unhappiness are related more to the way we perceive things and the domain of the mind.

If we compare these two kinds of happiness and suffering—one depending mainly on the body and one depending mainly on the mind—we can see that the mind clearly has the greater capacity to affect us. If you live in the wealthier parts of the world, you can be surrounded by every comfort and convenience, and yet in your minds you are still unhappy. So it stands to reason that when it comes to beating your problems, it can only be achieved by the mind itself. You cannot get rid of them by spending money, however hard you try. Pills and tranquillizers and even yoga or exercise programs will not work either. Of course, strategies like these might bring you some temporary relief and provide brief respite from the intense and turbulent thinking in your mind, but the underlying problem will still remain. If you don't know how to confront your difficulties and deal with them directly by using your intelligence, then just finding some temporary device to stop you thinking about your problems or help you avoid them for a while will not really be much of a solution.

It is our minds and our intelligence that we need to use. With problems that are in the realm of the mind, we need to get to the bottom of them, discover their causes, conditions, and effects and understand them more. It is vital that we deal with them directly like this, rather than simply ignoring them. Because if we do so, we can find a peace of mind and well-being that is steadfast and cannot be so easily disturbed.

INTERDEPENDENCE: A BROADER PERSPECTIVE ON LIFE

I often say that I find one of the most helpful things in this regard is the Buddhist view of interdependence. Now we shouldn't think of this as just a Buddhist practice; in fact it is a way all of us can view and see things. If we take the time to think about interdependence, we will find that it can definitely help us a great deal in our lives.

Interdependence explains how everything is affected by causes and conditions. Out of all the various changes that occur, none of them is the result of only one single cause or condition. On the contrary, there are countless causes and conditions that need to come together in order for things to happen. And these causes and conditions require their own particular causes and conditions, and so on, and so on. Interdependence therefore implies that there is a series of causes and conditions that combine to form new causes and conditions, which bring about changes, creating fresh causes and conditions. What's more, our own way of thinking is also a factor among all those changing causes and conditions.

When something happens to help or harm us in some way, and we experience pleasure or pain, it is not as a result of just one single cause or condition but because of a complex web of many interrelated causes and conditions. When we actually see this for ourselves, quite naturally it gives us a much broader perspective on things. Ordinarily, whenever we react with attachment or aversion and get upset, it is because we have a tendency to attribute our happiness or suffering to just a single cause. If something bad happens, we put it down to one factor alone and make that the target of our blame. When good things happen, we also tend to think it is due to just one thing. In reality, however, neither the good nor the bad things that happen to us are the result of just a single cause or condition. They are all the result of innumerable causes and conditions coming together, all depending on one another. If we can only recognize this, it can be so helpful. When we no longer have one specific object to blame as the source of our attachment or anger, it will reduce the strength of the emotions that is intensified by focusing on a single object.

DEPENDENCE ON OTHERS

The study of human physiology shows that when we suffer from some physical illness or pain, there is a natural reaction within the body that causes chemical substances, endorphins and enkephalins, to be released and so numb the pain. The body has a natural, instinctive response to pain and seeks to alleviate it. I think there is a parallel with the qualities of our mind that can relieve our inner suffering. When people are in trouble, quite naturally and spontaneously, we feel a sense of love and concern, and we try to help them out. When we support one another like that, it creates a feeling of mutual trust, so that whenever we ourselves face problems, we know we have someone we can rely on. Trustworthiness and a good heart; sincerity, honesty, and genuineness; affection and tenderness—these are really fundamental human qualities. If we possess them, people will readily trust us and befriend us, and whether we are actually facing difficulties or not, we will naturally feel more relaxed and at ease. Even if we do have problems and someone else cannot solve them for us, it does not seem to matter so much, because simply being able to talk with another person and share our problems will help. This is just our human nature.

Therefore when it comes to mental suffering, emotional and psychological difficulties, we have a natural tendency as human beings to care for one another, to be honest and friendly, and to help each other out. Quite naturally we have this tendency to act "like a good human being," and this is such a wonderful quality. It is so important that we recognize this positive tendency and acknowledge its value. We should not neglect or undervalue it but see just how important and necessary it is, because it will really help us to get through problems in life. This has nothing to do with past and future lives or with religion; it is something that is helpful whenever we face the difficulties of life.

If we think about our existence as human beings, from the moment we are born, all through the early years of our lives we are completely dependent on others for our survival. There is no way that we could survive by ourselves, and so there is a very special bond of intimacy that develops between a mother and her child. With certain animals, it is different. Take the case of sea turtles, for example. After the mother turtle has made her nest and laid her eggs, she has no further contact with her offspring. I think that if the young turtles were to meet their mother by accident, they probably would not feel the same affection as other animals, because they do not need to rely upon their mothers for survival. The mother simply lays her eggs, and when the young turtle is born, it just crawls into the sea. The mother does not need to teach the hatchling anything or give it milk or do anything else. So there is probably not such a strong feeling of closeness between the mother and her offspring. Maybe the young ones do not even recognize their mothers.

In the case of children, however, they have to depend on their parents for their survival, and so there is a natural feeling of love between them and their parents. This is what I think; it is quite possible that this is all inaccurate, but I feel that in the beginning this love we have for each other, this warmth and care, stems from our need to depend on each other for our survival.

Our mistake is that we have this love in the beginning, the mutual love between mother and child, but then gradually, as time goes by, we begin to value it less and less and even start to see it as unnecessary. We think we can take care of ourselves, and we don't need to depend on anyone else. Even though our presumed independence is an empty dream, we feel proud of ourselves, bold and confident. Then, instead of feeling love for others, we begin to feel jealous of them and try to harm and exploit them. This leads to all kinds of unhappiness in society and misery for us as individuals. We may feel as if there is no one we can trust, no one we can really depend on, and we begin to feel cut off from others, isolated and alone. Yet this situation is entirely of our own making. It runs counter to our true nature as human beings. It is all based on our own artificial expectations.

On top of that, because of all the economic development and advances in technology, there is every danger that we will increasingly place our hopes and trust in material things, like money and machines. We think that they will be able to protect us, give us security, and really help us in every way. But I feel that this attitude creates lots of problems.

So although interdependence is a Buddhist view, it is something we can all make use of in our daily lives. For example, when we are at school, we learn more about the nature of the world, and it gives us a much wider outlook on things. When we reflect on the nature of interdependence, it can also expand our minds and broaden our whole perspective and way of thinking. We begin to recognize, for example, how the positive tendencies we naturally possess as human beings are critical in our lives and of fundamental importance. Hand in hand with that, we can also come to a shrewder understanding about material progress, because however necessary and beneficial it may be, we must not place all our trust and hope in it. Instead, we should start to take charge of, and develop, the natural positive qualities we have as human beings. Then, I think, we will have happier lives.

This is not a matter of concern solely for people who have some religious belief. Everyone wants to be happy; nobody wants to suffer; and we all possess these positive human qualities. So you could call this "secular ethics."

THE REAL ESSENCE OF RELIGION

If we do have some faith in a religion, but we are content simply to think of ourselves as believers because it was our parents' religion, and we do not take any interest in what it has to say or what its practices might be, then we will not really derive much benefit from it. If we think religion is only about performing rituals and saying prayers, then there will be no real connection between the periods we think of as "practice" and the rest of our daily lives. If we look into the major faith traditions, as I always say, we find that they all teach the same virtues of love, compassion, tolerance, contentment, and ethical conduct. This is the real meaning and heart of religion. Religion is not just about saying prayers in a temple. It is about how we lead our daily lives and about just that—being loving, compassionate, tolerant, contented, and ethical. So if we consider ourselves religious people, we need to understand the real essence of religion—not placing too much importance on prayers and rituals but more on the conduct of our daily lives. Whether we are Christian, Muslim, Buddhist, Hindu, Jewish, or followers of any other faith, we need to apply the teachings in our daily lives and interactions, and that is the most important point.

Some people actually believe that religion has nothing to do with daily life. But they must have a very narrow view of what religion is. If we think of religion as rituals and prayers that are performed in a temple, then it is true that there might not be much connection with everyday life. But what is the whole reason behind these rituals and prayers? It is to increase our love, compassion, tolerance, and the like. So if we are someone who follows a particular religion, we need to understand that religion's teachings, take an interest in them, and be able to apply them to our daily lives. I feel that this is a crucial principle.

All the different religious traditions that exist in this world are more or less equal in their capacity to make us into good human beings. Of course, there are differences in terms of their philosophical views, but variety is there in order to accommodate diverse mentalities and beliefs. Given that there is such a range of temperaments and inclinations, one view will seem more appropriate and rational to one person, and another view will clearly be the most relevant and effective for someone else. In this respect, the different faith traditions are like varieties of medicine. It is just that medicines treat the sicknesses of the body, and religions heal the sicknesses of the mind. When we are choosing a medicine, the only important consideration is which illness it cures. We don't need to pay too much attention to the price or the ingredients. Nor do we need to explain such details when we give the medicine to the patient. The only important factor at that point is whether the medicine will help cure the illness or not. Anything else is simply irrelevant.

In the same way, the various religious traditions have divergent philosophical views, but the real aim of all these views is simply to benefit a person's mind. And from this perspective, they are all equal. Philosophical views differ, and some are more elaborate than others, but you cannot really say there are "good" and "bad" views. It is more a question of what a person is best suited to. If you consider the more elaborate views to be the best and most profound, then they *are* the best for you, as an individual. The point is that whichever view fits your particular temperament and beliefs will be of the greatest benefit.

THE ESSENCE OF THE BUDDHADHARMA

Let us look at Buddhism in particular. You might wonder, What is the essence of the Buddhist teachings? Usually I explain it like this: "the conduct is nonviolence, and the view is interdependence." When we talk about nonviolence—in other words, refraining from harm—it is sometimes very difficult to determine whether an action is harmful or not by considering only its outward appearance. The key factor is the motivation behind it. Any action of the body, speech, or mind that is motivated by a wish to benefit others is by its very nature nonharming. But if our basic intentions are cruel, say we want to trick someone and exploit them, our behavior can give every appearance of being harmless, with charming words and handsome gifts, but the action itself will be harmful. Why? Because it is done with a negative motivation. Therefore the distinction between harmful and nonharmful actions must be based primarily on the motivation behind them. I think we can say that the *conduct of nonviolence* means actions that are motivated by compassion or the wish to benefit others. With this motivation in our hearts, at best we should actually help others, but if we are unable to help them, at least we should do them no harm.

Then, the view of interdependence reveals in fact how happiness and suffering come about. It shows us how all our feelings of happiness and suffering, and all inner experiences and outer circumstances, arise because of the coming together of particular causes and conditions. So the view of interdependence explains the logic behind the conduct of nonviolence. How? Because the feelings of pleasure and pain that we experience depend on certain conditions, which are intimately bound up with our conduct. If we act negatively, we will experience suffering. If we act positively, the result will turn out well. This is the way things occur, in dependence on causes and conditions. So if we do not want to suffer, we have to avoid doing anything harmful to others and try to help them instead.

Now, if we continue and extend the practice of nonviolence, eventually it leads to bodhichitta and to cherishing others more than ourselves. And if we take the view of interdependence further and deeper, in time it leads to the view of emptiness, the understanding that all phenomena are devoid of any true reality. This is what is called *emptiness of which compassion is the very essence,* and if we can put it into practice, our whole way of thinking will undergo a tremendous shift. Quite naturally our lives will become much more meaningful. We will begin to work for the benefit of others. And should we encounter any unavoidable difficulties, we will no longer suffer in our minds, or at least we will suffer less than we did before. We might even come to accept the suffering, so that even though we are obliged to endure physical pain, in our minds we have the serenity to be able to deal with it and turn it into something with a greater purpose.

Let me give you an example. In 1958, when many monasteries in Kham and Amdo had already been destroyed and many lamas and khenpos were being imprisoned, a khenpo who was an outstanding practitioner was sentenced to death by firing squad. At the moment of his execution, just before he was killed, he said the following prayer:

> Therefore, O compassionate and noble master,
> May all the negativity and obscurations of beings, my past mothers,
> All their suffering, without exception, ripen on me here and now,
> And may I give them all my well-being, virtues, and merits,
> So that all beings may enjoy happiness![134]

He said this immediately before he was shot and killed. What this story shows is that, through practicing with skillful means and wisdom, we can bring about significant changes in our ways of thinking and develop extraordinary courage. We can even reach that point, like the khenpo, where we can transform any adversity into the path to enlightenment.

MAINTAINING THE AUTHENTICITY OF THE DHARMA

There is an important point I would like to make here, which applies not just to Buddhism but to any religious tradition. I think it is vital that we stay true to the authentic teachings of the original founder and the main disciples of the tradition. It is important that the tradition remains authentic and faithful to its origins.

There are a number of observations I would like to make in this regard. There was a time, for example, when Tibetan Buddhism was referred to in some Western books as "Lamaism." That is a mistake. Tibetan Buddhism is an authentic and verifiable tradition, which can be traced back to the great and learned masters of India. It is not something a few Tibetan lamas dreamt up themselves while freezing away in their caves! It is nothing less than the genuine Dharma of the Buddha, which originated in the noble land of India.

Then there are also people who refer to lamas as "living buddhas," an expression which probably comes from a Chinese translation. This is another big mistake. If it was coined out of a sense of devotion, of course that is good. However, if we look into the Buddhist scriptures, the original Sanskrit word for "lama" is *guru;* literally this means heavy, in the sense of being laden with precious qualities or with kindness. The Tibetan word *lama* means "the most unsurpassed," or someone who is worthy of respect and veneration. We don't find the term *living buddha* used anywhere nor does the word guru actually mean someone who is enlightened. I think the term living buddha must originate from a mistranslation from Chinese. It has ridiculous implications as well if "living buddhas" are seen to act just like ordinary people.

We also need to be aware of another phenomenon, "New Age" spirituality, which involves taking a little bit from various different religions and concocting a new brand of religion, which is really just someone's own invention. Of course, if people are honest and admit that it is the product of their own ingenuity, then it does not make such a big difference. But if they start improvising things and then try to pass them off as Buddhism or as Tibetan or as some extraordinarily swift form of the Vajrayana path, then we need to be extremely careful.

Some time ago, I met an Indian socialist, who told me that he was deeply interested in Buddhism, and it is true that he became especially fond of teachings like those on altruism and bodhichitta. But later on, when he came to the teachings on the hells, and particularly the explanation of the unbearable temperatures of the hot and cold hells, he became quite disturbed and would no longer listen! It is very difficult for us to get anywhere, I think, if we pick and choose from this ancient Buddhist tradition that has come down to us from the learned masters of India, and we take only the things that we like the sound of, while ignoring all the rest. Of course, if we find something that does not suit our own beliefs or experience, we can choose not to believe it, but we should not conclude that it is the Dharma that needs to change or call for some new and ad hoc form of Buddhism.

In fact I heard one story about a student who went to see a Tibetan lama and said, "Buddhism is wonderful, but there are certain things about Buddhism that just don't fit my way of thinking." The lama replied, "Well? Who's forcing you to become a Buddhist? If it doesn't suit you, forget it!" That's really true, I think. We need to keep Buddhism authentic. We need to keep to the original teachings spoken by our kind teacher, the Lord Buddha, and those teachings contained in the works of the learned masters of India, as well as the writings of the learned and accomplished masters of the different schools of Tibetan Buddhism—Sakya, Geluk, Kagyü, and Nyingma. That is extremely important.

What we should bear in mind is that it is quite possible that some of these teachings will not make sense to us immediately. In fact, there are different categories of knowable phenomena. There is what is *immediately apparent* to us and directly perceivable; there are things that are *partially hidden;* and finally things that are *extremely hidden.* It is very difficult for us to comprehend the things in this latter category by trying to reason them out with our intelligence. Yet if we believe only in things that are immediately observable and apparent, even the state of buddhahood becomes quite improbable! We can accept the general notion, but it becomes rather difficult to accept it just as it is taught. Therefore, since there are some things that are extremely hidden, when we find that there is something that does not make sense to us immediately, we need to investigate what is written in the texts and then reflect on it by applying our logical reasoning. Yet, still there will be some things that we cannot fathom even by reasoning, and it would be a little arrogant of us to dismiss them out of hand. We don't have the ability to perceive absolutely everything, including all hidden phenomena. There are many things that are hidden from our direct perception, so we cannot simply say that we don't believe in them, because that would just be presumptuous and prejudiced. The main point I am making here is how important it is to follow the original and authentic teachings.

This concludes the general introduction for the new people who arrived today. Now we will continue where we left off in the text of *Finding Comfort and Ease in Meditation on the Great Perfection.*

CHAPTER 18

THE WISDOM OF RIGPA

TWO METHODS TO REALIZE THE CLEAR LIGHT

Generally it is said that the profound path of Dzogpachenpo emphasizes the practice of the fourth empowerment. The four empowerments are: the elaborate vase empowerment, the unelaborate secret empowerment, the extremely unelaborate knowledge empowerment, and the utterly unelaborate word empowerment.

Now, in the teachings of the new translation schools of tantra, it is said that once "the actual clear light" has been made manifest, or "the learners' union" has been attained, there is no need to train in any new paths.[135] In other words, once the wisdom of the path of seeing according to the tantra system has arisen, or the state of "union" has been reached, we need only to familiarize ourselves with what we have realized. There is no need to train in, or develop, anything new.

According to the ancient translation school's system of nine successive vehicles, Dzogpachenpo is the vehicle that is the ultimate destination, while the previous eight vehicles, all of which base their approaches on the ordinary mind, are more like stages or steps along the path. So there are eight vehicles that serve to lead us to the ultimate destination and one vehicle that is the ultimate destination itself; at which point it is not the ordinary mind but wisdom that is taken as the path. This is why we say that Dzogchen emphasizes the fourth empowerment.

Among the miscellaneous writings of the omniscient Khedrup Jé, there is a text dealing with questions and answers, including the question of whether or not Dzogchen is a pure system. The answer he gives is that not only is Dzogchen a pure and authentic teaching, it is also an instruction on the very highest level of the completion stage practice according to the highest teachings of tantra. It is extremely profound, he says, but unfortunately its reputation has been harmed by the unethical conduct of some lay practitioners.[136]

In a similar vein, Khedrup Norzang Gyatso, in a guide to the generation stage practice of *Guhyasamaja,* explains that there are two ways to bring about the dawning of the fundamental mind of clear light. One method is to focus on and penetrate the vital points of the channels, wind energies, and essences; for example, in the completion stage practice associated with the father tantra *Guhyasamaja,* the clear light is realized through the yoga of the wind energies. The other method, he says, is that of the "ancient meditation traditions," by which he seems to mean both the Dzogchen tradition of the Nyingmapas and the Kagyü Mahamudra tradition. Through these ancient meditation traditions it is possible, he says, to actualize the clear light through nonconceptual meditation alone, without the need to work with the body's subtle channels, wind energies, and essences.

So this point is very clear. Keep in mind that Khedrup Jé was one of the most rigorous and outspoken writers in the Geluk tradition, expert at analyzing what is admissible or not, and yet still this is what he says in his miscellaneous writings. Likewise Khedrup Norzang Gyatso is famous as an exceptionally learned and accomplished master who attained the level of union during his lifetime. This was one point I wished to make.

RELYING ON THE AUTHENTIC WORKS OF THE TRADITION

When it comes to the numerous texts that explain the Dzogchen teachings, some of them are quite elaborate, and others are more concise. There are various instruction manuals on Dzogchen, for example, that accompany the many different cycles of terma revelations. In terms of the two approaches I mentioned earlier, the general approach related to the teachings as a whole and the approach that is more specific to certain individuals,[137] these instruction texts are often teachings given for the sake of individuals. They tend to consist of direct advice in the form of poetic verses or songs of experience, and they may not always provide a complete overview of the teachings. The real foundation for the teachings on Dzogchen is provided by the texts of Longchen Rabjam, particularly his *Seven Treasuries,* and also by the root text and commentary of the *Treasury of Precious Qualities,* composed by the second omniscient one, Jikmé Lingpa. In addition to these, there are the works of Rongzom Chökyi Zangpo, who, as we saw, lived three centuries before Longchenpa. These are the great works of the Dzogchen tradition, which means that we must definitely consult them.

The same principle holds true for all the schools of Tibetan Buddhism—Sakya, Geluk, Kagyü, or Nyingma. We cannot get a complete picture of a particular teaching simply by looking at brief instruction texts or pieces of advice taken from here and there. There will always be a danger of misunderstanding things and the possibility of going astray. Take the Geluk tradition, for example. If we are to gain a genuine understanding of the Geluk view, we have to rely primarily on the wonderful writings of the great Tsongkhapa. Otherwise, there is no guarantee that simply because someone claims to follow the Geluk view what he says will be correct. So this need to study the authoritative works of the tradition applies in the case of each of the schools, and it is something that we need to look into and think about seriously.

Even for us as individuals, if we are going to avoid pitfalls and mistakes in our own practice, we need to have a thorough understanding of our own tradition, and therefore we must study its great treatises. This is also how I try to proceed myself. If we study only the shorter, simpler texts we might not glean such a complete understanding, and we might even come across things we have doubts about. But if we look into the major works, we can begin to see the logic and reasons behind things and have more appreciation for the crucial points. So, for this reason, I feel it is essential that we consult the main texts of our tradition.

THE WISDOM OF RIGPA

Now, there is another passage from the writings of Dodrup Jikmé Tenpé Nyima, which I would like to share with you at this point. He is talking about the wisdom of rigpa, the fundamental innate mind of clear light, but he is explaining it in the light of the terminology of the tantras of the new translation schools:[138]

> Regarding the wisdom of inner luminous awareness, *The Tantra of the Union of the Sun and Moon* states:
>
> In the jewel palace of the heart
> Is the radiance of the kaya uniting emptiness and clarity,
> Its faces and arms complete like a body enclosed within a vase,
> Abiding in its subtlemost form as the essence of clear light.
>
> As this says, there are coarse and subtle forms of the *avadhuti,* the central channel, and, within this "citadel" that has the nature of light, in the extremely subtle central channel, "the crystal tube" that is spoken of in the uncommon approach of this vehicle, is the glorious Samantabhadra, the teacher with no beginning and no end, the all-accomplishing wisdom king.

The coarse form of the central channel, or avadhuti, is the one mentioned in the highest yoga tantras, such as the *Guhyagarbha Tantra.* The subtler form is known as the crystal kati tube, or the channel of clear light. Dodrupchen says:

> It is the great mandala in which all that appears and exists is of equal taste...

All the phenomena of samsara and nirvana arise from the fundamental innate mind of clear light, and in this respect they are all equal. Pure phenomena have the nature of wisdom, whereas impure phenomena are temporary and adventitious. But this is the only difference. They are both equal in being the display of the clear light. The text continues:

> ...it is the enlightened state that does not arise from the ordinary mind, the fundamental condition that is not fabricated by conceptual thought, utterly pure buddhahood that has never been stained by any faults and has always been present. In other classes of tantra,

this is referred to as the fundamental mind that is "all-empty." Thus, in this context, fundamental mind and uncompounded wisdom refer to the same thing.

I have already discussed how *uncompounded* is to be explained in this context. When we find *fundamental mind* in texts of the new translation traditions, the word *mind (sem)* is used in its broadest sense to include wisdom, and in this sense we can say that it is present even at the level of buddhahood. This is not *sem* in the sense of the ordinary mind that is to be distinguished from the pure awareness of rigpa.

Even in the Nyingma tradition the word *sem* does not always mean the ordinary impure mind. In one of the mahayoga tantras of Yangdak, *The King of Herukas,* for example, *sem* is used in connection with the practice of the six yogas. So we cannot say that *sem* always refers to the impure mind. Dodrupchen Jikmé Tenpé Nyima resumes:

> It has always been present, never changing its status.

The ordinary mind comes into being and then ceases and changes, but this is different. It cannot alter or change its status.

> Always free, it can never become confused.

In its essence, it has always been free, timelessly, and so it is not possible for it ever to become confused.

> It cannot undergo birth and death.

We cannot use terms like *birth* and *death* in reference to the fundamental innate mind of clear light. The coarse ordinary mind does have a beginning and an end. It is like the elements of earth, water, fire, and wind, which can arise and cease to be. Yet the element of space, out of which they all arise and into which they are all absorbed, is itself beyond arising and ceasing. Likewise, the fundamental innate mind of clear light is beyond all arising and ceasing.

In our ordinary state of mind, which is the coarser level of consciousness, and even in the thick of thoughts and emotions like attachment and aversion, there is still a quality of rigpa, or awareness. So in that sense these states are pervaded by an aspect of rigpa awareness, but still the nature of our minds is obscured. As Jikmé Tenpé Nyima says:

> Although that is its nature, its own face is obscured by the three appearances and their conceptual thought states, and because of the 21,000 movements of the karmic wind, and so on, we cannot see its actual essence, which is why it is difficult for anyone to realize. As it says in the *Illusory Net:*
>
> > Emaho! Dharma that has been always secret,
> > Diverse in appearance and by nature secret,
> > By its very essence, completely secret,
> > Nothing else but extremely secret.
>
> That is why this is referred to as the "inner luminosity, the youthful vase body." Do not, however, misunderstand *buddha* as being something like a golden statue in a glass case.

The image of a body within a vase is used to illustrate how our nature is present within the inner luminosity; confined there, in a sense, until it is released.

THE INTRODUCTION TO RIGPA

The practice of trekchö in Dzogchen concerns the meditation on pure awareness, or rigpa. To be precise, it is cultivating familiarity with rigpa, once it has been distinguished from the ordinary mind. Now, how do we achieve this? At the moment the fundamental innate mind of clear light is a latent potential. In the unique language of Dzogchen, we would say that the rigpa of the ground, or the essential rigpa, is not manifest at the moment, as if it too was latent, and so what we are talking about here is the effulgent rigpa. This is the state in which thoughts are arising out of rigpa's pure awareness. There is movement in the mind, brought about by the three appearances and the eighty indicative conceptions, and so this is not the essential rigpa but the effulgent rigpa. When thoughts and emotions arise as the energy of rigpa, like all conscious states they are permeated by rigpa, "just as sesame seeds are permeated by oil." It does not matter what state of mind or what kind of thought or emotion we might be experiencing, there is still a quality of basic knowing or cognizance that is the aspect of rigpa awareness. And it is this aspect of awareness that is pointed out by an experienced teacher, when all the right conditions come together, to a student who has reached a certain level of spiritual maturity. So this introduction happens by means of the effulgent rigpa.

To begin with, students need to gain some understanding by studying and listening to the teachings. Then, by growing gradually more familiar and steadily gaining in experience, they will be able to recognize their own rigpa. When this happens, there is no other practice to do but abide continuously by rigpa and rigpa alone. This is accomplished through mindfulness. However, there are two kinds of mindfulness: contrived and natural. This practice cannot be achieved through a contrived mindfulness, because that would only lead us to thoughts such as, "Now I am meditating on Dzogchen" or "Now I am sustaining rigpa," so bringing us back into the realm of the ordinary mind.

As soon as the mind is disturbed by ordinary notions and clinging, we are back at the coarse level of the ordinary mind. When this happens, and the coarse ordinary mind is manifest, we need to use whatever understanding we have of the difference between the ordinary mind and rigpa in order to return to the aspect of awareness. This does not happen by trying to direct the mind toward rigpa with mindfulness, like shooting an arrow at a target, but just by remaining naturally and gently in the essence of awareness itself. In fact, this is beyond words, thoughts, and expression and is difficult to communicate or to understand straightaway.

The introduction to rigpa takes place in a context such as receiving the "empowerment of the energy of rigpa," *rigpé tsal wang,* from a qualified master. But there are different ways for recognition to occur, and in the case of the most capable students, there is not much need for formal rituals.

Let me tell you a story that will illustrate this. Khenpo Münsel was an incredible Dzogchen master who passed away only a few years ago.[139] Someone I know who lives in Lhasa went to Khenpo Münsel to request an introduction to the nature of mind. When he arrived in Khenpo Münsel's presence, he immediately felt an intense devotion, so strong that it brought tears to his eyes. Khenpo Münsel was simply sitting there, reciting prayers, and he did not give him any formal instruction at all. But then, after a while, he turned to him and said, "Now you have received the pointing out instructions. You have received 'the empowerment of the energy of rigpa.' Go and meditate on this." This shows how students of the very highest caliber do not need to rely on rituals.

In the case of students of medium capacity, there is the formal introduction that is given according to texts such as *Yeshe Lama*, which I myself received from Dilgo Khyentse Rinpoche.[140] There is a certain physical posture to be adopted, and the lama gives the introduction by, for example, uttering the syllable "Phat!" or by using some other method that—because it is unusual or unfamiliar and because it happens all of a sudden—causes the mind immediately to go blank, without any thought process. There is a statement about this, which I heard from Khenpo Rinchen.[141] Some say it comes from Sakya Pandita Künga Gyaltsen, but others claim it does not. It goes like this: "In the gap between past and future thought, the clear light nature of mind dawns uninterruptedly."[142] When the past thought has ceased, and the future thought has not yet risen, there is a moment in which there is no clinging and no thought of "It is like this" or "It is like that." There is just a pure awareness, which is basic clarity and knowing. This is the effulgent rigpa. It is an aspect of rigpa and not the essential rigpa. If the right conditions combine, we can have this experience, and, through it, we can recognize rigpa. This recognition comes about through receiving blessings.

There was a lama I knew who came from Kham and who belonged to the Kagyü tradition, although he practiced Dzogchen meditation. He really was an exceptional master, but unfortunately he passed away not so long ago. He told me that when he was young, he received the instructions on Mahamudra and Dzogchen, but while he was doing the preliminary practices, he attempted to deceive his teacher. He had to get up early in the mornings to perform prostrations. They had no butter lamps, and it was still dark. His teacher would sit somewhere nearby, meditating and reciting his practice, and he had to do his prostrations in a corner that was pitch dark. But instead of prostrating, he simply sat there on his knees and banged his fists against the floor from time to time, to simulate the sound of someone prostrating. For a while, he carried on deceiving his teacher like this, and, of course, he did not gain even the slightest realization.

One day, some time after his teacher had passed away, he suddenly had a very vivid memory of him and was overcome with deep devotion. In fact, he felt such intense and one-pointed faith and devotion for his master, it was as if he fainted. When he recovered, he thought, "Ah! This must be what they call rigpa. This must be the clear light of Mahamudra." He took this feeling or experience, and the more he deepened it through practice, the clearer and clearer it grew. He persevered in this practice for a long time, to the extent that he experienced such clarity, he told me, that he even gained some slight memory of his past lives. He had not developed any realization at all when he was first introduced by his teacher, because at that time he was still trying to deceive him. But later on, by practicing assiduously over time, he gradually gained some measure of realization. So in some cases, this kind of experience comes only after long periods of sustained practice.

As we have seen, when we use the terms *rigpa* and an *aspect of rigpa,* we mean, respectively, the essential rigpa and the effulgent rigpa. Once we have recognized the aspect of rigpa, we need to prolong the natural, effortless kind of mindfulness. At the beginning we will not be able to stay mindful for very long. But gradually, over time, we will develop the ability to remain mindful for longer and longer periods and our experience will deepen; then our awareness does not chase after and get entangled in objects of thought and perception but abides, without losing its ground. When this happens, the ordinary mind is put out of business and made jobless, which means that the wind energies that cause it to move also naturally begin to change and lose their strength. As a result conceptual thoughts cease, and we reach a meditation that is entirely nonconceptual, or "thought free." All the various degrees of the ordinary mind and the different levels of wind energy that support it—coarse, subtle, and extremely subtle—all fade and dissolve into the state of clear light.

I would like to read now from an instruction on the view of Dzogchen[143] by Tulku Tsullo:

> Well then, you might ask, when do we gain freedom from the ordinary mind and the various thought states that obscure the very face of the wisdom of rigpa, so that the wisdom of the dharmakaya can be laid bare? And what is the actual nature of this wisdom? Most Dzogchen practitioners these days do not have even a conceptual understanding of this, and so some take it to be mere stillness of mind in which there is no mental activity at all. Some set their sights on the vivid clarity and awareness of mind that is accomplished through shamatha and is unstained by coarser types of thinking. Some take pride in thinking that, when they remain and recognize their coarser thoughts as well as the slightly subtler thought of wishing to suppress them, this is the supreme view of Dzogchen. Then there are even others who assert that the coarse type of nonconceptuality—where there is freedom from the most obvious, wilder thoughts but which is still within the domain of the karmic winds and conceptions—is indivisible, permanent, single, and real, and that this is the supreme view of the great secret path. Thus there are a great many people who have got things completely upside down and make unrelated assertions, like trying to point out a hat by describing a shoe. When there are approaches as untrustworthy and unreliable as these, it shows how very important it is to get rid of doubts and misconceptions.
>
> So let me just say a little, according to the advice of my qualified teacher, who was able to discern unerringly the vision of the earlier and later omniscient ones, Longchen Rabjam and Jikmé Lingpa, the great pioneers who commented independently on the meaning of the excellent teachings of the Great Perfection according to both kama and terma. That is, as long as the subtle habitual tendencies of the three appearances and

> the conceptual thought states have not ceased, the dharmakaya wisdom that abides as the ground will not manifest. The ceasing of all the karmic winds, thought states, and habitual tendencies of the three appearances occurs when we get close to abandoning the aggregates of the illusory body, and the dissolution of the elements takes place. From the moment when the earth element dissolves into water until the wind element dissolves into consciousness and consciousness dissolves into appearance, the white experience of appearance dawns. The thirty-three thought states related to anger cease. When appearance dissolves into increase, the red experience of increase dawns, and the forty thought states associated with desire come to an end. Then when increase dissolves into near-attainment, the black experience of near-attainment dawns, and the seven thought states associated with delusion cease. Following this, when near-attainment has dissolved into space, and when the previous experiences of one's own mindstream have been absorbed and future ones not yet risen, this marks the dawning of the bardo of dharmata. It is at that moment that all the karmic winds, thought states, and subtle habitual tendencies of the three appearances are brought to an end in the central channel at the heart, and the fundamental ultimate wisdom, the rigpa that naturally abides within the ground, which dwells within the extremely subtle channel of light, the "supremely victorious golden sun," is made manifest.

Basically, the context here is the introduction to the fundamental innate mind of clear light, or the essential rigpa. This is what we must make manifest, and as we have seen, there are two ways in which this can be achieved. One method is to penetrate the vital points within the channels, wind energies, and essences and so cause the three appearances and the wind energies that serve as their mounts to cease. The other method does not require us to work with the channels, wind energies, and essences but is based on the fact that an aspect of rigpa awareness, or clear light, pervades all states of consciousness; and right now, while the ordinary mind and this rigpa are mixed together, we can make a clear separation between mind and rigpa and direct the mind toward the aspect of awareness, lay it bare, and sustain it continuously. As we do this, we will grow closer and closer to rigpa, and the power and momentum of ordinary states of mind will diminish. But of course, there are many factors that have to come together for this to happen. It is not just about focusing our mind, we also need to receive blessings and to go through the preliminary practices and the like.

In order to realize rigpa like this, we need to gather the accumulations of merit and wisdom and purify our obscurations. But we also need to go further and abandon all nine types of action—the outer, inner, and secret actions of the body, speech, and mind.[144] This includes setting aside positive actions of the body, such as prostrating and circumambulating, and of course the negative actions associated with doing business, making money, and the like. As regards the speech, it means setting aside not just negative forms of speech but even prayers and recitations of different kinds. In terms of the mind, it means to set aside, of course, thoughts of attachment and aversion but also anything else besides this practice. To do anything else at that point would be to take a wrong path, and, as it is said, "We need to pacify the distractions of false paths." So at this stage, there is not even any meditation on compassion or cultivation of devotion and so on, because they are not the focus at that particular time. When we abandon the nine types of action, we need to practice with real dedication. It is not easy at all. A lot of people think that Dzogchen is really easy, but it is not. Or, of course, it could be that it is just me who finds it difficult! Realistically, though, this is the pinnacle of all the vehicles and that can only mean that it is extremely difficult and not easy at all. This is something we need to be clear about from the outset.

In Dzogchen, the unique pith instruction on gathering the accumulations and purifying the obscurations is the practice of "separating samsara and nirvana"—*khordé rushen.* This is also a way to cultivate renunciation and destroy discursive thinking and concepts. Then there are the preliminaries of the body, speech, and mind and what is called "searching for the hidden flaw of mind" by examining where it comes from, where it remains, and where it goes—which is a way, as we saw, of cultivating the view of emptiness.

THE IMPORTANCE OF THE MIDDLE WAY VIEW

When it comes to ascertaining the view, there are those with higher faculties, such as King Udayana. When he was shown a drawing of the wheel of existence with the twelve links of dependent origination, he understood dependent origination in progressive and reverse order, and this alone, it is said, was enough for him to realize the truth.[145] There is also the story of one of Milarepa's close disciples, who was an ordinary shepherd boy when he met Milarepa.[146] He felt so happy in Milarepa's presence that he stayed there for a while, and Milarepa asked him, "Where is the 'I'? What is the shape of the consciousness that thinks 'I am'? What is its color?" The disciple went home and thought intently about these questions. Then the next day he came back to Milarepa and said, "There is no 'I' at all." This was the kind of teaching designed to suit a particular individual. All the right conditions came together for the student, and when he searched for the object behind the imputation and labeling, he realized the view of emptiness.

In this regard, Tulku Tsullo wrote:[147]

> Certain individuals have the capacity to come to a definitive understanding through the subtlemost logical reasoning. Through simply being taught the investigation of whether mind has color, shape, and so on or the reasoning of mind's absence of origin, location, and destination, they can use the subtle logic that refutes all the objects of refutation, even down to the subtlest, to establish mind's absence of true reality. Therefore, through the force of such reasoning, individuals with supreme faculties can realize how all phenomena are emptiness, while for the likes of us it is extremely important to come to an understanding of emptiness just as it is taught in the Middle Way, by studying and reflecting on the Middle Way scriptures and comprehending all the logical arguments that prove the absence of true reality.

So he insists on the central importance of understanding the view of the Middle Way. Later in the same text, he explains why it is not sufficient simply to recognize rigpa and sustain it in practice and why it is also necessary to cultivate the view of emptiness:[148]

> The reason awareness and emptiness must be united is that unless we meditate on emptiness with rigpa's pure awareness, merely realizing the essence of rigpa alone will not be enough to cut through samsaric existence at its roots. Even in the bardo of dharmata, the rigpa that abides as the ground manifests, but since this rigpa has no realization of emptiness, it does not counteract our clinging to reality and patterns of grasping, and therefore it does not cut samsara's roots. Thus the clinging to reality that is the root of samsaric existence cannot be severed merely through the manifestation of the rigpa of the ground. When the rigpa of the ground manifests at the time of the bardo of dharmata for ordinary beings who have not embarked upon the path, it is perceived neither as real nor as lacking true reality but as vague and indeterminate, and it was with this in mind that the later omniscient one, Jikmé Lingpa, referred to it using the term *ignorance*.

In other words, even the mother luminosity is mixed with ignorance. The text continues:

> Therefore, whether in sutra or in tantra, there is consensus that the only direct antidote to the ignorance of clinging to things as real—which lies at the root of our karma and disturbing emotions—is the wisdom that realizes emptiness. So for Dzogchen practitioners, too, it is extremely important to realize emptiness. *The Reverberation of Sound*[149] says:
>
> > Nonexistent therefore appearing, appearing therefore empty,
> > The inseparable union of appearance and emptiness with its branches.
>
> And Zilnön Zhepa Tsal[150] said:

How could liberation be attained without realizing emptiness?
And how could emptiness be realized without the Great
Perfection?
Who but I offers praise such as this?

We need a special form of wisdom—the wisdom that realizes emptiness—to act as the direct antidote to the cognitive obscurations. Without this wisdom, which can be realized through the Great Perfection, in other words, through the realization of the fundamental innate mind of clear light, we will not have the direct antidote to the cognitive obscurations. So this point is conclusive. The text continues:

And the lord of the victorious ones, Longchenpa, also said:

These outer appearances are not mind,
They are the magical manifestation of mind.

By saying this he taught that all phenomena are emptiness and merely the manifestation or magical creation of thoughts in the mind. They are not established from their own side.

The view of the Middle Way that is common to both sutra and tantra establishes how all phenomena are merely names and verbal designations. As it says in *The Sutra Requested by Upali:*

All kinds of variety, lovely flowers in bloom,
A golden palace gleaming and delightful,
Even such as these have no ultimate creator,
They are imputed by the power of thought;
The whole world is imputed by the power of thought.

When we understand that things are only imputed by the power of our thoughts, we can see how they have no existence in their own right, other than that which we ascribe to them. In Dzogchen, we say that all phenomena are the energy of rigpa. All phenomena, pure or impure, are not outside the domain of rigpa; they are its manifestation or display. If we come to see this, it definitely has a real and significant impact on our usual tendency to view the objects of our attachment and aversion as real and solid.[151]

THE ESSENCE, PRIMORDIAL PURITY

Tulku Tsullo's text also speaks about the nature of rigpa and so discusses the fundamental innate mind of clear light, or the rigpa of the ground. It is introduced in terms of three qualities: its essence, its nature, and its compassionate energy.

> Furthermore, the *empty essence* is primordial purity, *ka dak*. It refers to the empty aspect of the wisdom of empty clear light, the universal monarch who creates all samsara and nirvana, free from the very beginning and uncompounded. If we explain this further, just as *ka* is the "original" or the very first of the thirty Tibetan consonants, the wisdom of clear light has always been "pure" *(dak)* from its very origin or primordial beginning. It is unstained by all the adventitious concepts, thoughts, and emotions of the ordinary mind, both subtle and coarse—and the various impure negative actions they give rise to—as well as the coarse and subtle virtuous states of mind, such as devotion and the various pure positive actions they inspire, and all the neutral intentions and the behavior they motivate, such as ordinary work and everyday actions. It is also untainted by the ignorance of believing there is some inherent identity to phenomena or to the self, and the habitual tendencies of such clinging, as well as the karmic winds upon which they ride. Therefore this clear light is called primordially pure and empty.[152]

It is called *primordial purity* because it is free from adventitious defilements and because it is empty of inherent existence. That is the empty essence. A number of important related terms are also explained at this point:[153]

> Since this wisdom or rigpa remains continuously, without being destroyed or undergoing arising and ceasing or birth and death, in the way that the ordinary mind or an individual does, it is called *innate* or *permanent*. Since it is not created by karmic winds or thought states, it is called *uncompounded wisdom*. Since it cannot be harmed by the mind and mental states and cannot be bound by whatever adventitious virtuous or nonvirtuous thoughts may occur or whatever kind of movement there may be in the mind—positive or negative, coarse or subtle—it is called *unimpeded*. Although the ordinary mind of beings falls into one-sided positions, such as being virtuous, nonvirtuous, or neutral, this wisdom or rigpa is beyond any such limitation or position and does not fall into being virtuous, nonvirtuous, or neutral, so it is called *great evenness*.[154]

The text goes on to define other terms such as *uncontrived, self-luminous, clear light, the wisdom of coemergent great bliss, the wisdom of inner clarity, wisdom that is beyond the ordinary mind, the nature of the five wisdoms,* and *the dharmakaya of the ground.*

To sum up, it seems there are two ways to understand "the essence that is primordial purity." The first is that it is "empty" of all adventitious states, up to, and including, the three appearances, and it is never stained by them. The second is that it is free of the conceptual elaborations associated with the four or the eight extremes.

THE NATURE, SPONTANEOUS PRESENCE

"The nature that is spontaneous presence" is not like the empty aspect, primordial purity, but is what produces all samsara and nirvana. As Longchenpa says in *The Wish-Fulfilling Treasury*, it is the basis for karma, disturbing emotions, and the phenomena of samsara but not in an entirely dependent way.[155] The adventitious phenomena are not part of the nature of the clear light, and therefore it is said that although it provides a basis for them, they are not entirely dependent on it. It is similar to clouds in the sky. In some sense, they depend upon the sky, but no matter how dense they are, clouds never become part of the nature of the sky itself. They can be separated. The sky and the clouds are both present but without touching or becoming part of one another. By contrast, the phenomena of nirvana depend on the clear light nature inseparably, just like the sun and its rays. The kayas and wisdoms have always been part of this nature and are never separate from it. To put it simply, the spontaneously present or perfect nature is the basis out of which all pure and impure phenomena can arise.

Within the ground of being, the three qualities of the essence, nature, and compassionate energy are all united, but conceptually we make distinctions between them and speak of the essence that is primordial purity and the nature that is spontaneous presence. The term *spontaneously present* indicates that this is the nature out of which all the phenomena of samsara and nirvana arise and into which they are all absorbed.

ALL-PERVASIVE COMPASSIONATE ENERGY

Turning to the all-pervasive compassionate energy, Tulku Tsullo says:[156]

> The manifest power of that wisdom is capable of arising as anything whatsoever, and therefore this compassionate energy pervades all phenomena. All the pure phenomena of nirvana and impure phenomena of samsara—whatever there might be—are merely appearances arising to one's own mind. All the phenomena of samsara and nirvana are like this; there is not a single phenomenon in samsara or nirvana that is not like this and that exists from its own side. The nature of conceptual ideas evaluating phenomena and also nonconceptual states of mind is the wisdom of rigpa's pure awareness. Therefore, in short, all the phenomena of samsara and nirvana are but a display arising through the creative power of the wisdom of rigpa within our own minds.

To sum up, I think the most important points to understand are the essence that is primordial purity and the nature that is spontaneous presence and how, on the basis of these two, all the pure and impure phenomena of samsara and nirvana arise.

SOME KEY POINTS OF DZOGCHEN PRACTICE

At the moment we may not be able to realize the meaning of all of this exactly as it is explained, but still we can arrive at some degree of understanding. Then, at that point, there is no need to analyze with the conceptual mind. It is more a matter of resting in a state free from conceptual thoughts. In Mahamudra meditation, in meditation on "the inseparability of samsara and nirvana," in the Geluk Mahamudra tradition of Panchen Lozang Chökyi Gyaltsen,[157] and in Dzogchen meditation, the real emphasis is on nonconceptual meditation. There is no analysis with the ordinary intellectual mind.

When the mind rests in a thought-free state, in this context it is sometimes described as being "wonderstruck"—*hedewa.*[158] But hedewa, being astonished or struck by wonder, is not sufficient in and of itself. Simply to stay in this wonderstruck state and have some slight awareness of thoughts and movement in the mind does not qualify at all as recognizing the Dzogchen view. Nor does a state in which the coarser movements of thoughts and emotions have ceased, and there is some clarity of awareness—that is not the genuine Dzogchen view either. The main point is that while resting in that wonderstruck state, there must also be a quality of total and unimpeded clarity—*zang thal.* As it says in *Hitting the Essence in Three Words:* "Struck by wonder, and yet all is transparent and clear." This can only come through experience, as well as through receiving the blessings of one's teacher.

We spoke earlier about the liberation of thoughts and emotions and the different modes, such as: primordial liberation, self-liberation, naked liberation, complete liberation, and liberation from extremes.[159] There are different stages to this liberation, as the practitioner trains in meditation and becomes increasingly familiar with the practice. In the beginning liberation occurs when we recognize thoughts, like recognizing a familiar friend or acquaintance. At this stage the coarser kind of thoughts and emotions arise. When they arise, we are aware that they have arisen, we recognize them just as we would recognize an old friend, and they are liberated. This is one mode of liberation. At the next stage, which is called *self-liberation,* when thoughts arise, they naturally have less power and naturally fade away, like a snake loosening its own knots, naturally and by itself. Then, when the experience of rigpa develops to its fullest, we reach the stage known as *beyond benefit and harm.* At this level, even if the slightest thought should occur, rigpa is laid bare and holds its own ground, so that the thought is not able to benefit or harm. It is like a thief entering an empty house: there is nothing to gain and nothing to lose. These are known as the three modes of liberation.[160]

When it comes to the practice itself, this can be explained in terms of the four *chokshak,* or ways of leaving things in their natural simplicity:[161]

View, like a mountain: leave it as it is.
Meditation, like the ocean: leave it as it is.
Action, appearances: leave them as they are.
Fruition, rigpa: leave it as it is.

There are different ways of explaining these chokshak, but in general we can relate them to view, meditation and action, and their result, which is the stage when the essence of rigpa is realized nakedly and directly. That is "fruition, rigpa: leave it as it is."

So this has been a basic introduction to Dzogchen, and it has just been a very general overview, addressed to a large audience. Actually, when you go through these practices, they are not taught as generally or as publicly as this, as these kinds of instructions must be given to smaller groups of students. The teachings on the practices from *khordé rushen* onward have to be given very carefully and precisely to people who are going to put them into practice. Teachings such as these cannot be given to large groups in a single session.

What I have shared with you here has been based mainly on the works of the two omniscient ones, Longchen Rabjam and Jikmé Lingpa, together with the clarifications of Dodrup Jikmé Tenpé Nyima and Tulku Tsullo. These are the writings that I myself find the most logical and helpful. When you practice individually, you should follow the guidance of your own teachers who will instruct you according to their own particular tradition of practice. I think that is best, but what I have said here may still be of some slight benefit in helping you develop a more general understanding.

At this point, His Holiness completed the oral transmission of Finding Comfort and Ease in Meditation on the Great Perfection.

CLOSING WORDS

This completes the text of *Finding Comfort and Ease in Meditation on the Great Perfection,* which includes a great deal of practical advice and exceptionally clear instructions on how to dispel hindrances and enhance one's practice.

With this, we have come to the end of these few days of teachings. Everything has gone very well, in the beginning, in the middle, and in the end. You have all listened with great interest and diligence. You may not have understood every single thing I have said, and of course you do not understand my words directly, so it may have been tiring at times. But everyone has made a real effort and listened attentively, so I feel that it will definitely have planted some positive seeds for the future.

To sum up, I think the main point, ultimately, is to try and be a good human being. Not only will this bring us happiness, but it will also be of real benefit to society. This is the way to give meaning to this life of ours. And whether you believe in future lives or not, you will be doing the best possible thing for the sake of all your lives to come.

I also wish to thank all those who have worked and persevered to make this event possible, those who gave it their support, and the inhabitants of this area who gave us such a warm welcome. Everyone collaborated in a very positive spirit, and I thank you all. I hope we will meet again. Some of us will surely meet again, others will not. At any rate, as the Buddha said, it is up to us to travel the path. It is entirely in our hands: we are our own guide and our own protector. So be diligent in your spiritual practice. Thank you.

FINDING COMFORT AND EASE IN MEDITATION ON THE GREAT PERFECTION

BY LONGCHEN RABJAM

In Sanskrit: *Mahasandhi dhyana vishranta nama*
In Tibetan: *rdzogs pa chen po bsam gtan ngal gso zhes bya ba*
In English: *Finding Comfort and Ease in Meditation on the Great Perfection*

Homage to the glorious Samantabhadra!

Homage to the primordial nature, sphere of purity, equal to space,
Supreme Dharma, unfluctuating, utterly free of conceptual elaboration,
The clear light nature of mind, essence of awakening,
The perfect ground, beyond any transition or change!

In order that you might realize the wisdom of your own self-knowing awareness,
The exceedingly wondrous wisdom mind of all the victorious ones,
I have gathered the quintessence of tantras, oral transmissions, and pith instructions
And offer this explanation according to the way it is practiced.
So listen well!

I. LOCATIONS FOR CULTIVATING SAMADHI

On mountaintops, in secluded forests, and on islands, and the like,
Places that are agreeable to the mind and well suited to the season,
Cultivate tranquil samadhi, which is single-pointed and unwavering—
Clear light, which is free from the slightest conceptual elaboration.

This is achieved naturally when three pure factors come together:
The ideal location, individual, and Dharma to be practiced.

First of all, the location must be one that is secluded and agreeable,
Somewhere conducive to spiritual practice in the different seasons.
In *summer,* meditate in cooler dwellings and cooler locations,
In places near to glaciers, or on mountaintops, and the like,
In simple dwellings made out of reeds, bamboo, or straw.

In the *autumn,* adjust your diet, your clothing, and your conduct,
And stay in a region and dwelling of moderate temperature,
Such as a forest, or a mountainside, or a building made of stone.

In *winter,* stay somewhere warmer at a lower altitude,
Such as a forest, a rocky cave, or a hollow in the earth,
And adjust your diet, clothing, bedding, and the rest.

In the *spring,* stay in the mountains or on the edges of a forest,
On a deserted island or in buildings with mild and even temperature,
With diet, clothing, and conduct all suitably attuned—this is crucially important.

There is an important interconnection between outer and inner,
So keep to inspiring and secluded places that you find uplifting.
High among the mountains the mind grows clear and expansive,
The perfect place to bring freshness when dull and to practice the generation phase.

Snowclad regions help make samadhi clear and awareness bright and lucid,
Ideal for cultivating vipashyana and where obstacles are few.

Forests bring stillness of mind and help us develop mental stability,
So they are ideal places for cultivating shamatha with a sense of ease.

Below rocky cliffs a vivid sense of impermanence and disenchantment dawns,
Clear and inspired, helping us to achieve the union of shamatha and vipashyana.

On the banks of a river, our attention becomes well focused,
And the wish to escape samsara comes rapid and afresh.

Charnel grounds are powerful places for swift accomplishment,
Ideal for the generation or completion phases, it is said.
Villages, markets, empty houses, solitary trees, and the like,
Which are frequented by humans and nonhuman demons,
Are distracting for beginners and can bring many obstacles
But for stable practitioners, they are a support, regarded as supreme.

Temples and shrines, inhabited by *gyalpo* and *gongpo* spirits,
Can disturb the mind and incite thoughts of anger and aversion.

Caverns in the earth and such places, haunted by the *senmo* demonesses,
Cause passionate desire to arise and bring excessive dullness and agitation.

Solitary trees and other places, which are inhabited by *mamos* and *dakinis,*
As well as boulders and mountain spurs, where the *mutsen* and *theu'rang* reside,
Contribute, it is believed, to mental turmoil and bring all manner of obstacles.

The lands of outcasts, *nagas, nyen,* and local spirits,
By the lakeside or in meadows, forests, and such places,
Adorned with beautiful flowers, plants, and trees,
Are pleasant enough at first but later prove disruptive.

In short, all the areas and dwelling places that seem agreeable at first
But not so once you come to know them are sites of lesser
accomplishment.
Whereas those that seem frightening and unpleasant at first
But prove agreeable once you have grown accustomed to them
Are powerfully transformative, bringing great accomplishments without
obstacle.
And everywhere else in between is neutral, neither beneficial nor harmful.

As our minds are affected by the places in which we stay,
This can make our practice grow stronger or make it weaker,
So it is said that to examine locations is of crucial importance.

Moreover, there are four types of place based on the four activities:
Peaceful places, where mind naturally becomes focused and still,
Expansive places, delighting the mind, which are awesome and inspiring,
Magnetizing places, where mind feels captivated and develops attachment,
And *wrathful* places, where mind is disturbed by feelings of fear and dread.
Further divisions can be made, countless and beyond measure,
But in this context, for samadhi, peaceful places are the best,
And so, fearing an excess of words, I will elaborate no further.

In such a peaceful place, the meditation dwelling should be isolated,
As this will suit the development of concentration in the mind.
The ideal dwelling is one that is open at the sides and has a clear view.

For nighttime yoga, practice inside a circular "dark house,"
In a high place, and in the middle of the central chamber,
With your pillow to the north, lying down in the posture of nirvana.

The location for practicing the yoga of light during the daytime
Should be mild in temperature and should have an entrance
With a broad, unobstructed view onto glaciers, waterfalls, forests,
or valleys,
And the vast and open sky, so that mind becomes clear and bright.

When cultivating shamatha, a solitary hut surrounded by a fence
Is the ideal place for stillness of mind naturally to arise.
For vipashyana, it is important to have a clear, inspiring view
And to be constantly cheerful and well attuned to the seasons.

Low-lying and shaded areas, such as forests and ravines,
Are ideal for practicing shamatha, whereas higher regions,
Such as among snowy mountains, are ideal for vipashyana—
It is important that you know these different specifications.

To put it simply, any region or retreat house,
Where renunciation and disenchantment arise, attention is well focused,
And samadhi grows in strength—any such place of virtuous activity—
Is said to be the equal of the place where the essence of enlightenment was attained.
Whereas any place in which virtues decline, mental afflictions increase,
And one is overcome by distractions and the affairs of this life,
Is a demonic haunt of evil actions, only to be avoided by the wise.

Since these points were taught by Padmasambhava,
They should be learned by all who wish for liberation.

This concludes the first section, being an explanation of the locations for cultivating samadhi, from Finding Comfort and Ease in Meditation on the Great Perfection.

II. THE MEDITATOR

Secondly, as an individual who takes up the practice,
You must have faith, perseverance, renunciation, and a sense of disenchantment.
You must be saddened and wearied by samsara and strive for freedom.
Renouncing the concerns of this life and seeking eventual enlightenment,
You must leave distractions and busyness far behind, and have few mental afflictions,

Be easy-going and tolerant, and have pure perception and great devotion,
As well as stability of mind,[162] and deep respect toward the teachings—
[Practitioners such as this will accomplish the supreme liberation!][163]

You must serve, in the best possible way, a noble teacher
And purify your mind through study, reflection, and meditation.
In particular, you should spend your days and nights
Diligently applying yourself to the essential instructions of the oral lineage.

Without becoming distracted for a moment by ordinary concerns,
Diligently apply yourself to the profound innermost meaning.
Never transgressing the precepts of shravakas, bodhisattvas, and vidyadharas,
With your own mind under control, help others in any way you can,
And take whatever you experience onto the path to liberation.

As a beginner, it is most important that you secure your own well-being,
Guarding your mind in solitude, abandoning distractions and busyness,
Avoiding unfavorable situations, and subduing the mental afflictions with appropriate antidotes.
Ensuring that your view and conduct are in harmony, enthusiastically devote yourself to meditation.
Whenever any of the ordinary five poisons arise, in that very moment,
Catch them with mindfulness and, without distraction, apply the antidotes.

With conscientiousness, introspective vigilance, self-restraint, and a sense of dignity, bring your own mind under control.
See the equality of praise and blame, approval and disapproval, good and bad reputation,
For they are just like illusions or dreams and have no true existence.
Learn to bear them patiently, as if they were mere echoes,
And sever at its root the mind that clings to an "I" or a self.

In short, by never transgressing the Dharma in all that you do,
Bring your mind under control, do no harm to others,

And without succumbing, even for an instant, to the mental afflictions,
Devote your days and nights to virtue—this is crucial!

Nowadays, when people are so unruly,
It is vital that you first achieve your own well-being in solitude.
Just as a bird cannot fly without both wings,
The welfare of others cannot be accomplished without the higher faculties of perception,
So strive diligently for your own well-being, while mentally considering the welfare of others.

Without letting your mind be deceived by the devious maras of distraction and busyness,
It is vital that you apply yourself to the practice—
Do not cause yourself to suffer regrets at the time of death!

Therefore, inspect your mind, make it ready now,
And consider this: Were you to die now, what would become of you?
Without any assurance as to where you'd go or what might happen,[164]
To spend your days and nights in the grips of confusion and distraction,
Is to squander and make meaningless the freedoms and advantages.
Meditate therefore on the essential meaning, alone and in solitude.
For it is now that a long-term strategy is really needed.
How can you be sure where you will go in future?
You must diligently apply yourself this very day!
These delusory appearances of samsara are like treacherous pathways.
Keep this in mind: You must find the methods to free yourself.
For if you remain deluded now, you'll wander in delusion forever.
So arouse perseverance and keep this in your heart.

The ocean of mental afflictions and the sea of self-grasping are difficult to cross,
But now that you have the vessel of the freedoms and advantages, use it to reach the distant shore!

Now, when through the force of your merit, you have gained this
opportunity—
Access to the paths of liberation and enlightenment, so rare to find—
Strive from the depths of your heart to bring about benefit and happiness!

Life is impermanent and changes from one moment to the next,
And we expertly deceive ourselves with distractions, postponing virtuous
practice.
When we have long become accustomed to delusion,
In each moment we're naturally drawn into the mental afflictions,
And even if we apply ourselves to merit and virtue,
We find they do not easily arise.
Strive, therefore, to avert the miseries brought about by your own
actions!
There is not the slightest joy to be found within the states of samsara.
The sufferings of conditioned existence, if you think of them, are impossible to bear.
Therefore apply yourself, right now, to the means for gaining freedom.
If you do not earnestly devote yourself to the essential meaning,
The state of leisure and intermittent Dharma will bring no benefit.
So develop a strong sense of weariness for all that is impermanent,
And, without being distracted even for an instant, generate enthusiasm
for the practice!

If you realize this at the very outset,
You will swiftly achieve the state of a sublime one!
Accomplishing your own welfare, the welfare of others will come
naturally,
And you will find the supreme path of liberation from the states
of samsara.
When everything that you do is in accordance with the Dharma,
Then you are one who has the basis for attaining enlightenment.

This concludes the second section, being an explanation of the individual practitioner, the meditator, from Finding Comfort and Ease in Meditation on the Great Perfection.

III. THE DHARMA TO BE PRACTICED

In this section there are three parts: the preliminary practices, the main practices, and the concluding practices.

THE PRELIMINARY PRACTICES

The General and Specific Preliminaries

Reflection on impermanence and feeling disenchanted are the general preliminaries
That radically counteract our attachment to the things of this life.
And compassion and bodhichitta are the specific preliminaries
That transform all spiritual practice into the path of Mahayana.
Train therefore at the outset in both these preliminaries.

The Special, Supreme Preliminaries

Afterward, there are the special, supreme preliminary practices.
Having received all the empowerments, there are two aspects to the generation stage:

[1] Imagining your own body as the deity and the surrounding environment and sentient beings also as the deity
Counteracts attachment to our ordinary perception.

[2] By practicing the profound path of guru yoga,
Blessings beyond measure arise through the force of realization,
All obstacles are dispelled and the two types of siddhi are achieved.
Therefore, after the general and specific preliminaries, practice the two supreme preliminaries.

Boundless qualities arise as a result of these four preliminaries:
Your mind enters the unerring path,
You reach the supreme path of liberation,
Realization of the natural condition swiftly arises,
It becomes easy to train in the main practices, with no obstacles,

Accomplishments are readily achieved, and so on.
Therefore it is crucial to train in these preliminaries.

THE MAIN PRACTICE

The main practice is the recognition of the natural condition,
Through meditation involving bliss, clarity, and nonconceptuality.
The clear light primordial wisdom, free of conceptual elaboration,
Arises as the fundamental innate mind.

The Method of Great Bliss

Firstly, there is the introduction through the method of great bliss.
After practicing the preliminaries described above, consider this:
Through the center of the four chakras, the three channels rise like pillars:
The right channel white, the left red, and the central channel deep blue and hollow.
The top of the central channel is at the Brahma aperture, and its bottom is at the secret place.

Inside the central channel at the level of the navel visualize an *A*,
Blazing with fire, and at the crown a *Ham* from which nectar descends,
Filling the four chakras and the whole interior of the body.
As your body becomes suffused with bliss, the nectar from the *Ham*
Flows continuously down into the syllable *Bam* at your heart.
Meditate on this until the experience of bliss arises.

Then the *Bam* becomes smaller and smaller,
Until your mind settles in a state beyond any conceptual imagery or elaboration.
Through this method attention is focused and calm abiding arises by way of bliss.
Then a state of awareness arises, which is utterly inexpressible,
Space-like, and beyond the ordinary mind.

This is the clear light great perfection of bliss and emptiness,
The nature of reality, radiant and inconceivable.

As you become familiar with this, four types of experience will arise:
All your perceptions will dawn as an experience of bliss,
You will never be separated from the blissful state, day or night,
Your mind will remain unperturbed by painful feelings of attachment, aversion, and the like,
And you will gain the wisdom of understanding the meaning of the words of Dharma.

As you continue to practice, limitless qualities, such as clairvoyance and other kinds of extraordinary perception,
Will arise in your mind, just like the rising sun.
This is an exceptionally profound and crucial instruction.

The Method of Clarity

Secondly, for the introduction using the method of clarity,
Begin with the preliminaries just as before.
Visualize the three main channels, with the *roma* and *kyangma* channels curving and entering the central channel
At their lower ends and their upper ends going directly through the nostrils.
Breathe out the stale air three times, expel all illnesses, destructive influences, negativity, and obscurations.
As you slowly inhale, the entire world with all its inhabitants melts into light
And is drawn through the nostrils into the central channel by way of the *roma* and *kyangma*.
Then that light dissolves into an orb of light, one inch in diameter, in the center of your heart,
As you hold your breath for as long as you can.

Joining the upper and lower wind energies together, hold your breath for a while and retain a little air when exhaling.
It is very important that you allow your breathing to be slow and gentle.
Moreover, imagine all the sublime qualities of the buddhas and so on
Dissolving into your heart, without being distracted elsewhere.

With this technique, mental clarity, radiance, and stability arise.
Afterward, imagine light flowing out from the light at your heart,
Blazing inside the four chakras within your body
And extending out to fill the whole world with light.

By meditating on this day and night for several days,
Your dreams will cease and you will see everything, inside and outside,
Pervaded by the appearance of five-colored light and
The light of the moon, blazing fire, fireflies, stars, and so on.
By focusing your mind on the state of clarity, calm abiding will arise.

Then, as you draw the light back in, imagine the light at your heart
Growing smaller and smaller until your mind settles in a state of emptiness.
Without focusing on anything, an empty, clear, and radiant state of mind
Will naturally arise, free of the extremes of elaboration.
This fundamental wisdom of clarity and emptiness
Is the way of abiding of the natural great perfection.

When you grow familiar with this, four types of meditative experience will arise:
Everything that arises will seem intangible, unimpeded, and luminous;
Day and night, you will remain in a state of luminosity;
Your mind will be clear and radiant, unmoved by discursive thoughts;
And wisdom will overflow from within, free of any dualistic grasping.

In addition, familiarization with this practice brings extraordinary powers of perception
And the achievement of miraculous abilities and clairvoyance,

Including the ability to see unimpededly through solid objects.
This is an exceptionally profound and quintessential instruction.

The Method of Nonconceptuality

Thirdly, there is introduction through the method of nonconceptuality,
Which is preceded by the preliminary practices as before.
The three aspects of the main practice are
Projection, presence, and purification.

For *projection,* the clear light nature of your mind is visualized at your heart
As the syllable *Ha* or as an orb of light one inch in diameter.
As you recite *Ha* forcefully twenty-one times,
The object of your visualization emerges from the crown of your head and is projected far out into space,
Where it ascends higher and higher until it is no longer visible,
And you rest with your body and mind deeply relaxed.
In that moment the stream of your thoughts ceases,
And you remain in a state that is inexpressible by speech or thought.
An experience arises that cannot be objectified and that is beyond the realm of ordinary thought.

For *presence,* turn your back to the sun
And gently rest your gaze in the clear sky.
Breathe as softly as you can, hardly feeling the movement of the air.
Then a state of nonconceptuality, free of elaboration, will arise from within,
And a space-like experience will naturally occur.

For *purification,* direct your gaze undistractedly into the sky,
Settle your mind in a state of clarity, without projecting or withdrawing,
And imagine the entire environment, including earth, stones, and mountains, and all beings,

As transparent and merging with space.
While experiencing even your own body as insubstantial,
Rest in a state in which mind is indivisible from space.
With both body and mind deeply relaxed in this space-like state
In which there is no separation between outside, inside, and in-between,
And memories, thoughts, and mental activity are all naturally pacified,
Let the mind remain naturally, just as it is, without projecting or withdrawing.

At that time, there will arise a space-like realization of the nonduality
Of the nature of reality and the mind that is inconceivable and ineffable—
This is the essence of the victorious ones of the past, present, and future.

By familiarizing yourself with this, four types of meditative experience arise:
Your entire perception will seem even, lacking any coarser concepts or ideas;
Day and night, you will never be separated from a state of nonconceptuality;
The five poisons will naturally be pacified, making your mindstream gentler;
And you will experience all phenomena as being just like space.
By familiarizing yourself like this with the three types of nonconceptuality,
You will accomplish the sublime qualities of clairvoyance, extraordinary perception, and samadhi.
Through the union of skillful means and wisdom and of calm abiding and insight,
You will accomplish your own and others' temporal and ultimate well-being.

THE CONCLUDING PRACTICES

Thirdly, the concluding practices are of four kinds:
Meditative experience, enhancement, realization, and the fruition.

Meditative Experience

Of the two types of meditative experience, the flawless ones were explained above.
Flawed meditative experiences occur due to grasping and clinging to the respective experiences—
Attachment to bliss, attachment to clarity, and attachment to nonconceptuality,
Involving clinging to extremes, compulsive thinking, and contamination from the ordinary mental poisons.

Perverted bliss involves seminal emission, ordinary desire,
Unhappiness, and excessive laxity.
Perverted clarity involves disturbed wind energy, ordinary aggression,
Coarse thinking, and excessive agitation and proliferation of thought.
Perverted nonconceptuality involves ordinary delusion,
Mental dullness, sleepiness, and lethargy, as well as lack of discernment.
Should any of these flawed inverse experiences arise, recognize them
And correct them with the appropriate antidotes.

Enhancement

Enhancement includes methods for correcting errors and for improvement.
There are three methods for correction:
The *superior method* is to correct errors through the view, by recognizing how all phenomena
Are mental designations, like apparitions without any identifiable essence,
Even and equal, like space, free from clinging and empty of inherent existence,
And in that state beyond grasping and fixation, to reach a final decision.

Errors and obscurations dawn as the great nature of reality,
Obstacles spur us on to virtue, and adversity aids enlightenment.
On the basis of fundamental bliss, mental well-being constantly arises.

The *intermediate approach* is to correct errors by means of meditation,
To make mind clear, transform one's consciousness, and hold it with mindfulness
And, without distraction, to settle in a state of bliss, clarity, and nonconceptuality.
Since distraction and lack of attention are defects,
It is crucial to rest in a state that is undistracted even for a moment.

To counteract seminal emission, visualize a *Hum* in a vajra vase,
From which fire consumes all the elements inside the body,
And then meditate in a state of nothing whatsoever.
This is also a profound practice for cases of emission due to illness and harmful influences.
Once clinging to bliss has been eliminated, meditate on emptiness.
Look piercingly into the mind that is experiencing ordinary desire
And by resting in an uncontrived and uncorrupted state free of hope and fear,
Desire will be freed by itself, and the wisdom of bliss and emptiness will dawn.

Unhappiness is a problem that comes from degeneration of the vital essence.
To remedy it, practice the blissful meditation of blazing and dripping.
If mental dullness predominates, it is the fault of a failure to separate the pure essence from impure residue.
To remedy it, sit upright in an erect posture,
Joining the upper and lower wind energies, hold your breath, and imagine the inside of your heart filled with light,
And meditate on the universe, luminous and empty, being filled with light.

If you fall into clinging to clarity, train in great nongrasping.
If your mind is unclear and drowsy, meditate on radiance and clarity.
If your mind is excited and agitated, close your eyes and visualize inside your heart

Light, a syllable, a lotus, a sword,
Or a double vajra descending lower and lower
From the inside of your heart
Until it descends all the way down to the golden ground at the base of the universe.
This infallible technique is sure to dispel [agitation].

When your mind is caught up in ordinary hostility, direct your attention right at it,
And it will be released into the luminous and empty state of mirror-like wisdom.

When a state of nonconceptuality arises, purify it with the technique of nongrasping.
Recognize the mind of delusion and examine it directly.
In that instant, it will be freed by itself and dawn as the wisdom of the basic space of reality (dharmadhatu).

When your mind is dull, lethargic, and undiscerning,
Visualize light inside your heart ascending and emerging through your Brahma aperture
And hovering in the space about a fathom above your head.
This is an exceptionally profound point of instruction.

In general, it is crucial not to grasp onto anything at all.
If you are without hope and fear, you will be free from all kinds of hindrance.
Rest in the radiant state of the empty and clear nature of mind,
Without mentally projecting or withdrawing,
And you will definitely be freed from the treacherous pathways of hindrances and flaws.

The *lesser approach* is to correct errors by means of three kinds of conduct:
Gaze, material factors, and interdependence.

The general *gaze* is practiced while sitting in the seven-point posture of Vairochana:
With legs crossed, the eyes unmoving, breathing slowly and evenly,
With the head inclined, the tongue touching the palate,
And the eyes gazing down toward the tip of the nose, so that wind energies and mind are brought into a state of balance,
And flawless meditation arises without dullness or agitation.
Since all the defects occur due to imbalances in the body,
Which disturb the channels, wind energies, and essences,
It is important to rest evenly without any such disturbance.
Moreover, since qualities arise when the channels, energies, and essences
Are steady and functioning in the proper way,
It is ever so crucial to understand this vital point.

Even more than for other yogic exercises and physical training,
It is particularly important to practice this slowly, gently, and in a balanced way.
It is crucial that you practice according to your physical constitution,
Countering the gentle with the rough and the rough with the gentle.
Specifically, for bliss the crucial points are crossing your arms,
Lowering your gaze, and focusing your attention on the bliss itself.
For clarity, place your hands on your knees,
Breathe slowly, and gaze directly into space.
Nonconceptuality is achieved simply through sitting in the seven-point posture.

As for *material factors,* take the support of seasonal locations, companions,
Food, drink, and so on in order to help meditative experience.

As for *interdependence,* in the case of seminal emission,
By tying around the waist a three-stranded thread woven by a young girl
And consecrated by reciting mantras, the bindu can be retained.
If discursive thoughts proliferate, take pills made of sandalwood powder, saffron, and melted fat,

And nonconceptuality will be achieved.
It is said in the tantras that when the mind becomes drowsy,
Samadhi will be achieved by ingesting pills of saffron, camphor, and bodhichitta.

To increase the experience of flawless bliss, clarity, and nonconceptuality,
It is said to be best to focus the attention on some object.
If at first you meditate by focusing upon an object,
Later you will naturally reach a state beyond focus.
This point is extremely profound and sublime,
So all you fortunate ones should take it to heart!
To reject a practice by saying, "It is conceptual!" is the path of fools,
A tendency of the inexperienced and something to be avoided.

In particular, a sublime practice for *enhancing bliss* entails drawing the lower wind energies upward,
Pulling the essences *(bindu)* up from the secret place,
Dissolving them into the crown,
And resting in a state beyond any focus whatsoever.

After that, hold the upper and lower wind energies joined together,
And, while focusing your attention at the heart, rest in the unborn state.
This is to remain in the state of bliss and clarity free from conceptual elaboration.

From time to time, practice the crucial points of the yogic exercises in accordance with the visual transmission,
Including descent and reversal, drawing upward and diffusion, and final resolution,
By shaking in the lion posture and so on.

Descent involves adopting the mudra of embracing
And shaking the upper parts of the body and pressing down on the lower parts.

Bodhichitta descends from a visualized syllable *Ham,*
And when it reaches the secret place attention is focused on the bliss.
Reversal means to draw it upward,
Pressing the hands down on the hollows and joining the "ocean" against the "rocky shore."[165]
Drawing the lower wind energies *upward,* press your tongue against the palate.
Roll your eyes back and turn your head as if you were trembling.
For the visualization, imagine the bindus, strung together as if by a gossamer thread,
Dissolving one into another, up to the crown of the head.

Diffusion entails flexing your arms and legs powerfully as if drawing a bow,
Then exhaling with a hissing noise, the tip of the tongue pressed against the teeth.

Final resolution entails lying on your back, breathing gently with the mind at ease.
Not thinking of anything at all nor clinging to anything whatsoever,
Rest in the natural state, free from any conceptual elaboration,
And you will achieve the great bliss of enlightenment without any hindrance.

A sublime method for *enhancing clarity* with the breath
Entails alternating gentle and forceful breaths
And in particular to alternate breathing in and holding the breath and breathing out and holding.
It is important to combine this with the crucial point of [the breath being] slow and gentle.

Although there are teachings on many techniques,
Including counting, color, touch, and shape,
This is an essential instruction in which one method accomplishes all,
So to train like this is the sovereign of all key points.

For the body, the crucial point is not to move, like before.[166]
Let your breath be very slow, passing evenly through the mouth and both nostrils,
And rest effortlessly in a state of ordinary, natural release.
For the mind, the crucial point is not to grasp onto anything, but be natural.

Afterward, lie down on your back with your limbs outstretched.
Utter a forceful "Ha!" and direct your attention toward the center of the sky.
Undistractedly, without projecting or gathering your thoughts, rest gently and naturally.

By resting in the primordial state, in which breath and mind are released by themselves,
Boundless sublime qualities can arise without any hindrance.
The body feels light, there is no movement [of breath],[167] and conceptual elaboration is pacified.
The mind becomes very clear and radiant and extraordinary powers of perception arise.
"Speed walking" is accomplished, the body becomes lustrous, samadhi arises,
And the signs of the wind energies and mind entering the central channel arise.[168]
This is a most profound and sublime crucial point and extremely secret.

As for *enhancing* space-like *nonconceptuality*,
Relax your body and mind from deep within and focus single-pointedly on the object of meditation.
By focusing on that alone, without being distracted by anything else,
Other discursive thoughts will dissolve into that state.
Even discursive thoughts pertaining to the meditative object will be fully pacified,
And then realization in which there is no grasping onto appearances will arise.

This is a crucial point. Moreover, you should train like this:
At times, focus your attention outside, exhale,
And by holding your breath, nonconceptuality will arise.
From time to time, hold your breath inside and focus directly and without distraction,
On some object of meditation in the upper or lower part of the body.

At other times, allow your mind to settle by itself with no object
And remain in a state without grasping onto objective appearances.
This wisdom mind of the nonconceptual dharmakaya
Will arise naturally from within by relying on the key instructions.

As for the general enhancement of bliss, clarity, and nonconceptuality,
To gather the accumulations, purify the obscurations, cultivate the generation and completion phases,
And practice the profound path of guru yoga is praised as supreme.
This, the ultimate and most crucial of instructions,
Should be taken to heart by all those fortunate ones who long for liberation.

Realization

The realization that arises from meditating in these ways
Is of one equal taste and cannot be differentiated.
The three approaches all come together in a single destination,
Just like separate rivers converging in the ocean.

Whichever of the three techniques you practice—whether you cultivate bliss, clarity, or nonconceptuality—
When mind's ordinary activity is pacified thoroughly and dissolves into
The space-like state of the unborn nature of mind,
Bodhichitta, which is free from the conceptual notions of existence or nonexistence,
The sun of natural clear light, will dawn from deep within.
This unchanging realization, in which there is nothing to achieve and nothing to eliminate,

Is the nature of the essence of the buddhas—the sugatagarbha—as vast as space.

At that time, in the ocean of samadhi transcending calm abiding and clear seeing,
One-pointed, radiant, clear, and immaculate,
Everything appears without bias or clinging, like reflections devoid of inherent nature,
All phenomena are inseparably united in the essence of realization.
And there is no grasping onto appearances, which are illusory and empty.
This inseparable unity, the vast expanse of realization,
Clear light arising through the crucial points, dawns from deep within.

Naturally arising wisdom, inspired by the blessings of the lama,
Is seen when you have transcended verbal expression and conceptual ideas.
What is seen in this way, at that time,
Is beyond the three times, beyond outer and inner,[169] and beyond any division or exclusion.

It is the transcendent perfection of wisdom *(prajnaparamita)* and the Middle Way,
It is the pacification of conceptual elaborations and suffering, Mahamudra,
The essential nature of phenomena, the Great Perfection,
Primordial cessation in which all dharmas are exhausted, the fundamental nature of things,
And the clear light nature of mind, naturally arisen wisdom.
Although they are given different names, in essence they are one.

Bodhichitta, the nature of mind, which is beyond words and concepts,
Is the space-like nonduality of samsara and nirvana,
Beyond clinging to any position at all, and beyond the traps of philosophical constructs,

It transcends limitations and duality and is the supreme state of equalness
and perfection.
This is to be comprehended thoroughly by the yogins
In the vast expanse of the wisdom mind of the victorious ones, free of
extremes.

Fruition

As you reach the culmination of these practices, the stages of fruition are
as follows:
In the shorter term, through the union of bliss, clarity, and non-
conceptuality,
You will achieve clairvoyance, extraordinary powers of perception, and
boundless qualities,
And ultimately, you will achieve the wish-fulfilling three kayas and all
the qualities of the victorious ones,
Spontaneously bringing about your own and others' welfare.

This completes the third section, describing the stages of the samadhi to be practiced from Finding Comfort and Ease in Meditation on the Great Perfection.

DEDICATION

Through the merit of explaining the vast and profound,
The essential meaning of this approach to the Dharma and tranquillity,
May all beings attain the two sublime aspects of awakening
And gain the limitless wealth of wish-fulfilling enlightened activity!

The heir to the victorious ones, Drimé Özer, composed this
Clear explanation for the sake of future generations,
By synthesizing the key points of his own practical experience,
On the slopes of Gangri Thökar.

All who seek liberation should apply themselves
To practicing in accordance with this text,
And, with abundant benefits on a temporal and ultimate level, for both themselves and others,
They will swiftly find happiness and joy in the realm of supreme bliss!

This completes the text Finding Comfort and Ease in Meditation on the Great Perfection, *which was composed on the slopes of Gangri Thökar by the yogin Drimé Özer, a follower of Tsokyé Dorjé, the great and glorious master of Oddiyana.*

May it be virtuous! May it be virtuous! May it be virtuous!

APPENDIX

HISTORICAL PERSPECTIVES

ON BOTH A HISTORICAL and spiritual plane, the events that took place at Lerab Ling as a prelude to His Holiness' public teachings in September 2000 were remarkable and unique. For two weeks prior to the Dalai Lama's arrival at Lerab Ling, monks from the Namgyal monastery performed a complete *drupchen* and *mendrup* of Vajrakilaya, according to the Yang Nying Pudri terma revelation of Tertön Sogyal, Lerab Lingpa. Having presided over the final session of the drupchen, on the next day His Holiness conferred the empowerment of Yang Nying Pudri. What follows below is His Holiness' own account of the background and significance of these events, along with some notes on the history of this revelation, its connection with the Dalai Lamas, and the benefits of the drupchen and mendrup.

On September 19th, His Holiness granted the empowerment of Vajrakilaya to one thousand four hundred people, headed by Kyabjé Trulshik Rinpoche and including lamas, geshes, monks and nuns, practitioners from all the Rigpa centers around the world, members of other Buddhist centers in Europe, some of the Dalai Lama's close associates, and a number of activists for Tibet. The setting was the large tent, decorated like a temple, in which the drupchen and mendrup had taken place. A majestic atmosphere prevailed as His Holiness spoke of the historic connections of this practice and its importance for the flourishing of the Dharma, the Tibetan people, the Tibetan government, and his own long life.

HIS HOLINESS THE DALAI LAMA

The main purpose behind us gathering here today at Lerab Ling, the center established by Sogyal Rinpoche, is for the empowerment into the profound terma cycle of Vajrakilaya, as revealed by the great Lerab Lingpa. This comes at the end of the drupchen and the mendrup rituals for the consecration of the amrita, or nectar. I have been asked to give this Vajrakilaya empowerment by Sogyal Rinpoche and his students, because it forms a regular part of the practice schedule for the Rigpa sangha. And so I agreed to their request.

I take it that most of you here have, to some extent, trained your minds already in the more ordinary stages of Buddhist practice. By this, I mean that there are two aspects that I see as fundamental in order to train our minds as Buddhist practitioners. One is the profound view of the Middle Way, the Madhyamaka view of emptiness, that is common to both the sutra and the tantra vehicles. The other aspect is the altruistic motivation of compassion—the sincere desire that we hold in our hearts to be of true benefit to all beings. These two, the view and the motivation, are fundamental.

THE HISTORY OF THE TRANSMISSION

Now the deity known as "the great and glorious one," Vajrakumara or Vajrakilaya, is a deity associated with the general principle of the five buddha families of the mandala. Vajrakilaya is associated specifically with the karma, or activity, family, which brings about the accomplishment of the practitioner's ultimate goal. In the cycle of the Kagyé, the eight great mandalas of the Nyingma school, Vajrakilaya also functions as this deity of activity. And so the mandala of Vajrakilaya, among all the different cycles of Vajrayana practice, is particularly identified with the power and strength of that enlightened activity and with its ability to avert unfavorable circumstances and obstacles and remove negativity. This is held to be the speciality of Vajrakilaya practice.

The empowerment that I am offering to you today is for the cycle of Vajrakilaya known as Yang Nying Pudri, *The Razor of the Innermost Essence,* revealed by Lerab Lingpa, who was a great tertön, a discoverer of hidden treasures, during the time of my predecessor, the Thirteenth Dalai Lama. In fact, there was a very strong connection between Lerab Lingpa and the Thirteenth Dalai Lama. When this terma was revealed by Lerab Lingpa, it was prophesied to him that the Thirteenth Dalai Lama was to be the *chödak,* the custodian of these teachings. The task of the chödak was to receive the teachings from the tertön and propagate them. This explains why the Thirteenth Dalai Lama composed the manual of liturgies that is used to perform the drupchen associated with the Yang Nying Pudri cycle. So there was a very strong and powerful connection between the Thirteenth Dalai Lama and the tertön Lerab Lingpa.

To this day the monks of my personal chapel, the Namgyal Dratsang, perform the mendrup, the consecration of medicine, and the drupchen, the intensive group practice, for this cycle of Vajrakilaya every year as part of our annual schedule of practices. This is because the powerful connection with this terma of Vajrakilaya and its discoverer Lerab Lingpa did not solely apply to the Thirteenth Dalai Lama but to the entire lineage of the Dalai Lamas. And so we maintain this practice on an annual basis to the present day.

When I was in Tibet, on occasion I participated in some of the rituals associated with this form of Vajrakilaya. But curiously, although at that point I had not received either the empowerment or any instructions, or made it in any way part of my personal practice, I definitely felt that I had a karmic connection with this practice. This continued to intrigue me, even while I was in Tibet.

Later on, in exile, when I was attempting to formulate the cycle of practices for the Namgyal Dratsang, I felt that this ritual of Vajrakilaya, the Yang Nying Pudri cycle, needed to be brought into the cycle of annual practices; thus I was put in the position of needing to seek for myself the empowerment, oral transmissions, and teachings, which I had not yet received in this lifetime. So I began to investigate which teacher would be best suited to approach to grant me the practice of Vajrakilaya according to Lerab Lingpa.

So important did this become for me that I consulted my senior tutor, who many of you will remember, Kyabjé Ling Rinpoche. For me personally, he is like Vajradhara, the primordial buddha. And when

I explained the situation to this great master, he said to me, "In order for the teachings and the Tibetan people to benefit, it is important that the Dalai Lama's life be as long as possible and that his activities flourish as much as possible, in any of his incarnations. If you, as the present holder of the title of Dalai Lama, have decided that it is important for you to receive this practice, then you should follow that impulse. You should follow that through, because this indicates that it is very important and highly significant. No one who's at all concerned will have any problem with you seeking out those teachings when they understand the importance for you personally and how much your personal welfare influences the Buddhadharma and the nation of Tibet."

So I took Ling Rinpoche's vajra words to heart, and I started looking for the most appropriate master from whom to receive these teachings. Eventually I decided that Kyabjé Dilgo Khyentse Rinpoche was the most qualified, because of the very personal and intimate nature of the transmission that he had received,[170] and because of his extraordinary qualities as a vajra holder and master of these teachings. I requested that he bestow on me the empowerment and transmissions, which he did. Then, since I had received the actual transmission, I undertook some formal practice on my own.

PURE PERCEPTION

As you have requested the empowerment for this Vajrakilaya cycle revealed by Lerab Lingpa, I would ask that all of you gathered here cultivate a feeling of unwavering faith in these teachings and a real sense of samaya commitment, of establishing a deep connection with them. As much as you can, evoke a sense of pure perception. In order to receive the teachings of the secret mantra vehicle in the spirit they are given, the way we listen to them is by letting go of all clinging to ordinary perceptions and instead arousing in ourselves a sense of perceiving things from the point of view of the deity. We might describe it as a state of divine perception, in the sense that our ordinary way of looking at things is no longer functioning. In its place, we keep clearly in mind an attitude—a way of looking at everything—that possesses the nature of the deity. If we continue as we are in an ordinary frame of mind, without letting go of our ordinary patterns of perception and reaction and the like, and we approach the teachings from that viewpoint, somehow I feel it simply will not work. We will not truly receive the teachings as long as we relate to them from a purely ordinary point of view.

When we speak of pure perception, it implies that all phenomena, whether they are nominally pure or impure, are by their very nature shunyata, or emptiness. What I am referring to here is that view of shunyata, or the emptiness that is the nature of all phenomena, be they pure or impure on the relative level. Ordinary beings such as ourselves are said to have an impure state of perception, because our minds are immersed in cognitive and emotional obscurations. But if we consider things from the point of view of the nature of our mind, which is inherently and totally pure—what the teachings refer to as the fundamental innate mind of clear light, or ground luminosity—from that perspective, we understand that the capacity to experience the four kayas of buddhahood is already present within us.

When we understand that key point, then our perspective changes, and we realize that our ordinary perceptions, which are based upon our present state of confusion, do not truly exist as they seem. They are purely adventitious and superficial, and the fundamental innate mind of clear light, the nature of mind, is completely unaffected and unsullied by these adventitious factors. They have nothing to do with the actual nature of our mind as it is, because that nature is not sullied by such superficial manifestations. It is with the confidence that comes with such a view that we can arouse a state of perception that is not ordinary, but divine, and which pertains to the deity rather than to ordinary ways of seeing things. In a way, it is quite automatic. Once we understand things from the point of view of the nature of mind, then the confidence that gives us means that our ordinary way of perceiving things simply ceases, as a matter of course. And in its stead there arises this divine state of perception, this way of seeing things from the point of view of their innate purity.

Before we begin the empowerment then, let me emphasize that the way you approach such a transmission is not to think of the teacher who is conferring the empowerment as being the ordinary human individual that you see sitting in front of you. Rather, in your mind, you identify the vajra master who is bestowing such an empowerment with the central deity of the mandala, in this case the entire mandala of Vajrakilaya. You have a feeling of trust and conviction that the vajra master is indistinguishable from the deity. That is the kind of attitude with which you approach an empowerment of this nature.

At the conclusion of the empowerment, His Holiness stated:

Now I have completed this empowerment of Vajrakilaya, this terma treasure revealed by Lerab Lingpa, with which I have such a strong connection due to my own personal aspirations and motivation. Those of you who have received this empowerment are now authorized to do the practice. I would encourage you to do so, using either the more extensive rituals or the very concise daily practice, and learning how to apply all the different levels of significance of the Vajrakilaya practice. What is most important in the case of such practice is the experience of the union of rigpa and shunyata. That is the ultimate stage of the practice and is therefore the most important to focus on. Yet, along with it, there is the meditation and the mantra associated with this deity, and it would be a very good idea, I think, having received this empowerment, if you kept this up on a regular basis, reciting the mantra, and performing the meditation as regularly as possible without a break or interruption, and without letting it simply peter out.

As I mentioned earlier, there is a strong connection between this practice and the Buddhadharma and the Tibetan nation in general. And so when you carry out this practice, I would ask that, in addition to your own aspirations and dedication, you specifically focus upon the teachings of the Tibetan Buddhist tradition and the fate of the Tibetan nation, by including prayers and aspirations for the welfare of the Tibetan people and for the spread and flourishing of these teachings.

THE HISTORY OF THE TERMA REVELATION

As His Holiness explains, the Yang Nying Pudri is a terma treasure that was revealed by Lerab Lingpa. In the Nyingma tradition, the teachings are passed down through two transmissions: the long, continuous lineage of kama and the short lineage of terma, the treasures concealed by Guru Padmasambhava to be discovered later by the treasure revealers or *tertöns,* who are emanations of his close disciples.[171] Tertön Sogyal, Lerab Lingpa (1856–1927), was the incarnation of Nanam Dorjé Dudjom, one of Padmasambhava's closest disciples who attained siddhis through his practice of Vajrakilaya and was able to move, unhindered, through space like the wind and to pass through solid rock. Tertön Sogyal was a prolific tertön, whose collected revelations fill twenty volumes. He was a student of Nyoshul Lungtok, Jamyang Khyentse Wangpo, Mipham Rinpoche, and Jamgön Kongtrul and also received teachings from Nyala Pema Düdul and Patrul Rinpoche. His own disciples included the Thirteenth Dalai Lama Thupten Gyatso (1876–1933), the third Dodrupchen Jikmé Tenpé Nyima (1865–1926), and Jamyang Khyentse Chökyi Lodrö (1893–1959). Five volumes of his revelations are dedicated entirely to termas of Vajrakilaya; one of them, *The Razor of the Innermost Essence*—Yang Nying Pudri—was destined to become particularly renowned.

Tertön Sogyal's biography, which was written by Tulku Tsullo, describes how the terma was revealed. In the autumn of 1895, Tertön Sogyal went with Jamgön Kongtrul to Tsadra Rinchen Drak, a sacred site closely linked with both Jamgön Kongtrul and Chokgyur Dechen Lingpa, and one of the twenty-five holy places of east Tibet, representing "the wisdom mind of enlightened qualities." There, high up on the hillside, Tertön Sogyal approached "The Cave that Delights the Awesome Heruka," where, his biography recounts:

> The outline of the terma door stood out clearly in the rock face, and when he saw this, he became as if excited and flung a stone at it. At once the earth shook with a great crashing sound, as though a whole mountain were subsiding. An aperture in the rock gaped open, and an exquisite fragrance flooded out to fill the air. Tertön Sogyal plunged his hand into the opening and withdrew a *kutsap*—a representation of Guru Rinpoche—in a striding posture and gripping vajra and phurba, and along with it, the casket containing the terma of Yang Nying Pudri. Wrapping

them carefully in silk so that no one might see, he placed them in the terma chest held by his consort. The terma trove in the rock was also full of amrita, but he said that it was not his to take and he would not remove it. However, his consort pleaded with him insistently, and to avoid disappointing her, he took some of this amrita, which liberates when tasted, and left the remaining treasure just as he had found it. He offered a substitute for the terma and closed the door and sealed it well. Then Jamgön Kongtrul Rinpoche approached the site, and together, in joyful gratitude, they all celebrated a tsok feast, offered tormas to please the terma guardians, and made prayers of dedication and auspiciousness on a grand scale, aspiring to benefit the Dharma and all living beings.

THE CONNECTION WITH THE THIRTEENTH AND FOURTEENTH DALAI LAMAS

In 1898 Tertön Sogyal traveled to Lhasa to meet the Dalai Lama. His first, momentous, meeting with the Dalai Lama had been ten years earlier, when, it was said, "their wisdom minds instantly merged as one." Now, following a proclamation of the Nechung oracle, Tertön Sogyal offered the complete cycle of empowerment, transmission, and instruction of the Yang Nying Pudri to the Dalai Lama.

Early the next morning, the Dalai Lama records a vivid dream, in which he found himself before the palace of Guru Rinpoche, where he was met by two celestial beings, singing prophetic verses about this practice of Vajrakilaya. They told him that desire, anger, and ignorance would be eliminated, obstacles overcome and attainments realized, if he performed a thousand tsok offerings according to the Yang Nying Pudri practice. The Dalai Lama's biography explains: "He awoke, remembering the words very clearly. The Dalai Lama and Lerab Lingpa then decoded their meaning together. And he accomplished the thousand tsok offerings of Vajrakilaya, as the prophecy made clear was the right thing to do."

Tertön Sogyal then gave the Yang Nying Pudri empowerment to the monks of the Namgyal Dratsang in the Potala Palace, who have maintained this practice ever since. In 1899 the mendrup was performed as part of the Mönlam Chenmo, the annual Great Prayer Festival at the New Year in Lhasa, and woodblocks for the entire cycle were carved. The Thirteenth Dalai Lama arranged the Yang Nying Pudri for practice as a drupchen and so composed the text *Treasury of Wishes for the Benefit of Self and Others* that was used by the Namgyal monks at Lerab Ling.

As His Holiness the Dalai Lama explains, it was Kyabjé Dilgo Khyentse Rinpoche who offered him the empowerment of Yang Nying Pudri. In 1990, at Rigpa's summer retreat at Prapoutel in France, Khyentse Rinpoche explained:

> It was said in the prediction associated with this terma that the chödak and holder of this teaching would be the Thirteenth Dalai Lama, an incarnation of the King Trisong Detsen. So Tertön Sogyal transmitted this teaching to him, and he made it one of his central practices. Through its blessing and activity, the realm of Ganden Phodrang entered a period of great stability and expansion. Many of the disciples of Tertön Sogyal took this sadhana as their principal practice. His Holiness the Fourteenth Dalai Lama told me that it is one of his main practices.[172]

Lerab Lingpa had three reincarnations. Sogyal Rinpoche is one of them, and another was Khenpo Jikmé Phüntsok Rinpoche, who said when he visited Lerab Ling in 1993:

> The main holder of this teaching was the Thirteenth Dalai Lama, who wrote a structure and the prayers necessary to make it into a drupchen and used to practice it in the Potala. The Fourteenth Dalai Lama was not able to practice it when he first came out of Tibet, but he has reestablished this drupchen, and it is now practiced in Dharamsala. This must be one of His Holiness' main practices, because when I went to Dharamsala in 1990, immediately he said there should be a Yang Nying Pudri tsok offering the next day. During the tsok, when I saw how familiar His Holiness was with the mudras and all the details of the practice, I said to my attendant, "We have been doing this all our lives, but still we are not as proficient in it as His Holiness."

THE NAMGYAL MONASTERY AND THE DRUPCHEN

The monks of the Namgyal Dratsang, who performed the drupchen and mendrup at Lerab Ling, have always assisted the Dalai Lamas in their public and private religious activities and performed rituals on their behalf and for the welfare of Tibet. Founded by the saintly Gendün Gyatso (1476–1542), the Second Dalai Lama, the Namgyal College, given the name Phende Lekshé Ling—*Elegant Abode of Peace and Prosperity*—grew to great prominence during the time of the Fifth Dalai Lama Ngawang Lozang Gyatso (1617–82), when it moved into the Potala Palace. A particularly close association developed between the monastery and the Thirteenth Dalai Lama, which has continued during the time of the present Dalai Lama. In exile, the Namgyal Dratsang was reconstituted in Dharamsala, next to His Holiness' residence, and the monks follow a monastic study program introduced by His Holiness himself. Renowned for their expertise in ritual practice, they frequently accompany the Dalai Lama on his visits abroad; for example, whenever he grants the empowerment of Kalachakra.

In Dharamsala, the Namgyal Dratsang received the empowerment of the Yang Nying Pudri from Kyabjé Kalu Rinpoche, the activity emanation of Jamgön Kongtrul, and more recently from Kyabjé Trulshik Rinpoche. Every year, for ten days in the second Tibetan month, the drupchen is practiced at the monastery; when it was performed at Lerab Ling, it was the first time that the complete drupchen and mendrup had been executed outside Tibet or the Himalayan region.

A drupchen, literally "vast accomplishment," is a form of intensive group practice that epitomizes the depth, power, and precision of the Vajrayana, drawing together the entire range of its skillful methods—mystical, ritual, and artistic—and including: the creation of the mandala house; the complete sadhana practice with visualization, mudra, chant, and music; continuous day and night practice of mantra; the creation of tormas and offerings, with sacred substances and precious relics; the tsok feast; the sacred dance of *cham;* as well as the construction of the sand mandala. All blend to create the transcendent environment of the pure realm of the deity and awaken, for all those taking part, the pure perception of this world as a sacred realm. So it is said that several days participating in a drupchen can yield the same results as years of solitary retreat, and great contemporary masters such as Kyabjé Dilgo Khyentse Rinpoche have made a point of encouraging and reviving the practice of drupchen, because of its power of transformation in this degenerate age.

On the morning after his arrival at Lerab Ling, His Holiness the Dalai Lama joined in the concluding session of the drupchen. This session included "the receiving of the siddhis," a practice for gathering the spirit of abundance, and the consecration by His Holiness of the amrita that had been prepared during the mendrup.

THE SIGNIFICANCE AND BENEFITS OF THE MENDRUP

During a mendrup ritual, large quantities of amrita—sacred spiritual medicine—are fermented and consecrated. The Sanskrit word *amrita* means "deathless"; in Tibetan it is *dütsi,* because, it is said, "it is the medicine that overcomes the fearful state of death." *The Tantra of the Secret Cycle* elaborates:

> To samsara which is like mara *(dü)*
> When the elixir *(tsi)* of the truth of Dharma is applied,
> It is called nectar *(dütsi)*.

The medicinal nectar of amrita effects healing and attainment on every dimension. The Thirteenth Dalai Lama wrote: "All the siddhis, it is said, including the accomplishment of the vajra body of immortality, come as a result of the qualities of amrita." *The Eight Volumes on Nectar* explain:

> Curing the four hundred and twenty-four illnesses
> And destroying the four maras,
> It is the essence supreme, the king of medicines.

Composed of "a hundred major and a thousand minor ingredients," the five hundred kilos of amrita created at Lerab Ling included *arura* and other medicinal ingredients of every conceivable kind, along with countless holy relics and precious substances of buddhas, siddhas, and saints provided by different masters and monasteries all over the Himalayas.

The mendrup is a ritual that is held to bring enormous benefit for all who take part and bestows a powerful blessing on the site where it takes place. Guru Padmasambhava explains:

> Sacred medicinal substances to be offered to the buddhas,
> Elixirs that invoke the masters and yidam deities—
> These are the heart essence of the dakinis.
> When ingested, their benefits are beyond all description:
>
> You gain the qualities of the five kayas of a buddha.
> Externally, diseases and physical obstacles are all destroyed;
> Internally, the poisons of five negative emotions are purified
> And impairments and breakages of samaya are healed;
> Secretly, you will realize self-arising wisdom.
>
> Should a shravaka or pratyekabuddha
> Take this nectar, they will attain the tenth stage
> And become a "great bodhisattva" on the Mahayana path.
>
> Offer this medicine to the masters,
> And great blessings are received.
> Offer it to the yidam deities,
> And powerful siddhis are attained.
> Offer it to the buddhas,
> And their compassion is invoked.
> Offer it to the dakas and dakinis,
> And they will deliver a prophecy.
>
> Should a yogin, or anyone, eat this nectar,
> Externally, illness and harmful influence,
> Negative acts and obscurations, all are purified.
> Internally, the samadhi of the generation stage
> Becomes vivid and clear.

Secretly, your awareness attains
The state of dharmakaya.
And all impairments of vows and
Errors in the practice are amended.

Merely by holding this medicine,
All danger of premature death is eliminated,
And the deadliest poison is counteracted.
By applying it on the body,
Sickness and harmful influence are dispelled.
By burning it as incense,
Negative forces and obstacle-makers are chased away.

The place where this practice is performed
Becomes the equal of the Cool Grove Charnel Ground.
Countless dakas and dakinis will gather there
And infuse the area with their blessings.
Rains will fall on time and resources abound.
Anyone who later uses this place for retreat
Will easily attain the state of samadhi.

Should anyone about to die
Take some of this sacred nectar,
He or she will gain the level of vidyadhara
Regardless of what kind of life was led.
Indeed, it is a substance sacred and supreme.[173]

These explanations above suggest the deep significance of the empowerment, drupchen, and mendrup that took place at Lerab Ling. Through his own special connection with this practice, His Holiness wove together and brought alive the links between Lerab Lingpa, the Thirteenth Dalai Lama, the Namgyal monastery, himself, Sogyal Rinpoche, and all those who took part. Through this powerful practice, the blessing of the buddhas was invoked for Tibet, its people, and its destiny, as well as for the future of Buddhism in Europe and the West. By conferring this empowerment on the site of its construction,

His Holiness also blessed the future temple at Lerab Ling. As it happened, His Holiness' public teachings and the events described here had an additional resonance for members of Rigpa, as they occurred during the twenty-fifth year since Sogyal Rinpoche started to teach in the West and Rigpa's work began. What took place in 2000 will always remain a landmark in Rigpa's history and an unforgettable blessing, inspiration, and encouragement for its endeavors in the future.

At the very end of his arrangement of the Yang Nying Pudri drupchen, the Thirteenth Dalai Lama made the following dedication:

> Though the power of this,
> May the precious teachings of the Buddha, the source of benefit and happiness,
> Spread and flourish in all places and times without sectarian bias.
> May those who uphold the teachings enjoy long life.
> May all negative forces that cause wrong actions be banished.
> May we enjoy the wonderful experience of lasting happiness.
> May the doorways be open to ordinary and extraordinary spiritual paths.
> May all that is excellent unfold just as we would wish and bring benefit and happiness everywhere!

NOTES

1 The centers inviting His Holiness and forming the Association Golfe du Lion were Lerab Ling, Kagyü Rintchen Tcheu Ling (a center founded in Montpellier by Kyabjé Kalu Rinpoche in 1975), Kagyü Yi Ong Tcheu Ling, Jardin du Dharma, and Jardin de Claire Lumière.

2 See Sogyal Rinpoche, *The Tibetan Book of Living and Dying*, rev. ed. (San Francisco: Harper, 1992; San Francisco: Harper, 2002; London: Rider, 2002), p. 155. Rider revised edition cited.

3 The biography of Longchenpa can be found in Nyoshul Khenpo, *A Marvelous Garland of Rare Gems, Biographies of Masters of Awareness in the Dzogchen Lineage* (Junction City: Padma Publishing), pp. 98–161; see also Tulku Thondup, *Masters of Meditation and Miracles* (Boston: Shambhala, 1996), pp. 109–17.

4 See Nyoshul Khenpo, *Marvelous Garland of Rare Gems*, pp. 141, 145.

5 Nyoshul Khenpo, *Marvelous Garland of Rare Gems*, pp. xxiv–v.

6 From *Ngal gso skor gsum gyi spyi don legs bshad rgya mtsho*, pp. 223–24. The eight similes of illusoriness, given in the order in which they appear in the text, are as follows: dream, magical illusion, hallucination, mirage, reflection of the moon in water, echo, city of gandharvas, and phantom or apparition.

7 See H.H. the Dalai Lama, *Dzogchen, the Heart Essence of the Great Perfection* (Ithaca: Snow Lion, 2001).

8 Lamas present at these teachings included: Kyabjé Trulshik Rinpoche, Dagyab Rinpoche, Kyongla Rinpoche, Dagpo Rinpoche, Ato Rinpoche, Thamtog Rinpoche, Dzigar Kongtrul Rinpoche, Tsoknyi Rinpoche, Khamtrul Rinpoche, Pema Wangyal Rinpoche, Rangdrol Rinpoche, Sogyal Rinpoche, Jadho Rinpoche, Gyari Rinpoche, Lelung Rinpoche, the Nechung Oracle, Namgyal Khensur Rinpoche, Gomang Khensur Rinpoche, Geshe Thubten Ngawang, and Geshe Lobsang Tengye, plus a number of other geshes, monks, and nuns.

9 H.H. the Dalai Lama, while giving the empowerment of Rigdzin Dungdrup in Dharamsala, India, on March 21, 2004. Quoted in *A Great Treasure of Blessings, A Book of Prayers to Guru Rinpoche* (London: The Tertön Sogyal Trust, 2004), pp. 13–14.

10 See The Fourteenth Dalai Lama, *Kindness, Clarity and Insight,* trans. and ed. Jeffrey Hopkins and Elizabeth Napper (1984; Ithaca: Snow Lion, 2006), 1984 ed., pp. 220–21; 2006 ed., p. 249; see also Dalai Lama, *Dzogchen,* p. 120.

11 During his long career as scriptwriter, dramatist, and author, Jean-Claude Carrière won a number of awards and worked with the most celebrated figures in film and theater. Besides his long-standing collaboration with Luis Buñuel, he also worked with Jean-Luc Godard, Milos Forman, Volker Schlöndorff, Andrzej Wajda, Louis Malle, and Nagisha Oshima and, in the theater, with Peter Brook and Jean-Louis Barrault. He is the screenwriter for more than forty films, including *The Return of Martin Guerre, The Unbearable Lightness of Being, The Mahabharata,* and *Belle de Jour.* His passionate interest in Eastern culture led him to meet the Dalai Lama a number of times; their conversations in Dharamsala became the book *The Power of Buddhism* (*La Force du Boudhisme,* Paris: Robert Laffont, 1994).

12 This verse comes from *The Diamond Cutter Sutra,* Vajracchedika, *'Phags pa shes rab kyi pha rol tu phyin pa rdo rje gcod pa:* skar ma rab rib mar me dang// sgyu ma zil pa chu bur dang// rmi lam glog dang sprin lta bu// 'dus byas de ltar blta bar bya.

13 Maitreya, *The Ornament of Clear Realization,* v. 1.

14 Nagarjuna, *Fundamentals of the Middle Way,* 1.1–2, for translation see The Dalai Lama, *The Essence of the Heart Sutra,* trans. Geshe Thupten Jinpa (Boston: Wisdom, 2002), p. 122.

15 *Nges legs:* definitive goodness. *An Encyclopaedic Tibetan-English Dictionary* (Beijing: Nationalities Publishing House, 2001) says: "Continuous happiness: the state of liberation, and omniscience." See Jeffrey Hopkins, trans., *Buddhist Advice for Living and Liberation: Nagarjuna's Precious Garland* (Ithaca: Snow Lion, 1998), p. 46.

16 To take an ordinary example, if you have a correct perception (valid cognition) of a fire, its immediate result might be that you could make a cup of tea. This is the "uninterrupted or direct effect or fruit" of that valid perception. However, this perception can lead to numerous other benefits, which are indirectly linked to the perception but are interrupted by other states of mind in between. So the attainment of higher rebirth, liberation, and so on are said to be "interrupted or indirect fruits" of valid perception or valid cognition.

17 "In this, there is not a thing to be removed, nor the slightest thing to be added." Maitreya, *The Ornament of Clear Realization,* V:21.

18 The four reasonings *(rigs pa bzhi)* are the reasoning of: dependency, functionality,

nature, and establishing logical feasibility: *(ltos pa'i rigs pa dang, bya ba byed pa'i rigs pa dang, chos nyid kyi rigs pa, 'thad pa sgrub pa'i rigs pa).*

19 His Holiness is referring to the practice of Dzogchen, the Great Perfection. As Dodrupchen Jikmé Tenpé Nyima says: "Generally speaking, in the instructions on Dzogchen, profound and special aspects are endless." The key point, however, is the differentiation between the ordinary mind and rigpa. As Jikmé Lingpa puts it in his *Treasury of Precious Qualities:* "Rigpa, which transcends the ordinary mind, is the special feature of the natural Dzogpachenpo." In *rdzogs chen skor,* p. 554.

20 His Holiness' explanation of this topic, given in a teaching in New York in 1991, is quoted in Sogyal Rinpoche, *Tibetan Book of Living and Dying,* rev. ed. (San Francisco: Harper, 2002), pp. 93–94.

21 "Nontransferable actions" *(mi g.yo ba'i las)* are the meditations of the four dhyanas and four formless absorptions. They are called *nontransferable* because they can only result in rebirth within the corresponding form and formless realms and cannot be "transferred" to produce a result in any other realm.

22 The five disturbing or deluded views are: the view of the transitory collection *('jig tshogs la lta ba),* which means regarding the five aggregates as "I" and "mine"; the view of extremes *(mthar 'dzin pa'i lta ba),* meaning eternalism and nihilism; wrong views *(log lta);* the view of ethical superiority *(tshul khrims dang brtul zhugs mchog 'dzin);* and the view of doctrinal superiority *(lta ba mchog 'dzin).*

23 This is a quotation from the *Eight Thousand Verse Prajñaparamita Sutra.* See E. Conze, *The Perfection of Wisdom in 8,000 Lines and Its Verse Summary* (Delhi: Sri Satguru Publications, 1994), p. 84.

24 Dza Patrul Rinpoche (1808–87) was one of the greatest Tibetan masters of the nineteenth century and the author of one of the most widely read works in Tibetan literature, *The Words of My Perfect Teacher.* His biography appears in Nyoshul Khenpo's *A Marvelous Garland of Rare Gems,* pp. 223–38.

25 The sublime ones (Skt. *arya,* Tib. *'phags pa*) are beings who possess a direct realization of the nature of reality and who have transcended samsara.

26 The higher states of existence *(mngon mtho)* are the higher realms within samsara—the realms of the human beings and the gods.

27 According to Patrul Rinpoche, the explanation of four different types of nirvana is exclusive to the Madhyamaka tradition. *Natural nirvana* is the nature of phenomena, free from any conceptual elaboration. *Nonabiding nirvana* is the nirvana of the buddhas and bodhisattvas, beyond the extremes of samsaric existence and quiescence. *Nirvana with remainder* refers to the result of an arhat who has transcended suffering but not yet abandoned the psychophysical aggregates and still experiences the effects of past karma.

Nirvana without remainder is attained when the arhat relinquishes the aggregates and enters the realm of cessation.

28 The four maras are: the mara of the aggregates, referring to the five psychophysical aggregates, the mara of the afflictions, the mara of the Lord of Death, which is death itself, and the devaputra mara, which means distraction and desire and attachment.

29 "The four" refers to the *four maras.* "The six" refers to the *six fortunes (bskal pa drug):* (1) The perfect power of mastering what is desirable; (2) the perfect body of excellence of the marks and signs; (3) the perfect wealth of immeasurable things, such as the retinue; (4) perfect fame; (5) the perfect wisdom of knowing things as they are and all that there is; and (6) the perfect diligence of accomplishing the benefit of beings. The final syllable in *Chomdendé,* i.e., dé, means "transcending," signifying that the Buddha has transcended the extremes of existence and quiescence.

30 The "vehicles leading from the origin" are the three vehicles of the shravakas, pratyekabuddhas, and bodhisattvas. They are so called because they lead us along the path to the result of liberation from samsara by abandoning all the actions and kleshas that are the cause or "origin" of suffering. The "vehicles of Vedic asceticism" are the vehicles of the three outer classes of tantra—kriya, charya, and yoga. They are so called because they stress aspects of ascetic conduct, such as ritual purification and cleanliness, and in this respect they are similar to the Vedic tradition of the brahmins. The "vehicles of supreme and powerful transformative methods" are the vehicles of the three inner tantras—mahayoga, anuyoga, and atiyoga. They are so called because they include powerful methods for transforming all phenomena into great purity and equalness. See Zenkar Rinpoche, *A Brief Presentation of the Nine Yanas,* www.lotsawahouse.org/nine_yanas.html.

31 Aryadeva's *Four Hundred Verses,* VIII:15.

32 Although it is traditional to speak of eighteen schools, there are several different lists, and it is likely there were actually many more. Among the main groups into which they were divided were the Mahasamghika, Sarvastivadin, and Sthavira.

33 Jé Tsongkhapa, from *The Prayer of the Virtuous Beginning, Middle, and End (Thog ma dang bar dang mtha' mar dge ba'i smon lam):* ji ltar thos pa'i don la rigs pa bzhis// nyin dang mtshan du tshul bzhin rab brtags nas//bsam bya'i gnas la bsams las byung ba yi//rnam dpyod blo yis the tshom chod par shog.

34 *An Encyclopaedic Tibetan-English Dictionary* explains these three qualities of learning, sanctity, and kind-heartedness: "Learning means having no confusion about objects of knowledge, sanctity means possessing pure discipline with regard to faults of body, speech, or mind, and kind-heartedness means that one's altruistic commitment to act on behalf of others is impeccable."

35 A portrait of Rongzom Chökyi Zangpo's life is given by Dudjom Rinpoche, who says of him: "He was renowned as the supreme mahapandita of Tibet...an unrivaled master of the teaching of the Ancient Translation School of the secret mantra. With respect to the different sutras, tantras, and treatises, he mastered all those which are knowable." Atisha (982–1054) met him and is said to have called him "infallible." Rongzom's commentary on *The Secret Essence Tantra* begins with the verse: "The nature of the Three Jewels is the enlightened mind," and so it became known as *The Jewel Commentary. The Entrance to the Way of the Mahayana* is among his best-known writings. As well as his remarkable scholarship, he also manifested many signs of his deep realization. The historian Gö Lotsawa said of him: "In this snowland of Tibet no scholar has appeared who has been his equal." See Dudjom Rinpoche, *The Nyingma School of Tibetan Buddhism, Its Fundamentals and History*, trans. and ed. Gyurme Dorje (Boston: Wisdom, 1991), pp. 703–9.

36 Longchenpa and Butön both passed away in 1364, seven years after the birth of Tsongkhapa in 1357. Butön Rinchen Drup was a famous Tibetan scholar and historian, best known for his efforts to compile the Kangyur, the canonical teachings of the Buddha in Tibetan translation.

37 Jamgön Mipham Rinpoche (1846–1912).

38 *Kun bzang smon lam gyi rnam bshad kun bzang nye lam.* Tsultrim Zangpo (1884–1957), also known as Tulku Tsullo, one of the most exceptional Tibetan scholars of recent times, was an important student of Tertön Sogyal Lerab Lingpa, as well as the author of his secret biography and a lineage holder of his terma teachings. He was also a student of the Third Dodrupchen Jikmé Tenpé Nyima and of Amnye Khenpo Damchö Özer of Dodrupchen Monastery. Khenpo Damchö said of him on one occasion, "I am just a dog, but I have a lion for a student." Although it was notoriously difficult to meet Dodrup Jikmé Tenpé Nyima in his later years, Tsullo was able to do so because of his work as a scribe. He copied many texts for Dodrupchen Rinpoche's personal library and used the work as an opportunity to get access to him and to receive clarifications. Tulku Tsullo's main residence was at Shugjung *(shugs 'byung)* monastery in the Do Valley, which is located about fifteen to twenty miles from Dodrupchen Monastery and belongs to the Northern Treasures *(byang gter)* tradition. Tsultrim Zangpo was a monk who upheld the Vinaya, as well as an accomplished tantric practitioner. Those who saw him say that he possessed a statuesque demeanor, seated in meditation posture, hardly ever moving, and with an impressive white beard. Among his writings is a two-volume commentary on Ngari Panchen's *Ascertainment of the Three Types of Vows (Sdom gsum rnam nges),* as well as several texts on Dzogchen, including an instruction manual *(khrid yig)* for the *Gongpa Zangthal* and the commentary on the famous *Prayer of Kuntuzangpo.* His other writings include a commentary to Padmasambhava's *Garland of*

Views and many works related to the tantras of the new translation tradition. He was the root teacher of Khordong Tertrul Chimé Rigdzin, popularly known as "C.R. Lama" (1922–2002), and also of Tulku Gyenlo and Zhichen Öntrul, who passed away recently in Tibet. From information kindly provided by Tulku Thondup Rinpoche.

39 The collected works of Tulku Tsullo were published in eight volumes from woodblocks kept at his monastery of Shugjung in East Tibet. A full list of the contents *(dkar chag)* of these volumes is available online at www.lotsawa-house.org/school/tsullo_index.html.

40 These lines are by Gungthang Tenpé Drönmé (1762–1823) from a prayer for the flourishing of the teachings of Tsongkhapa, known as *blo bzang rgyal bstan ma*. Gungthang Tenpé Drönmé's biography can be found in Thupten Jinpa and Jas Elsner, *Songs of Spiritual Experience* (Boston: Shambhala, 2000), pp. 223–24.

41 From his *Rtogs brjod mdun legs ma,* a short autobiographical work in which Tsongkhapa traces the development of his realization through his practice of sutra and tantra.

42 According to the *Tshig mdzod chen mo,* the Six Ornaments who adorn the world of Jambudvipa are Nagarjuna and Aryadeva, the ornaments to the Middle Way; Asanga and Vasubandhu, the ornaments to the Abhidharma teachings; and Dignaga and Dharmakirti, the ornaments to the teachings on Pramana, or valid cognition. The Two Supreme Ones are Shakyaprabha and Gunaprabha, who were both extremely learned in the teachings on monastic discipline as taught in the Vinaya.

43 This refers to a saying from *The Seven Points of Training the Mind,* in the sixth point, concerning the commitments of mind training. The gist is to "avoid ridiculing and insulting others out of a sense of superiority." See Thupten Jinpa, trans. and ed., *Mind Training, The Great Collection* (Boston: Wisdom, 2006), p. 121.

44 Drakyap Rinpoche was an incarnate lama from the Penpo region near Lhasa, who was considered to be an emanation of the great Kadam teacher, Potowa. He passed away at the end of the 1980s, and his incarnation is currently studying in Sera monastery.

45 The wisdom that is realized directly at the moment of the path of seeing.

46 This is from *Uttaratantra Shastra,* 1:51:3.

47 *las mtha' rnam 'byed,* Skt. *karmantavibhanga.*

48 See Dalai Lama, *Dzogchen,* passim, especially pp. 176–77, 183–84.

49 The Sanskrit word *kaya* literally means "body." According to the Mahayana teachings, buddhahood is described in terms of two, three, four, or five kayas. The two kayas are dharmakaya (body of truth) and rupakaya (body of form). The rupakaya can be divided into sambhogakaya (body of perfect enjoyment)

and nirmanakaya (body of manifestation), to make three kayas. With the addition of the svabhavikakaya (body of suchness), there come to be four buddha bodies. The five kayas consist of the first three kayas together with the abhisambodhikaya (body of complete awakening) and the vajrakaya (immutable vajra body). The enlightened bodies of the buddhas are regarded as the supports for their enlightened wisdom, just as our ordinary bodies may be said to provide a support for our ordinary consciousness.

50 The full title of this text is: *Words of the Vidyadharas: An Instruction Manual on Generation, Completion, and the Great Perfection for the Great Compassionate One, Liberation of Samsara into Basic Space (Thugs rje chen po 'khor ba dbyings sgrol gyi bskyed rdzogs rdzogs pa chen po'i khrid yig rigs 'dzin zhal lung).*

51 sangs rgyas gzhan nas re ba'i mkhas rlom gyi/ stong bshad shar 'drer nub tu glud gtong tshul/ mthong tshe zag bcas phung po 'od sku ru/ grol 'di gsang chen rnying ma'i khyad par chos. From *Words of the Vidyadharas,* p. 150.

52 Khenpo Achung (1918–98) came from the famous Lumorap monastery in Nyarong, which is closely associated with the great Nyingma foundation of Mindroling in Central Tibet. He had many disciples in the area around Tromge, Nyarong, and Kandze. Khenpo Achung attained the rainbow body on a hillside above Lumorap in September 1998. Apart from reports in the regional press, this was the subject of an article, "The Rainbow Body," in *Institute of Noetic Sciences Review* 59 (March–May 2002); it was also mentioned by Matthew T. Kapstein in *The Presence of Light: Divine Radiance and Religious Experience* (University of Chicago Press, 2004).

53 dpe mthong tsam la rang bzo'i rtsal bshad kyis/ gzhan 'drid bum stong gcig nas gcig 'byo ba'i/ rnam thar ma yin dmar 'khrid rgyud thog tu/ bkal ba'i nyams myong gdengs tshad cung zad mchis/ zab don 'di ko thub bstan de srid bar/ gnas shing bdag 'dra'i dad pa'i las can la/ phan phyir ston zla ltar dkar lhag bsam gyis/ bskrun las chos brgyad nyon mongs can gyis min/ From *Words of the Vidyadharas,* pp. 149–50.

54 gnyis pa dngos gzhi la skyon ye nas ka dag tu ston pa khreg chod kyi lam dang/ yon tan ye nas lhun grub tu rdzogs pa thod rgal gyi lam gnyis… From *Words of the Vidyadharas,* p. 88.

55 The eight extremes, which are referred to by Nagarjuna in the opening verse of his most famous work, the *Mula-madhyamaka-karika,* are arising and ceasing, permanence and nonexistence, coming and going, multiplicity and singularity.

56 The extrinsic emptiness or "other empty" *(gzhan stong)* tradition of Madhyamaka, which is most closely associated with the Jonang school of Tibetan Buddhism, maintains that the absolute is not empty of itself *(rang stong)* but is empty of all other relative phenomena. The "intrinsic emptiness" tradition holds that the absolute truth is empty even of itself.

57 This quotation appears in Chandrakirti's *Clear Words (Prasannapada)* at the end of the thirteenth chapter.

58 phung po rnam dpyad stong pa nyid// chu shing bzhin du snying po med// rnam pa kun gyi mchog ldan pa'i// stong nyid de ltar ma yin no. See Khedrup Norsang Gyatso, *The Ornament of Stainless Light: An Exposition of the Kalachakra Tantra,* translated by Gavin Kilty (Boston: Wisdom, 2004), pp. 567–69. From *A Short Teaching on Our Assertions Concerning the View,* P4580, Tengyur, vol. *bu*, f. 23b1.

59 A brief biographical note on Khedrup Norzang Gyatso (1423–1513) appears in Khedrup Norsang Gyatso, *Ornament of Stainless Light,* p. xv.

60 His Holiness discussed "uncompounded clear light" and the "permanent" status of the enlightened activity of the buddhas in the teaching he gave in London in 1984 on *Hitting the Essence in Three Words.* See *Dalai Lama, Dzogchen,* pp. 52–53.

61 Longchenpa describes *alaya* in this way: "It is unenlightenment and a neutral state, which belongs to the category of mind and mental events, and it has become the foundation of all karmas and 'traces' of samsara and nirvana."

62 In these verses a number of nonhuman beings and spirits are named.

63 *Maitreya, Ornament of Clear Realization,* 2:17d. According to Patrul Rinpoche's commentary *('bru 'grel)* this means that a place where enlightenment has been attained or where someone on the path of meditation has resided is worthy of veneration. See *Sher phyin mngon rtogs rgyan rtsa 'grel* (si khron mi rigs dpe skrun khang, 1997), p. 521.

64 *'dun pa sgyur la rang sor bzhag.* This is another slogan from point six of *The Seven Points of Training the Mind,* which concerns the commitments of training the mind. Other translations are: "Transform your attitudes, but remain as you are," or "Shift your priorities, but stay as you are."

65 The eight worldly concerns or preoccupations are: wanting to be praised and not wanting to be criticized, wanting happiness and not wanting suffering, wanting gain and not wanting loss, and wanting fame and approval and not wanting rejection and disgrace.

66 From *Song of the Eastern Snow Mountain (Shar gangs ri ma),* a praise to Tsongkhapa by the First Dalai Lama, Gendün Drup.

67 *Mahayanasutralamkara* 17:10: bshes gnyen dul ba zhi zhing nyer zhi ba//yon tan lhag pa brtson bcas lung gis phyug//de nyid rab tu rtogs pa smra mkhas ldan//brtse ba'i bdag nyid skyo ba spangs la (b)sten.

68 See Tsong-kha-pa, *The Great Treatise on the Stages of the Path to Enlightenment,* vol. 1, trans. Lamrim Chenmo Translation Committee (Ithaca: Snow Lion, 2000), p. 71.

69 *Disciplined* refers to the training in discipline *(shila), peaceful* to the training in

meditation *(samadhi),* and *serene* to the training in wisdom *(prajna).* Tsong-kha-pa, *Great Treatise on the Stages of the Path,* vol. 1, pp. 71–72.

70 His Holiness is following closely a section from Tsongkhapa's *The Great Treatise on the Stages of the Path,* vol. 1, p. 86. This is the quote from Gunaprabha's *Vinaya-sutra.* He also goes on to include the quotation from the *Ratnamegha Sutra.*

71 These lines come from Ashvaghosha's *Fifty Stanzas on the Guru (Guru-pancashika),* v. 24: rigs pa yis ni mi nus na// mi nus de la tshig gis sbyang. They are quoted in Tsongkhapa's *The Great Treatise on the Stages of the Path,* vol. 1, p. 86.

72 The twelve links of dependent origination are: (1) ignorance, (2) karmic formations, (3) consciousness, (4) name and form, (5) the six sense media (ayatana), (6) contact, (7) sensation, (8) craving, (9) grasping, (10) becoming, (11) rebirth, (12) old age and death. The progressive order of these twelve links describes the origination of the samsaric process and their reverse order describes its cessation.

73 The word *ordinary (rang rgyud pa)* here means an emotion that continues on its own track, without being addressed by a remedy or dealt with in some way.

74 Shantideva, *Bodhicharyavatara,* 6:90.

75 Chandrakirti, *Introduction to the Middle Way,* 6:120: nyon mongs skyon rnams ma lus 'jig tshogs la// lta las byung bar blo yis mthong gyur zhing // bdag ni 'di yi yul du rtogs byas nas// rnal 'byor pa yis bdag ni 'gog par byed.

76 This line is from Jamyang Zhepa's *Root Text of Philosophical Tenets (Grub mtha' rtsa ba),* chap. 1: bdag lta'i zhen yul grub 'gog phyi nang gnyis.

77 His Holiness is referring to the research carried out by psychologist Dr. Larry Scherwitz, who taped the conversations of six hundred men, a third of whom were suffering from heart disease and the rest of whom were healthy. He found that men who used the words "I," "me," "my," and "mine" most often had the highest risk of heart trouble. He concluded that the level of self-reference in someone's speech patterns seems to be an indicator of the high risk of heart disease and stress-related illnesses.

78 Nagarjuna, *Ratnavali,* 2:69: g.yan pa 'phrugs na bder 'gyur ba// de bas g.yan pa med pa bde// de bzhin 'jig rten 'dod ldan bde// 'dod pa med pa de bas bde.

79 This classification seems to come from *Lankavatara Sutra.*

80 *gtad so.* The commentary spells this as *brten so;* it is taken to mean "assurance, reliability."

81 This is the theory that phenomena arise by themselves, uncaused. In Tibetan literature this position is mostly attributed to the nihilist Charvaka school of Indian philosophy.

82 The teachings on the gradual path *(lam rim)* categorize beings according to three levels of spiritual capacity. Those of lesser capacity are inspired by a wish to attain the higher states within samsara as human beings or as gods. Beings of middling capacity, the followers of the shravaka and pratyekabuddha paths, seek liberation from samsara for themselves alone. Those of greater capacity, the bodhisattvas, are motivated by the wish to lead all beings to perfect buddhahood.

83 The translation of this line is based on His Holiness' commentary.

84 Shantideva, *Bodhicharyavatara,* 8:129.

85 Shantideva, *Bodhicharyavatara,* 8:130.

86 Verse 483.

87 Shantideva, *Bodhicharyavatara,* 3:21.

88 Shantideva, *Bodhicharyavatara,* 10:55.

89 So called because they were lay practitioners as opposed to monks.

90 There are four kinds of nirmanakaya, the aspect of buddhahood that manifests out of compassion to help ordinary beings: artisan, birth, great enlightenment, and supreme. A supreme nirmanakaya, such as the Buddha Shakyamuni, always displays the twelve deeds: (1) the descent from Tushita, the Joyous pure land, (2) entering the mother's womb, (3) taking birth in the Lumbini garden, (4) becoming skilled in various arts, (5) delighting in the company of royal consorts, (6) developing renunciation and becoming ordained, (7) practicing austerities for six years, (8) proceeding to the foot of the bodhi tree, (9) overcoming Mara's hosts, (10) becoming fully enlightened, (11) turning the wheel of Dharma, and (12) passing into mahaparinirvana in the city of Kushinagara.

91 Shantideva, *Bodhicharyavatara,* 10:55.

92 The original source for what follows is Tsongkhapa's *Basic Path to Awakening (Byang chub gzhung lam).*

93 The exact question is: *"Have you heard the teachings of the bodhisattva pitaka or a summary of them?"* In this context summary refers to Asanga's *Bodhisattva Stages* and the discipline chapter in particular.

94 From Samantabhadra's *Aspiration to Good Actions.*

95 *Venerable one* is the term used when the teacher is a monk of senior rank; other terms are employed if the teacher is a householder or monk of lower seniority. This is explained by Tsongkhapa in *Byang chub gzhung lam,* p. 36a.

96 The "potential of the family" of the bodhisattvas is equivalent to the buddha nature. All beings possess this potential, but in most cases it lies dormant. When an individual meets the right conditions, it is awakened and he or she pursues the bodhisattva path.

97 Chapter 5, verse 31: sangs rgyas byang chub sems dpa' dag//kun du thogs

med gzigs par ldan//de dag thams cad spyan snga na//rtag par bdag ni gnas so zhes.

98 At this juncture, His Holiness stood up on the throne.

99 These are the final two verses from the prayer, *Words of Truth,* composed by His Holiness in Dharamsala in 1960. The prayer is dedicated to restoring peace, the Buddhist teachings, and the culture and self-determination of the Tibetan people in their homeland.

100 On the Great Fifth Dalai Lama, see Dalai Lama, *Dzogchen,* pp. 22–25 and p. 229n4.

101 Tadrak Rinpoche *(stag brag rin po che ngag dbang gsung rab)* served as tutor to His Holiness the Dalai Lama and gave him his vows as a novice monk. He accepted the regentship of Tibet in 1941, resigning in 1950, aged seventy-five, when the Dalai Lama was offered full authority over Tibet. See W.D. Shakabpa, *Tibet: A Political History* (New York: Potala, 1984), p. 286.

102 From *Thugs sgrub yang snying kun 'dus kyi dbang chog padma dgyes pa'i 'jug ngogs,* Collected Works of Jamyang Khyentse Wangpo, Gangtok 1977 ed., vol. 12, p. 503.

103 His Holiness mentioned this in the context of having granted the empowerment of this practice at Lerab Ling four days earlier. (See appendix.)

104 *thugs rje chen po 'jig rten dbang phyug lha dgu.*

105 *khams gsum zil gnon.*

106 *Sixty Verses on Reasoning, Yuktishashtika,* v. 60.

107 His Holiness says: "In the context of sutra, wisdom refers to the wisdom realizing emptiness, and method refers to the practice of the six perfections." See The Dalai Lama, *The World of Tibetan Buddhism,* trans., ed., and ann. Geshe Thupten Jinpa (Boston: Wisdom, 1995), p. 99. Geshe Thupten Sönam adds an explanatory note on the accumulation of merit through skillful means: "It means arousing loving-kindness, compassion, and bodhichitta and training in the related skillful actions, such as generosity."

108 See Dalai Lama, *World of Tibetan Buddhism,* pp. 99–100; see also Dalai Lama, *Dzogchen,* pp. 154–55.

109 bla sgrub.

110 Enlightened body, speech, mind, qualities, activity, and basic space and wisdom.

111 *Dpal gsang ba'i snying po'i rgyud kyi spyi don nyung ngu'i ngag gis rnam par 'byed pa rin chen mdzod kyi lde mig,* in bka' 'bum (si khron mi rigs dpe skrun khang, 2003 version), vol. III (ga), p. 43.

112 "The four empties are respectively termed the empty, the very empty, the great empty and the all-empty and are also called the mind of radiant white appearance, the mind of radiant red or orange increase, the mind of radiant black near-attainment and the mind of clear light." See Daniel Cozort, *Highest*

Yoga Tantra (Ithaca: Snow Lion, 1986), pp. 73–76. "These subtle types of consciousness are to be used to realize emptiness, but they are not themselves emptinesses, nor realizations of emptiness." See *Highest Yoga Tantra*, p. 73.

113 The Prasangika or Consequence tradition is a subdivision of the Madhyamaka school of philosophy. A defining feature of this approach is its use of consequentialist arguments to establish the ultimate truth of emptiness beyond all conceptual elaboration. This approach was first explicitly formulated by the Indian scholar Buddhapalita and later elaborated upon and defended by Chandrakirti.

114 See Dalai Lama, *Dzogchen*, p. 172.

115 The Lamdré (Path with Its Result) teachings developed into two major lines of transmission: the general presentation known as *tsokshé* (Explanation for Assemblies) and the secret presentation known as *lopshé* (Explanation for Private Disciples). As H.H. Sakya Trizin explains: "In the early Sakya tradition, Lamdré was actually one teaching. Later, during the time of Muchen Könchok Gyaltsen, when he gave Lamdré teachings, he gave the most esoteric, essential, and important teachings to his innermost disciples in his private room, whereas for the assemblies he gave the common teachings. Since then there have been two Lamdré." Tsarchen Losal Gyatso (1502–67) was an important master of the Sakya tradition, the founder of the Dar Drangmo Ché monastery and the Tsar school of the Sakya order and holder of the Lamdré Lopshé transmission. A number of his writings survive, especially his compositions on the Hevajra visualization and on the Vajrayogini teachings. His biography was written by the Fifth Dalai Lama. His chief disciples were Mangtö Ludrup Gyatso, Yol Khenchen Zhönnu Lodrö, the Third Dalai Lama Sönam Gyatso, Zhalu Khenchen Khyentse Wangchuk, and Bokarwa Maitri Döndrup Gyaltsen. Information kindly provided by Tibetan Buddhist Resource Center. On Mangtö Ludrup Gyatso, see Dalai Lama, *Dzogchen*, p. 234n44.

116 See Dalai Lama, *Dzogchen*, p. 262.

117 Chapter 3, verse 11. See Dalai Lama, *World of Tibetan Buddhism*, p. 148; see also Dalai Lama, *Dzogchen*, p. 238n82.

118 Jikmé Tenpé Nyima, *Dpal gsang ba'i snying po'i rgyud kyi spyi don nyung ngu'i ngag gis rnam par 'byed pa rin chen mdzod kyi lde mig*, p. 43.

119 *chos nyid kyi sku*. According to Khenpo Namdrol Rinpoche this refers to the svabhavikakaya *(ngo bo nyid kyi sku)*.

120 Jikmé Tenpé Nyima, *Dpal gsang ba'i snying po'i rgyud kyi spyi don nyung ngu'i ngag gis rnam par 'byed pa rin chen mdzod kyi lde mig*, p. 45.

121 Tarthang edition, p. 1180.

122 Tarthang edition, p. 1182.

123 Tarthang edition, pp. 1182–83. *The Fine Array of Jewels (Nor bu bkra bkod)* is

one of the seventeen tantras of the innermost, unexcelled class of the pith instruction category of Dzogchen.

124 Tarthang edition, pp. 1186–87.

125 Tarthang edition, vol. e, p. 151.

126 Tarthang edition, vol. e, p. 151.

127 Tarthang edition, vol. wam, p. 221.

128 Tarthang edition, pp. 234–35.

129 Rdo grub chen 'jigs med bstan pa'i nyi ma'i gsung 'bum (si khron mi rigs dpe skrun khang), vol. 2, p. 27.

130 Verse 80.

131 Verse 81a.

132 Here, His Holiness briefly related this to the need to study *The Seven Treasuries.*

133 These are the first three of the six stages of the completion stage according to the *Guhyasamaja Tantra,* when distinguished according to results.

134 From *Bla ma mchod pa'i cho ga* by Panchen Lozang Chökyi Gyaltsen (1570–1662): des na rje btsun bla ma thugs rje can// ma gyur 'gro ba'i sdig sgrib sdug bsngal kun// ma lus da lta bdag la smin pa dang// bdag gi bde dge gzhan la btang ba yis// 'gro kun bde dang ldan par shog.

135 On "the actual clear light" or "meaning clear light," see Cozort, *Highest Yoga Tantra,* pp. 66, 106–10: see also Yangchen Gawai Lodoe, *Paths and Grounds of Guhyasamaja According to Arya Nagarjuna* (Dharamsala: Library of Tibetan Works and Archives, 1995), pp. 75–80. On "the learner's union," or "trainees' state of union," see *Highest Yoga Tantra,* pp. 66, 111–14 and *Paths and Grounds of Guhyasamaja,* pp. 90–96. The latter quotes *The Five Levels (rim lnga):* "Abiding in the meditative stabilization of the state of union, he/she does not train in any further [new paths]."

136 Khedrup Jé's response is quoted in Dalai Lama, *Kindness, Clarity and Insight,* pp. 203–5; 2006 ed., pp. 231–32. It is from mkhas grub dge legs dpal bzang po'i gsung thor bu'i gras rnams phyogs gcig tu bsdebs pa, *The Collected Works of the Lord Mkhas-grub rJe dGe-legs-dpal-bzang-po* (New Delhi: 1980), 125.1–6.3.

137 *The Collected Works of the Lord Mkhas-grub rJe,* p. 129.

138 From Dodrupchen Jikmé Tenpé Nyima's *Collected Works: sgrub brtson rnal 'byor gyi dbang po padma maha sukha'i bzhed skong du gdams pa, rdo grub chen 'jigs med bstan pa'i nyi ma'i gsung 'bum* (si khron mi rigs dpe skrun khang, 2003), vol. 2, pp. 15–16.

139 Golok Khenchen Münsel (1916–93). His life is described by Nyoshul Khenpo in *A Marvelous Garland of Rare Gems,* pp. 524–26.

140 The *Triyik Yeshé Lama* was composed by Jikmé Lingpa (1730–98) and, as

Tulku Thondup Rinpoche observes, "has become the most comprehensive manual of Dzogpachenpo meditation in the Nyingma tradition." Based on the innermost, unexcelled cycle of the category of pith instructions, it incorporates the essence of the Dzogchen tantras and presents primarily the practical instructions for trekchö and tögal, along with instructions for liberation in the bardo states and liberation in pure nirmanakaya realms.

141 Born in eastern Tibet, Khenpo Rinchen taught at Dzongsar monastery before fleeing into exile in India. He became the teacher of H.H. Sakya Trizin and served as the main Sakya khenpo at the Tibetan Institute in Sarnath, as well as head khenpo at the Sakya monastery in Puruwala. During the Kalachakra empowerment in Bodhgaya in 1974, he was praised by H.H. the Dalai Lama as a teacher who had mastered the scholarship of all four schools of Tibetan Buddhism. His Holiness also spoke of Khenpo Rinchen at Lerab Ling in 2000: "I think there are hardly any teachers, Geluk, Nyingma, Kagyü, or Sakya, who know the teachings of all the other schools. From my own experience, I can say that the late Khenpo Rinchen was one who did: he really was an excellent master."

142 See Dalai Lama, *Dzogchen*, p. 234n45; see also Dalai Lama, *World of Tibetan Buddhism*, p. 151.

143 Its full title is *Ornament to the Wisdom Mind of Samantabhadra: A Secret Instruction Directly Revealing the View of the Clear Light Dzogpachenpo and Dispelling All Wrong Views*. In Tibetan: *'Od gsal rdzogs pa chen po'i lta ba dmar 'byin gsang khrid log rtog kun sel kun bzang dgongs rgyan*. It appears in volume *kha* of Tsultrim Zangpo's collected works. The extract given here begins on page 9a.

144 The nine actions of the three doors; all outer, inner, and secret activities of body, speech, and mind. Three concern the body: (1) outwardly, all worldly, distracting activities, (2) inwardly, all ordinary virtuous deeds such as prostrations and circumambulations, and (3) secretly, all unnecessary movements that scatter one's practice. Three concern speech: (1) outwardly, all worldly, deluded conversations, (2) inwardly, all liturgies and recitations, and (3) secretly, any talking whatsoever. Three concern the mind: (1) outwardly, all worldly, deluded thoughts, (2) inwardly, all mental activity focused on visualizations of the development and the completion stages, and (3) secretly, all movements of the mind.

145 See The Dalai Lama, *The Meaning of Life*, trans. and ed. Jeffrey Hopkins (Boston: Wisdom, 1992), p. 43.

146 See Milarepa, *The Hundred Thousand Songs of Milarepa*, trans. and ann. Garma C.C. Chang (Boston: Shambhala, 1999), pp. 122–30.

147 Tsultrim Zangpo, *Ornament to the Wisdom Mind*, p. 6a.

148 Tsultrim Zangpo, *Ornament to the Wisdom Mind*, p. 33b.

149 The root tantra of the seventeen tantras of the innermost, unexcelled class of the pith instructions of Dzogchen, *Sgra thal 'gyur rtsa ba'i rgyud.*

150 A secret name of the Great Fifth Dalai Lama.

151 In London in 1984, His Holiness quoted Dodrupchen: "In this respect, Dodrup Jikmé Tenpé Nyima says that once you understand all phenomena to be the energy, or the display, of this self-arising rigpa, then it is very straightforward to realize that all phenomena only seem to exist as a result of concepts, of them being labeled to be so." *Dzogchen,* p. 69. He has referred to this statement on a number of occasions, for instance, "Dodrup-chen says that when we are able to ascertain all appearing and occurring objects of knowledge as the sport of the basic mind, we perforce understand even better the position of the Consequence School that these exist only through the power of conceptuality." *Kindness, Clarity and Insight,* p. 214. See also *World of Tibetan Buddhism,* p. 120; and H.H. the Dalai Lama and Alexander Berzin, *The Gelug/Kagyü Tradition of Mahamudra* (Ithaca: Snow Lion, 1997), pp. 225–26.

152 Tsultrim Zangpo, *Ornament to the Wisdom Mind,* pp. 10b–11a.

153 Tsultrim Zangpo, *Ornament to the Wisdom Mind,* p. 11b.

154 The Tibetan terms are, respectively: *gnyug ma, rtag pa, 'dus ma byas pa'i ye shes, zang thal le, phyal ba chen po.* The terms in the following paragraph are: *ma bcos pa, rang gsal, 'od gsal, bde chen lhan skyes kyi ye shes, nang gsal gyi ye shes, sems las 'das pa'i ye shes, ye shes lnga'i rang bzhin, gzhi'i chos sku.*

155 Longchenpa, *Precious Wish-Fulfilling Treasury, A Treatise of Pith Instructions on the Greater Vehicle,* p. 152. "Furthermore, it [i.e., the ground] provides some basis for karma and the disturbing emotions and the phenomena of samsara but without them actually depending on it. These [phenomena] abide within the realm of the ground, without actually touching it or becoming part of it, just as clouds are, in some sense, 'supported by' the sky." de yang 'khor ba'i chos las dang nyon mongs pa rnams rten pa med pa'i tshul gyis brten pa ni/ nyi mkha'i ngos na sprin phung brten pa ltar/ gzhi la ma reg ma 'byar la de'i ngang la gnas pa ste.

156 Tsultrim Zangpo, *Ornament to the Wisdom Mind,* p. 14b.

157 The first Panchen Lama, Lozang Chökyi Gyaltsen, composed a famous root text, with an auto-commentary, on mahamudra, entitled: *Dge ldan bka' brgyud rin po che 'i phyag chen rtsa ba rgyal ba'i gzhung lam.* See Dalai Lama and Berzin, *The Gelug/Kagyü Tradition of Mahamudra.*

158 The Tibetan term is *had de ba.* See Dalai Lama, *Dzogchen,* pp. 66–67, 194–95.

159 The Tibetan terms are, respectively, *ye grol, rang drol, cer grol, rnam grol, mtha' grol.*

160 See Dalai Lama, *Dzogchen,* pp. 83–84, 186–87.

161 His Holiness discusses these in *Dzogchen,* pp. 50, 171, 196. Sometimes the

third chokshak, "action, appearances: leave them as they are," is given as "action, the pith instruction, leave it as it is."

162 As Professor H.V. Guenther noted, the word *bstan,* meaning "teachings," appears in the root text and also when the root text is given in the auto-commentary, *The Chariot of Utter Purity (Shing rta rnam dag);* but in commenting on this line, Longchenpa uses the word *brtan,* meaning "firm" or "stable." Both senses are incorporated into the translation. Cf. Longchenpa, *Kindly Bent to Ease Us,* trans. and ann. Herbert V. Guenther (Berkeley: Dharma Publishing, 1975–76), part 2, pp. 59, 103.

163 This line appears in the auto-commentary but not in the root text.

164 See note 80 above.

165 This section of the text describes certain advanced yogic postures, and the language used is metaphoric. For example, *ocean* signifies the abdomen, and *rocky shore* signifies the spine.

166 The commentary has a different version of this line: "The posture is as before, but in particular do not move your eyes."

167 The commentary says the movement of breath is imperceptible.

168 The commentary mentions that there are ten such signs.

169 The root text has *phyi nang* (outer and inner), but the same line appears in the commentary as *snga phyi* (earlier and later).

170 Dilgo Khyentse Rinpoche received the transmission from Jamyang Khyentse Chökyi Lodrö, who had received it from Tertön Sogyal himself.

171 See Tulku Thondup, *Hidden Teachings of Tibet: An Exploration of the Terma Tradition of the Nyingma School of Buddhism* (London: Wisdom, 1986). See also Andreas Doctor, *Tibetan Treasure Literature* (Ithaca: Snow Lion, 2005).

172 Kyabjé Dilgo Khyentse Rinpoche, August 17, 1990.

173 Quoted in a text in the Thirteenth Dalai Lama's *Collected Works* concerning *The Most Secret Cycle of the Mandala of Hayagriva* and the consecration of medicine, according to the pure visions of the Great Fifth Dalai Lama.

GLOSSARY

Some of the terms that appear in this book are listed below. Those marked with an asterisk have more than one English equivalent.

absolute truth *don dam bden pa*
actual clear light *don gyi 'od gsal*
affirming negation *ma yin dgag*
afflictions* *nyon mongs pa*
alaya* *kun gzhi*
all-penetrating* *zang thal*
analytical meditation *dpyad sgom*
appearances *snang ba*
appearances from the ground *gzhi snang*
attainment *thob pa*
basic space *dbyings*
basic space of reality *chos kyi dbyings*
bodhichitta *byang chub kyi sems*
body isolation *lus dben*
calm abiding* *zhi gnas*
cessation *'gog pa*
channels *rtsa*
clear light *'od gsal*
clear seeing* *lhag mthong*
coemergent wisdom of unchanging great bliss *mi 'gyur ba'i bde chen lhan cig skyes pa'i ye shes*

compassionate energy *thugs rje*
completion stage *rdzogs rim*
cognitive obscurations *shes bya'i sgrib pa*
conditioned *'dus byas*
confrontational antidote *sun 'byin pa'i gnyen po*
conscientiousness *bag yod*
consciousness *shes pa; rnam shes*
correct doubt *don 'gyur gyi the tshom*
definitive goodness *nges legs*
Dharma of realization *rtogs pa'i chos*
Dharma of transmission *lung gi chos*
dharmakaya of inward radiance *nang gsal chos sku*
direct fruits of valid cognition *bar du mi chod pa'i tshad ma'i 'bras bu*
display *rol pa*
disturbing emotions* *nyon mongs pa*
effulgent rigpa *rtsal gyi rig pa*
eight worldly preoccupations *'jig rten chos brgyad*
eighty indicative conceptions *rang bzhin brgyad cu'i kun rtog*
emotional obscurations* *nyon mongs pa'i sgrib pa*
empowerment of the energy of rigpa *rig pa'i rtsal dbang*
emptiness *stong pa nyid*
emptiness endowed with the supreme of all attributes *rnam kun mchog ldan gyi stong pa nyid*
energy* *rtsal*
essence *ngo bo*
essences *thig le*
essential rigpa *ngo bo'i rig pa*
extraordinary powers of perception *mngon shes*
freedom from conceptual elaboration *spros bral*
four empties *stong pa bzhi*
four ways of leaving things in their natural simplicity *cog bzhag bzhi*
fruition that is all-embracing spontaneous presence *'bras bu lhun grub sbubs*
fundamental innate mind of clear light *gnyug ma lhan cig skyes pa'i 'od gsal*
generation stage *bskyed rim*
Great Perfection *rdzogs pa chen po*
ground of all* *kun gzhi*

habitual tendencies *bag chags*
habitual tendencies of expression *mngon brjod kyi bag chags*
habitual tendencies of similar type *rigs mthun gyi bag chags*
habitual tendencies of the branches of conditioned existence *srid pa'i yan lag gi bag chags*
habitual tendencies of the transference of the three appearances *snang gsum 'pho ba'i bag chags*
habitual tendencies of the view of self *bdag lta'i bag chags*
higher absolute truth *lhag pa'i don dam bden pa*
higher relative truth *lhag pa'i kun rdzob bden pa*
highest yoga tantra *bla med rgyud*
ignorance *ma rig pa*
illusory body *sgyu lus*
incorrect doubt *don mi 'gyur gyi the tshom*
indirect fruits of valid cognition *bar du chod pa'i tshad ma'i 'bras bu*
inseparability of samsara and nirvana *'khor 'das dbyer med*
insight* *lhag mthong*
introspective vigilance *shes bzhin*
learners' union *slob pa'i zung 'jug*
learning, discipline, and kind-heartedness *mkhas btsun bzang gsum*
liberation beyond benefit and harm *phan gnod med pa'i grol ba*
Mahamudra *phyag rgya chen po*
meditative experience *nyams*
mental afflictions* *nyon mongs pa*
Middle Way *dbu ma*
mind isolation *sems dben*
Mind Only *sems tsam pa*
moral dignity *khrel yod*
mother luminosity *ma'i 'od gsal*
natural innate kaya *rang bzhin lhan cig skyes pa'i sku*
natural nirvana *rang bzhin myang 'das*
nature *rang bzhin*
near-attainment *nyer thob*
nirvana with remainder *lhag bcas myang 'das*
nirvana without remainder *lhag med myang 'das*
nonabiding nirvana *mi gnas pa'i myang 'das*

nonassociated formations *ldan min 'du byed*
nonimplicative negation *med dgag*
nontransferable actions *mi g.yo ba'i las*
obstructive forces *bdud*
other-empty *gzhan stong*
perceptions *'du shes*
personal selflessness *gang zag gi bdag med*
pith instruction *man ngag*
primordial purity *ka dag*
primordial wisdom* *ye shes*
postmeditation *rjes thob*
potential of the family *rigs*
qualities of basic space *dbyings kyi yon tan*
qualities of fruition *'bras bu'i yon tan*
reality *chos nyid*
realization *rtogs pa*
relative truth *kun rdzob bden pa*
rigpa of all-embracing spontaneous presence that is the ultimate state of freedom *mthar thug lhun grub sbubs kyi rig pa*
rigpa of the ground *gzhi'i rig pa*
samadhi *ting nge 'dzin*
sambhogakaya of outward radiance *phyi gsal longs sku*
searching for the hidden flaw of mind *sems kyi mtshang btsal ba*
self-arising wisdom *rang byung gi ye shes*
self-empty *rang stong*
self-liberation *rang grol*
self-restraint *ngo tsha shes*
selflessness of phenomena *chos kyi bdag med*
sensations *tshor ba*
separating samsara and nirvana *'khor 'das ru shan*
settling meditation *'jog sgom*
seven bountiful attributes of absolute truth *don dam dkor bdun*
shamatha* *zhi gnas*
speech isolation *ngag dben*
spontaneous presence *lhun grub*
suffering of change *'gyur ba'i sdug bsngal*

suffering of suffering *sdug bsngal gyi sdug bsngal*
thought states *kun rtog*
three continuums *rgyud gsum*
transcendent perfection of wisdom *shes rab kyi pha rol tu phyin pa*
uncertain doubt *cha mnyam gyi the tshom*
uncompounded* *'dus ma byas*
unconditioned* *'dus ma byas*
uncontrived *ma bcos pa*
unimpeded (clarity) *zang thal le*
untainted actions *zag med kyi las*
valid cognition *tshad ma*
valid direct perception *mngon sum tshad ma*
valid inference *rjes dpag tshad ma*
vehicles leading from the origin *kun 'byung 'dren pa'i theg pa*
vehicles of supreme and powerful transformative methods *dbang sgyur thabs kyi theg pa*
vehicles of Vedic asceticism *dka' thub rig byed kyi theg pa*
view of the transitory collection *'jig tshogs kyi lta ba*
wind energy *rlung*
wisdom* *ye shes; shes rab*
wisdom of one's own self-knowing awareness *so so rang rig pa'i ye shes*
wonderstruck *had de ba*
youthful vase body *gzhon nu bum sku*

BIBLIOGRAPHY

WORKS CITED BY HIS HOLINESS

SUTRAS AND TANTRAS

Guhyasamaja Tantra
Guhyasamajanamamahakalparaja
Gsang ba 'dus pa zhes bya ba brtag pa'i rgyal po chen po

Hevajra Tantra
Hevajratantraraja
Kye'i rdo rje zhes bya ba rgyud kyi rgyal po

Kalachakra Tantra
Shrikalachakranamatantraraja
Dpal dus kyi 'khor lo'i rgyud kyi rgyal po

Reverberation of Sound Root Tantra
Sgra thal 'gyur rtsa ba'i rgyud

Sutra of the Wisdom of Passing Beyond
Atajñananama-sutra
'Phags pa 'da' ka ye shes kyi mdo

Sutra Requested by Upali
Upalipariprccha-sutra
Nye bar 'khor gyis zhus pa'i mdo

Transcendent Wisdom in Eight Thousand Lines
Ashtasahasrikaprajñaparamitasutra
'Phags pa shes rab kyi pha rol tu phyin pa brgyad stong pa'i mdo

TREATISES AND COMMENTARIES

Aryadeva
Four Hundred Verses on the Middle Way
Chatuhshatakashastrakarika
Bstan bcos bzhi brgya pa zhes bya ba'i tshig le'ur byas pa

Asanga
Bodhisattva Stages
Bodhisattvabhumi
Byang chub sems dpa'i sa

Ashvaghosha
Fifty Stanzas on the Guru
Gurupanchashika
Bla ma lnga bcu pa

Chandrakirti
Introduction to the Middle Way
Madhyamakavatara
Dbu ma la 'jug pa

Clear Words
Prasannapada
Dbu ma rtsa ba'i 'grel pa tshig gsal ba

Dharmakirti
Commentary on "Valid Cognition"
Pramanavarttikakarika
Tshad ma rnam 'grel gyi tshig le'ur byas pa

Maitreya
Discriminating the Middle from the Extremes
Madhyantavibhanga
Dbus dang mtha' rnam par 'byed pa

Ornament of the Mahayana Sutras
Mahayanasutralamkara
Theg chen mdo sde rgyan

Ornament of Clear Realization
Abhisamayalamkara
Mngon par rtogs pa'i rgyan

Sublime Continuum of the Great Vehicle
Mahayana-uttaratantrashastra
Theg pa chen po rgyud bla ma'i bstan bcos

Nagabodhi
Analysis of Action
Karmantavibhanga
Las mtha' rnam 'byed

Nagarjuna
Fundamental Treatise on the Middle Way
Mulamadhyamakakarika
Dbu ma rtsa ba'i tshig le'ur byas pa

Precious Garland
Ratnavali
Rin chen phreng ba

Shantideva
The Way of the Bodhisattva
Bodhicharyavatara
Byang chub sems dpa'i spyod pa la 'jug pa

Compendium of Training
Shikshasamucchaya
Bslab pa kun las btus pa

Vasubandhu
Treasury of Knowledge
Abhidharmakoshakarika
Chos mngon pa'i mdzod kyi tshig le'ur byas pa

TIBETAN WORKS

Dodrupchen, Jikmé Tenpé Nyima
Advice to Fulfill the Wishes of the Diligent Practitioner, the Lord of Yogins, Padma Mahasukha
Sgrub brtson rnal 'byor gyi dbang po padma maha sukha'i bzhed skong du gdams pa, rdo grub chen 'jigs med bstan pa'i nyi ma'i gsung 'bum, published by si khron mi rigs dpe skrun khang, 2003, vol. 2, pp. 15–16.

Vajra Mortar: Words of Advice
Gdams ngag rdo rje'i gtun khung, vol. 2, pp. 25–31.

The Key to the Precious Treasury: A Brief Overview of the Glorious Secret Essence Tantra
Dpal gsang ba'i snying po'i rgyud kyi spyi don nyung ngu'i ngag gis rnam par 'byed pa rin chen mdzod kyi lde mig, vol. 3, pp. 1–206.

Great Fifth Dalai Lama
Words of the Vidyadharas: An Instruction Manual on Generation, Completion and the Great Perfection for the Great Compassionate One, Liberation of Samsara into Basic Space
Thugs rje chen po 'khor ba dbyings sgrol gyi bskyed rdzogs rdzogs pa chen po'i khrid yig rigs 'dzin zhal lung, Collected Works, vol. nang ga, pp. 51–152.

Jamyang Khyentse Wangpo
Entranceway Delighting Padmasambhava: The Empowerment Ritual for the Mind Sadhana of the Union of All the Innermost Essences
Thugs sgrub yang snying kun 'dus kyi dbang chog padma dgyes pa'i 'jug ngogs. Collected Works of Jamyang Khyentse Wangpo, Gangtok 1977 edition, vol. 12, p. 503.

Khedrup Norzang Gyatso
Ornament of Stainless Light: An Overview of the Kalachakra Tantra
Dus 'khor spyi don dri med 'od rgyan

Longchen Rabjam
from *The Trilogy of Finding Comfort and Ease (Ngal gso skor gsum):*

Finding Comfort and Ease in Meditation on the Great Perfection
Rdzogs pa chen po bsam gtan ngal gso
From Rdzogs pa chen po ngal gso skor gsum dang rang grol skor gsum: a reproduction of the A-'dzom Xylographic Edition, Gangtok 1999, vol. 3, pp. 1–24.

Chariot of Utter Purity: A Commentary on Finding Comfort and Ease in Meditation on the Great Perfection
Rdzogs pa chen po bsam gtan ngal gso'i 'grel pa shing rta rnam par dag pa vol. 3, pp. 35–126.

Ocean of Excellent Explanation: An Overview of the Trilogy of Comfort and Ease
Ngal gso skor gsum gyi spyi don legs bshad rgya mtsho
vol. 3, pp. 131–249.

from *The Seven Treasuries (Mdzod bdun):*

Precious Treasury of Philosophical Tenets Clarifying the Meaning of All Vehicles
Theg pa mtha' dag gi don gsal bar byed pa grub pa'i mtha' rin po che'i mdzod

Precious Wish-Fulfilling Treasury, A Treatise of Pith Instructions on the Greater Vehicle

Theg pa chen po'i man ngag gi bstan bcos yid bzhin rin po che'i mdzod

White Lotus: A Commentary on the Precious Wish-Fulfilling Treasury, A Treatise of Pith Instructions on the Greater Vehicle
Theg pa chen po'i man ngag gi bstan bcos yid bzhin rin po che'i mdzod kyi 'grel pa pad ma dkar po

Patrul Rinpoche
The Special Teaching of the Wise and Glorious King, with Its Commentary
Mkhas pa shri rgyal po'i khyad chos 'grel pa dang bcas pa
Collected Works, Dpal sprul o rgyan 'jigs med chos kyi dbang po'i gsung 'bum, published by Si khron mi rigs dpe skrun khang, 2003, vol. 4, pp. 737–54.

Tsongkhapa
The Basic Path to Awakening
Byang chub gzhung lam

Tsultrim Zangpo
Ornament to the Wisdom Mind of Samantabhadra: A Secret Instruction Directly Revealing the View of the Clear Light Dzogpachenpo and Dispelling All Wrong Views
'Od gsal rdzogs pa chen po'i lta ba dmar 'byin gsang khrid log rtog kun sel kun bzang dgongs rgyan, Collected Works, vol. kha.

SELECTED ENGLISH-LANGUAGE BIBLIOGRAPHY

BY HIS HOLINESS THE DALAI LAMA

Destructive Emotions, A Scientific Dialogue with His Holiness the Dalai Lama. Narrated by Daniel Goleman. New York: Bantam, 2003.

H.H. the Dalai Lama. *Dzogchen: The Heart Essence of the Great Perfection.* Translated by Geshe Thupten Jinpa and Richard Barron. Ithaca: Snow Lion, 2000.

Tenzin Gyatso, the Fourteenth Dalai Lama. *Essence of the Heart Sutra.* Translated and edited by Geshe Thupten Jinpa. Boston: Wisdom, 2002.

Tenzin Gyatso. *Flash of Lightning in the Dark of Night.* Boston: Shambhala, 1994.

His Holiness the Dalai Lama. *The Four Noble Truths.* Translated by Geshe Thupten Jinpa. Edited by Dominique Side. London: Thorsons, 1997.

H.H. the Dalai Lama and Alexander Berzin. *The Gelug/Kagyü Tradition of Mahamudra*. Ithaca: Snow Lion, 1997.

The Dalai Lama and Jeffrey Hopkins. *The Kalachakra Tantra*. Boston: Wisdom, 1989.

The Fourteenth Dalai Lama. *Kindness, Clarity and Insight*. Translated and edited by Jeffrey Hopkins and Elizabeth Napper. Ithaca: Snow Lion, 1984. New edition, 2006.

The Dalai Lama. *The Meaning of Life*. Translated and edited by Jeffrey Hopkins. Boston: Wisdom, 1992.

Tenzin Gyatso and Jean-Claude Carrière. *The Power of Buddhism*. Dublin: Gill & Macmillan, 1996.

His Holiness the Dalai Lama. *Practicing Wisdom, The Perfection of Shantideva's Bodhisattva Way*. Translated and edited by Geshe Thupten Jinpa. Boston: Wisdom, 2005.

His Holiness the Dalai Lama. *Transforming the Mind*. Translated by Geshe Thupten Jinpa. Edited by Dominique Side. London: Thorsons, 2000.

His Holiness the Dalai Lama. *The Universe in a Single Atom*. New York: Morgan Road Books, 2005.

The Dalai Lama. *The World of Tibetan Buddhism*. Translated, edited, and annotated by Geshe Thupten Jinpa. Boston: Wisdom, 1995.

ON BUDDHISM AND DZOGCHEN

Aryadeva. *Yogic Deeds of the Bodhisattvas*. Gyel-tsap on Aryadeva's Four Hundred. Commentary by Geshe Sonam Rinchen. Translated and edited by Ruth Sonam. Ithaca: Snow Lion, 1994.

Chökyi Nyima Rinpoche and Erik Pema Kunsang. *Indisputable Truth*. Rangjung Yeshe, 1996.

Cozort, Daniel. *Highest Yoga Tantra*. Ithaca: Snow Lion, 1986.

Deshung Rinpoche. *The Three Levels of Spiritual Perception*. Translated by Jared Rhoton. Boston: Wisdom, 1995.

Drubwang Tsoknyi Rinpoche. *Carefree Dignity*. Compiled and translated by Erik Pema Kunsang and Marcia Binder Schmidt. Edited by Kerry Moran. Boudhanath: Rangjung Yeshe, 1998.

Dudjom Rinpoche. *The Nyingma School of Tibetan Buddhism.* Translated and edited by Gyurme Dorje, with the collaboration of Matthew Kapstein. Boston: Wisdom, 1991.

Hopkins, Jeffrey. *Buddhist Advice for Living and Liberation: Nagarjuna's Precious Garland.* Ithaca: Snow Lion, 1998.

———. *Meditation on Emptiness.* Boston: Wisdom, 1983.

Khedrup Norsang Gyatso. *Ornament of Stainless Light: An Exposition of the Kalacakra Tantra.* Translated by Gavin Kilty. Boston: Wisdom, 2004.

Khenpo Ngawang Palzang. A *Guide to The Words of My Perfect Teacher.* Translated under the auspices of Dipamkara, in collaboration with the Padmakara Translation Group. Boston: Shambhala, 2004.

Longchen Rabjam. *The Precious Treasury of the Way of Abiding.* Translated under the direction of H.E. Chagdud Tulku Rinpoche by Richard Barron (Chökyi Nyima). Edited by Padma Translation Committee. Junction City: Padma Publishing, 1998.

———. *The Precious Treasury of the Basic Space of Phenomena & A Treasure Trove of Scriptural Transmission.* Translated under the direction of H.E. Chagdud Tulku Rinpoche by Richard Barron (Chökyi Nyima). Edited by Padma Translation Committee. Junction City: Padma Publishing, 2001.

Longchenpa. *Kindly Bent to Ease Us,* parts 1–3. Translated and annotated by Herbert V. Guenther. Berkeley: Dharma Publishing, 1975–76.

Maitreya. *Maitreya on Buddha Nature.* A new translation of Asanga's Mahayana Uttara Tantra Sastra by Ken and Katia Holmes. Forres: Altea, 1999.

Maitreyanatha / Aryasangha. *The Universal Vehicle Discourse Literature Together with Its Commentary by Vasubandhu.* New York: American Institute of Buddhist Studies, 2004.

Milarepa. *The Hundred Thousand Songs of Milarepa.* Translated and annotated by Garma C.C. Chang. Boston: Shambhala, 1999.

Mipham. *Mipham's Beacon of Certainty.* Translated by John Whitney Pettit. Boston: Wisdom, 1999.

Nagarjuna. *The Fundamental Wisdom of the Middle Way, Nagarjuna's Mulamadhyamakakarika.* Translation and commentary by Jay L. Garfield. New York: Oxford University Press, 1995.

Namkhai Norbu. Dzogchen, *The Self-Perfected State.* Edited by Adriano Clemente. Translated from the Italian by John Shane. London: Arkana, 1989.

Ngorchen Konchog Lhundrub. *The Beautiful Ornament of the Three Visions.* Translated by Lobsang Dagpa, Ngawang Samten Chophel, and Jared Rhoton. Singapore: Golden Vase, 1987; Ithaca: Snow Lion, 1991.

Nyoshul Khenpo. *A Marvelous Garland of Rare Gems, Biographies of Masters of Awareness in the Dzogchen Lineage.* Junction City: Padma Publishing, 2005.

Padmasambhava. *Advice from the Lotus Born.* Translated by Erik Pema Kunsang. Boudhanath: Rangjung Yeshe, 1994.

Patrul Rinpoche. *The Heart Treasure of the Enlightened Ones.* Commentary by Dilgo Khyentse. Translated by the Padmakara Translation Group. Boston: Shambhala, 1992.

Patrul Rinpoche. *The Words of My Perfect Teacher.* Translated by the Padmakara Translation Group. Boston: Shambhala, 1998.

Ringu Tulku. *The Ri-mé Philosophy of Jamgön Kongtrul the Great.* Boston: Shambhala, 2006.

Shantideva. *The Way of the Bodhisattva.* Translated by the Padmakara Translation Group. Boston: Shambhala, 1997.

Sogyal Rinpoche. *Dzogchen and Padmasambhava.* Santa Cruz: Rigpa, 1989.

———. *The Tibetan Book of Living and Dying.* San Francisco: Harper, 1992. Revised edition, San Francisco, Harper, 2002; London: Rider, 2002.

Takpo Tashi Namgyal. *Mahamudra: The Quintessence of Mind and Meditation.* Translated and annotated by Lobsang P. Lhalungpa. Foreword by C. Trungpa. Delhi: Motilal Banarsidass, 1993.

Thurman, R.A.F. *The Central Philosophy of Tibet: A Study and Translation of Jey Tsongkhapa's Essence of True Eloquence.* Princeton: Princeton University Press, 1991.

Tsele Natsok Rangdrol. *Circle of the Sun.* Translated by Erik Pema Kunsang. Boudhanath: Rangjung Yeshe, 1990.

Tsering, Geshe Tashi. *The Four Noble Truths.* Boston: Wisdom, 2005.

Tsong-kha-pa. *Great Treatise on the Stages of the Path to Enlightenment.* vols. 1–3. Translated by the Lamrim Chenmo Translation Committee. Ithaca: Snow Lion, vol. 1, 2000; vol. 2, 2004; vol. 3, 2002.

Tsongkhapa. *The Splendor of an Autumn Moon*. Translated by Gavin Kilty. Boston: Wisdom, 2001.

Tulku Thondup. *Buddha Mind*. Ithaca: Snow Lion, 1989.

———. *Masters of Meditation and Miracles*. Edited by Harold Talbott. Boston: Shambhala, 1996.

Tulku Urgyen Rinpoche. *As It Is,* vols. 1 and 2. Translated by Erik Pema Kunsang. Boudhanath: Rangjung Yeshe, 1999 & 2000.

———. *Rainbow Painting*. Translated by Erik Pema Kunsang. Boudhanath: Rangjung Yeshe, 1995.

Yangchen Gawai Lodoe. *Paths and Grounds of Guhyasamaja According to Arya Nagarjuna*. Dharamsala: Library of Tibetan Works and Archives, 1995.

Yongey Mingyur Rinpoche. *The Joy of Living: Unlocking the Secret and Science of Happiness*. New York: Harmony Books, 2007.

ACKNOWLEDGMENTS

WE WOULD LIKE TO EXPRESS our deepest gratitude to His Holiness the Dalai Lama for his kindness in granting the teachings at Lerab Ling in September 2000. We would also like to thank Sogyal Rinpoche for having played such a leading role in inviting His Holiness to give these teachings, and for his continuing inspiration.

With regard to His Holiness' visit to France 2000, we would like to pay homage to and thank Kyabjé Trulshik Rinpoche for his constant support and guidance, and thank equally Khamtrul Rinpoche, the Nechung Oracle, Jadho Rinpoche, and the monks of the Namgyal monastery, especially Tashi Dakpa-la, Pasang, and Namgyal.

We would like to give our heartfelt thanks to Tenzin Geyche Tethong and the Private Office of His Holiness the Dalai Lama, to Ven. Geshe Lhakdor-la, and to the Bureau du Tibet, and especially Kunzang Yuthok-la.

A special note of gratitude must be sounded for Lodi Gyari Rinpoche, His Holiness the Dalai Lama's Special Envoy, for his tireless work for Tibet, his service to His Holiness, and his constant help and advice to Rigpa at every level.

Our gratitude goes to Lama Seunam and Lama Tcheuky Sengue, and the members of the Association Golfe du Lion: Kagyü Rintchen Tcheu Ling, Kagu Yi-Ong Tcheu Ling, Jardin du Dharma, and Jardin de Claire Lumière, and we are most obliged to the Fédération du Bouddhisme Tibétain for their wise guidance.

Thanks go to those who played a key role in organizing this event, notably: Philip Philippou, Jean Lanoe, Olivier Fournier, Anne Wodrascka,

Herve Bienfait, Ian Maxwell, Mauro de March, Renate Handel, Laurence Bibas-Dahan, Seth Dye, Kimberly Poppe, Dominique Hilly, Tim Synge, Heidi Lindstedt, Pamela Truscott and many other Rigpa members too numerous to mention, including nearly four hundred volunteers.

We are grateful also to the Préfecture of Montpellier, the Mayors of Lodève, Roqueredonde, and the Larzac Plateau, and especially J.M. Barascut, Mayor of Les Rives.

For the translation work involved in this book, we would like to thank Matthieu Ricard, Richard Barron (Lama Chökyi Nyima), Adam Pearcey, Ane Samten Palmo, and Dominique Side. Grateful thanks also to B. Alan Wallace for his assistance in 2000. We would like to thank Ven. Geshe Lhakdor and Ven. Geshe Thupten Sönam for the transcription of the teachings into Tibetan. We are very deeply indebted to the kindness of Tulku Thondup Rinpoche, Ringu Tulku Rinpoche, Khenchen Namdrol, Geshe Thupten Jinpa, and Geshe Tashi Tsering, for their generous clarifications. The translators would like to pay tribute to the late Prof. H.V. Guenther's pioneering translation of *The Trilogy of Finding Comfort and Ease* published in 1975 as *Kindly Bent to Ease Us.*

In creating this book Susie Godfrey, David Haggerty, Ane Tsöndru, Sue Morrison, Andreas Schulz, Peter Fry, Sean Price, Mark and Jane Fulton, and Lorraine Velez have all played a vital part.

We also thank Tim McNeill and David Kittelstrom of Wisdom Publications for their gracious and expert advice.

As for any errors or inaccuracies which have crept into this work, the editor reserves the right to claim them entirely as his own.

The purpose of publishing this book has been to be of some small service to His Holiness the Dalai Lama, to make these teachings available, and to help them benefit as many as possible.

PATRICK GAFFNEY
RIGPA INTERNATIONAL

INDEX

S

ABOUT WISDOM PUBLICATIONS

Wisdom Publications, a nonprofit publisher, is dedicated to making available authentic works relating to Buddhism for the benefit of all. We publish books by ancient and modern masters in all traditions of Buddhism, translations of important texts, and original scholarship. Additionally, we offer books that explore East-West themes unfolding as traditional Buddhism encounters our modern culture in all its aspects. Our titles are published with the appreciation of Buddhism as a living philosophy, and with the special commitment to preserve and transmit important works from Buddhism's many traditions.

To learn more about Wisdom, or to browse books online, visit our website at www.wisdompubs.org.

You may request a copy of our catalog online or by writing to this address:

Wisdom Publications
199 Elm Street
Somerville, Massachusetts 02144 USA
Telephone: 617-776-7416
Fax: 617-776-7841
Email: info@wisdompubs.org
www.wisdompubs.org

THE WISDOM TRUST

As a nonprofit publisher, Wisdom is dedicated to the publication of Dharma books for the benefit of all sentient beings and dependent upon the kindness and generosity of sponsors in order to do so. If you would like to make a donation to Wisdom, you may do so through our website or our Somerville office. If you would like to help sponsor the publication of a book, please write or email us at the address above.

Thank you.

Wisdom is a nonprofit, charitable 501(c)(3) organization affiliated with the Foundation for the Preservation of the Mahayana Tradition (FPMT)

ALSO BY HIS HOLINESS THE DALAI LAMA

The Compassionate Life. Wisdom, 2003.

Essence of the Heart Sutra: The Dalai Lama's Heart of Wisdom Teachings. Translated and edited by Geshe Thupten Jinpa. Wisdom, 2002.

The Good Heart: A Buddhist Perspective on the Teachings of Jesus. Translated by Geshe Thupten Jinpa, introduction by Laurence Freeman, OSB. Wisdom, 1996.

Kalachakra Tantra: Rite of Initiation. Translated, edited, and introduced by Jeffrey Hopkins. Wisdom, 1999.

Imagine all the People: A Conversation with the Dalai Lama on Money, Politics, and Life as It Could Be. With Fabien Ouaki. Wisdom, 1999.

The Meaning of Life: Buddhist Perspectives on Cause and Effect. Edited and translated by Jeffrey Hopkins. Wisdom, 2000.

MindScience: An East-West Dialogue. With Herbert Benson, Robert A.F. Thurman, Howard E. Gardner, and Daniel Goleman. Wisdom, 1991.

Opening the Eye of New Awareness. Translated and introduced by Donald S. Lopez, Jr. Wisdom, 1999.

Practicing Wisdom: The Perfection of Shantideva's Bodhisattva Way. Translated and edited by Geshe Thupten Jinpa. Wisdom, 2005.

Sleeping, Dreaming, and Dying: An Exploration of Consciousness. Edited by Francisco J. Varela. Wisdom, 1997.

The World of Tibetan Buddhism: An Overview of Its Philosophy and Practice. Translated and edited by Geshe Thupten Jinpa, foreword by Richard Gere. Wisdom, 1995.